International Perspectives on Suburbanization

Also by Nicholas A. Phelps

POST-SUBURBAN EUROPE: Planning and Politics at the Margins of Europe's Capital Cities (*co-authored*)

THE NEW COMPETITION FOR INWARD INVESTMENT: Companies, Institutions and Regional Development (*co-edited*)

FDI AND THE GLOBAL ECONOMY: Corporate and Institutional Dynamics of Global-Localisation (*co-edited*)

MULTINATIONALS AND EUROPEAN INTEGRATION: Trade, Investment and regional Development

Also by Fulong Wu

MARGINALIZATION IN URBAN CHINA: Comparative Perspectives (*co-edited*)

CHINA'S URBAN POVERTY (*co-authored*)

CHINA'S EMERGING CITIES: The making of New Urbanism (*edited*)

URBAN DEVELOPMENT IN POST-REFORM CHINA: State, Market and Space (*co-authored*)

GLOBALIZATION AND THE CHINESE CITY (*edited*)

RESTRUCTURING THE CHINESE CITY: Changing Society, Economy and Space (*co-edited*)

GEODYNAMICS (*co-edited*)

International Perspectives on Suburbanization

A Post-Suburban World?

Edited By

Nicholas A. Phelps
University College London, UK

Fulong Wu
Cardiff University, UK

First published 2011 by
PALGRAVE MACMILLAN

Palgrave Macmillan in the UK is an imprint of Macmillan Publishers Limited,
registered in England, company number 785998, of Houndmills, Basingstoke,
Hampshire RG21 6XS.

Palgrave Macmillan in the US is a division of St Martin's Press LLC,
175 Fifth Avenue, New York, NY 10010.

Palgrave Macmillan is the global academic imprint of the above companies
and has companies and representatives throughout the world.

Palgrave® and Macmillan® are registered trademarks in the United States,
the United Kingdom, Europe and other countries

ISBN 978-0-230-27639-0   hardback

This book is printed on paper suitable for recycling and made from fully
managed and sustained forest sources. Logging, pulping and manufacturing
processes are expected to conform to the environmental regulations of the
country of origin.

A catalogue record for this book is available from the British Library.

Library of Congress Cataloging-in-Publication Data

International perspectives on suburbanization : a post-suburban world? /
    edited by Nicholas A. Phelps, Fulong Wu.
      p. cm.
    Summary: "New urban developments such as office blocks, warehouses
      and retail complexes are increasingly common in outer city regions
      across the world. This book examines the processes of post-
      suburbanization in international perspective, exploring how
      developments across the world might be considered post-suburban"
      – Provided by publisher.
    Includes bibliographical references and indexes.
    ISBN 978-0-230-27639-0
      1. Cities and towns. 2. Sociology, Urban. 3. Regional planning.
    I. Phelps, N. A. (Nicholas A.) II. Wu, Fulong.

    HT119.I58 2011
    307.76–dc22   2011012457

10   9   8   7   6   5   4   3   2   1
20 19 18 17 16 15 14 13 12 11

Printed and bound in Great Britain by
CPI Antony Rowe, Chippenham and Eastbourne

Contents

List of Figures

List of Maps

List of Tables

ix

Preface

This edited collection of papers represents a further development of a strand of research that dates back to work first published in 2001. That work, from a small Economic and Social Research Council (ESRC) funded study of a unique European network of self-styled edge cities (now defunct) prompted a broader interest in the urban geography and urban politics of settlements that whilst at the edge of major cities could not, for various reasons, quite be regarded as suburbs in the traditional sense. Further research funded by the British Academy extended and deepened this initial research. Together the materials from these projects were consolidated in Phelps, Parsons, Ballas and Dowling's *Post-Suburban Europe: Planning and Politics at the Margins of Europe's Capital Cities* (2006, Palgrave Macmillan).

The chapters in this book were originally presented at a one-day conference held at University College London on May 21, 2009 as part of a programme of research funded by the ESRC (RES 062-23-0924). Our thanks go to all who attended and contributed to discussion on the day and especially to Professor Sir Malcolm Grant, the Provost of University College London, for introducing the event and Andrew Wood for chairing one of the four sessions. That research, conducted through 2008–2009, was entitled 'Governing post-suburban growth' and sought to consider the different constellations of actors driving, and different political tensions regarding growth, in the development of six post-suburban settlements surrounding capital cities in unitary and federal states within market, mixed and transitional economy settings. This volume was intended – as part of this original research – to broaden the geographical scope of the research to include other potential examples of post-suburban growth and to generate critical discussion of the value of the term post-suburbia when set against a welter of existing terminology. As a result, only a very small sample of the original research is reported on this volume (notably that on Khimki).

Dr. Sonia Roitman was employed as the permanent researcher for this project and we are grateful for her energy in helping to liaise with contributors and organize parts of the day as well as her great work throughout the project. Sonia was instrumental in helping to secure a further small Abbey-UCL Collaboration Research Fund grant enabling the study of Pilar in Argentina in 2008, the results of which are reported in this volume. In connection with this we would like to thank Gabriel Fernández and Germán Leva at Quilmes University and Cynthia Goytia at Di Tella University for their assistance and hospitality during fieldwork. We are also grateful to Dr. Oleg Glubchikov who was also employed as a researcher for the case study of Khimki in Russia for the project and which is the subject of one of the chapters contained within this book. His continued involvement with and enthusiasm for the publication plans from the research project are much appreciated.

We grateful to Professor David Price and Susan Parkes at UCL for agreeing and arranging additional funds and assistance from University College London's own Sustainability 'Grand Challenge' initiative, which helped facilitate the one-day conference from which this book arises. We would also like to thank all the contributors. The quality of the papers and discussion made for an excellent day and their uniformly excellent and timely written contributions made the task of putting this volume together a simple one from an editorial point of view. In this last respect, the time, effort, patience and expertise of Philippa Grand and Olivia Middleton at Palgrave Macmillan publishers is greatly appreciated.

Nicholas A. Phelps (London)
Fulong Wu (London)

Notes on Contributors

David Bieri is Assistant Professor in Urban and Regional Planning at the University of Michigan, USA. From 1999 until 2006, he held positions at the Bank for International Settlements (BIS) in Basel, Switzerland. His main research interests are in economic geography and urban economics, in particular the analysis of locational sorting, non-market interactions and regional price levels.

Marco Bontje is Assistant Professor at the Department of Geography, Planning and International Development Studies of the University of Amsterdam, Netherlands. His main research interests are city-regional dynamics, polycentric urban regions, creative and knowledge-intensive industries and shrinking cities. He is co-author (with Sako Musterd) of *The Inventive City-Region*.

Joachim Burdack is Professor of Geography at the University of Leipzig, Germany, and head of department at the Leibniz-Institute for Regional Geography (IfL). He studied at the Freie Universität Berlin and at Indiana University (Bloomington, Indiana, USA). His current research interests include the development of metropolitan areas in Eastern and Western Europe, questions of regional development in Europe and the development of small cities.

Elisabeth Chaves is a PhD candidate in the School of Public and International Affairs at Virginia Polytechnic Institute and State University, USA. She also holds a J.D. from the University of San Diego School of Law. Her research focuses on the relationship of journals and politics, the changing materiality of discourse, the communication of scholarship, and the political economy of intellectual production.

Allan Cochrane is Professor of Urban Studies at the Open University, UK. He has researched and published on a wide range of topics relating to urban and regional politics and policy. He is author of *Understanding Urban Policy: a Critical Approach*, co-author of *Re Thinking the Region* and joint editor of *Comparing Welfare States* and of *Security: Welfare Crime and Society*.

Tommy Firman is Professor in the School of Architecture, Planning, and Policy Development at the Institute of Technology, Bandung, Indonesia. He has written numerous articles on urban and regional development and urbanization in Indonesia notably in the journals *Urban Studies, Cities, Habitat International, and Land Use Policy*. He has been a Fulbright Visiting Scholar at Massachusetts Institute of Technology (1994) and University of California at Berkeley (2005).

Oleg Golubchikov is a Research Associate at the School of Geography and the Environment of the University of Oxford, UK. His research interests are concerned with urban governance and spatial injustices, the transformation of post-socialist cities, and sustainable urbanism. He is author of *Green Homes: Towards Energy Efficient Housing in the United Nations Economic Commission for Europe Region.* (United Nations, 2009) and has published in the journals *Environment and Planning A, Geografiska Annaler B* and *European Planning Studies*.

Dirk Heinrichs works as a senior researcher at the Institute of Transport Research of the German Aerospace Centre in Berlin, Germany. He is a visiting lecturer at the Habitat Unit of the Technical University Berlin and the SPRING programme of the Technical University of Dortmund. He has several years of urban research and practical planning experience in Asia and Latin America. Most recently he coordinated the 'Risk Habitat Megacity' research initiative, carried out by a network of Latin American Universities and the German Helmholtz Association. His research interests focus on the linkages between land use change, housing policy and social-spatial segregation.

Andrew E.G. Jonas is Professor of Human Geography at the University of Hull, UK. His research on urban politics, labour control, urban sustainability and territorial governance has appeared in a wide range of journals in geography and the social sciences. He co-edited *The Urban Growth Machine: Critical Perspectives Two Decades Later* and *Interrogating Alterity: Alternative Economic and Political Spaces*.

Roger Keil is the Director of the City Institute at York University and Professor at the Faculty of Environmental Studies at York University, Toronto, Canada. Keil's current research is on global suburbanism. He is the co-editor of the *International Journal of Urban and Regional Research* (IJURR) and a co-founder of the International Network for Urban Research and Action (INURA).

Paul L. Knox is University Distinguished Professor and Senior Fellow for International Advancement at Virginia Tech, USA where he was Dean of the College of Architecture and Urban Studies from 1997 to 2006. His recent publications include *Metroburbia USA* and *Cities and Design*.

Yong-Sook Lee is Associate Professor, Department of Public Administration, Korea University. She specializes in regional economic development, industrial policy, and urban and regional planning. Her research foci include the role of the state in the globalizing cluster developments, global production networks in Asia, new urban developments in South Korea, and creative city policies in Asia.

Michael Lukas is a PhD student at the Helmholtz-Centre for Environmental Research – UFZ in Leipzig and the Christian-Albrechts-Universität zu Kiel, Germany. Previously he studied human geography (diploma degree, equivalent to an MSc/MA), sociology and political science in Bonn, Barcelona and Berlin and worked as freelance consultant in spatial and environmental planning in Santiago de Chile. His research interests are urban and environmental planning and governance, especially in Latin America.

Alla Makhrova is a principal research fellow at the Faculty of Geography of Lomonosov Moscow State University, Russia. Her research interests cover urbanization and cities, spatial planning, and residential property markets. She is co-author of *Moscow Capital City-Region at the Turn of the Century*, and *Moscow Oblast Today and Tomorrow: Tendencies and Perspectives of Spatial Development*, both in Russian.

Henning Nuissl is Professor of Applied Geography and Town Planning at the Humboldt-Universität zu Berlin, Germany. He is also a visiting research fellow with the Helmholtz-Centre for Environmental Research – UFZ in Leipzig, Germany. He has worked as a researcher in the field of spatial development for around 14 years and held guest professorships at Technische Universität Berlin and Potsdam University. Currently his major areas of interest are urban sprawl and land use change, regional development and urban and regional governance.

Nicholas Phelps is Professor of Urban and Regional Development at the Bartlett School of Planning, University College London, UK.

He is the author of *An Anatomy of Sprawl* and co-author of *Post-suburban Europe* (Palgrave Macmillan) and has published extensively on issues covering the economy, planning and politics of city-regions.

Sonia Roitman is a Postdoctoral Research Fellow at the Latin American Institute, Freie Universität Berlin. Her research and publications focus on social theory and segregation, gated communities and private governance, urban social inequalities and their impacts on the urban fabric, and land and housing policies.

HaeRan Shin is a Lecturer at the Bartlett School of Planning, University College London, UK. Her main academic interests have revolved around urban politics, planning theory, and immigrant studies. She has authored academic articles on the politics of culture-led urban regeneration, negotiation in planning, and the capability of Korean immigrant women and poverty.

André Sorensen is Associate Professor of Urban Geography in the Department of Geography and Programme in Planning, University of Toronto, Canada. He has published widely on Japanese urbanization, land development, and planning history. His *The Making of Urban Japan: Cities and Planning from Edo to the 21st Century* won the book prize of the International Planning History Association in 2004. In 2007 he was elected a Fellow of the University of Tokyo School of Engineering in recognition of his research on Japanese urbanism and urban planning.

Jon C. Teaford is Professor Emeritus of History at Purdue University, USA, where he taught American urban history for 32 years. He is the author of *Post-Suburbia: Government and Politics in the Edge Cities*, *The Metropolitan Revolution: The Rise of Post-Urban America*, and *The American Suburb: The Basics*.

Fulong Wu is Professor of East Asian Planning and Development at the School of City and Regional Planning, Cardiff University, UK. His research includes China's urban governance and transformation. He is co-editor of *Restructuring the Chinese City*; editor of *Globalization and the Chinese City*; *China's Emerging Cities*; and co-author of *Urban Development in Post-Reform China: State, Market, and Space*; *China's Urban Poverty* and co-editor of *Marginalization in China: Comparative Perspectives* (Palgrave Macmillan).

Douglas Young is Assistant Professor of Social Science and Coordinator of the Urban Studies Program at York University, Toronto, Canada. He is the co-author of *Changing Toronto: Governing Urban Neoliberalism* and co-editor of *In-between Infrastructure: Urban Connectivity in an Age of Vulnerability*. His research interests include legacies of modernism, urban infrastructure and suburban decline and renewal.

1
Introduction: International Perspectives on Suburbanization: A Post-suburban World?

Nicholas A. Phelps and Fulong Wu

1.1 Definitions

Definitions of cities and suburbs are rarely very precise and are rendered relative and arbitrary in geographical terms by the passage of time and in the manner in which their cultural meaning and socioeconomic content is socially constructed. Historically, in ancient and medieval times, the suburbs were composed of those usually noxious activities and disenfranchised citizens outside of the physical boundary of the city wall. In modern times, with the literal or figurative destruction of city walls, definitions of the suburbs are curious in their being incredibly vaguely defined in geographical terms and yet strongly invested with particular popular and academic meaning – a meaning, moreover, that is in some contrast to that historically, as a new found escape from the city. Indeed successive academic simplifications produced since the Chicago School models of the city have created their own misrecognitions of the character of the suburbs (Harris and Lewis, 1998). As we shall see, the term post-suburbia encounters many of the same problems when we try to use it to distinguish this potential class of settlements from those of cities and suburbs.

A new era?

The first and most obvious sense in which the terms post-suburbia has been used is to distinguish a new era of urbanization. This sense of a 'clean' break with suburbanization is perhaps most closely associated with the post-modern perspective evident in writings which focus on what might be regarded as the paradigmatic case of Los Angeles (Dear, 2004; Dear and Dahmann, 2008; Soja, 2000). Drawing on something of this perspective, Lucy and Philips (1997, p. 260) use the term to 'refer

1

to a time period which is succeeding the suburban era' in which there is a pattern of 'inner suburban population loss and relative income decline, suburban employment increase, suburban out commuting reduction, exurban population and income increase and farmland conversion' (Lucy and Philips, 1997, p. 259) to provide one of the most precise definitions that exists. It is also one that is exposed by the passing of time as one that inevitably is relative and, perhaps ultimately, arbitrary as they acknowledge when going on to note how in the US, 'the period of mature suburbs blends with the post-suburban era' (Lucy and Phillips, 1997, p. 261).

Viewed as a new era, post-suburbia is also relative when deployed in comparative perspective. Phelps et al (2006) refer to this as a 'temporal disparity': that is, there may be reasonably common urban forms – including post-suburban forms – emerging at different times in different national settings, leading, for example, to what Dick and Rimmer (1998) have depicted as periods of convergence and divergence in patterns and processes of urbanization in the West and in East Asia. In all of this it is little surprise then that Teaford's historical account in Chapter 2 serves to blur the boundaries between eras of suburbanization and post-suburbanization.

A new settlement space?

The weight of academic commentary has alighted instead on the idea that post-suburban settlement space is itself something new. Perhaps the most straightforward rendering of post-suburbia as a new form of settlement space are those which view it as the latest in a sequence of processes and patterns of urbanization. Thus Brake et al (2001, cited in Kraemer, 2005, p. 44) separate post-suburbia from preceding suburban developments when arguing that: 'in order to correctly define what really happens [in] "post" suburbanization, we should explicitly refer to the kind of urbanization that is taking place beyond the formerly suburbanized area, in the still rural hinterland'. Such definitions appear still to be rooted in the most predictable and linear processes of outward growth of the modern city-region, an assumption which for many no longer holds. Dear and Dahmann (2008, p. 269) submit not only that this logic has been reversed but that 'urban space, time and causality have been altered' in complex ways.

As a result, other definitions have gone further and see the essence of post-suburbia in terms of the very difficulty of defining it geographically, either by placing boundaries around it or locating it relative to cities and suburbs in the radial or concentric graphical renderings associated with the Chicago school. Whereas suburbs form part of, are integrated with, and can be planned as part of the monocentric city-region, post-suburbia is part of heavily urbanized regions in which there is fragmentation or 'splintering' (Graham and Marvin, 2001) of infrastructure and service provision related to the likes of public transportation, power and water supply and sewerage. Fishman compares the traditional suburb to what he terms the 'technoburb' arguing that the latter is 'at first ... impossible to comprehend. It has no clear boundaries' (Fishman, 1987, p. 203). He went on to describe how 'Unlike old cities, these new cities had no recognizable centres or peripheries; within regions that covered thousands of square miles they included formerly urban, suburban, and even rural elements; their only structure came from the patterns and intersections formed by the superhighway growth corridors that created and sustained them' (Fishman, 1991, pp. 234–235). In similar vein, Lang (2003) describes how 'edgeless cities' are 'not even easy to locate' because they 'spread almost imperceptibly throughout metropolitan areas, filling out central cities, occupying much of the space between more concentrated suburban business districts, and ringing the metropolitan areas' built-up periphery' (Lang, 2003, pp. 1–2). They form part of the restless urban or indeed 'metroburban' landscapes that Chaves, Knox and Bieri depict in Chapter 3.

Although unsatisfactory in many respects, notions of post-suburbia as new settlement space are perhaps the most intriguing for the way in which they set in train other questions regarding the political and social construction of places and their institutions (Phelps et al, 2010; Phelps and Wood, 2010).

New actors and forces in the production of the built environment?

The suburbs can be viewed as the collective expression of commonly held individual preferences of a growing affluent proportion of society in many nations (Bruegmann, 2005) so that suburbanization is truly likely to become a global phenomenon with a very similar logic. The interesting questions both about suburbia and post-suburbia in comparative perspective and in opposition to one another in any given nation is therefore how provision for this preference is mediated.

Here important lines of comparison emerge between regions of the world such as Europe and Latin America on the one hand and North America on the other hand in the historic role in the suburban location of provision for social housing and new towns made by local and central government. It would also be as well to be careful regarding generalizations within regions like East Asia, since it is apparent that residential suburbanization in the developmental state of Japan as described by Sorensen in Chapter 12 is rather different to the almost total state provision for mass residential demand and preference found in the new towns around Seoul as described by Yong-Sook Lee and HaeRan Shin in Chapter 13.

Private sector real estate, developer and construction industries have been at the heart of the suburbanization process. If we agree that our metropolitan regions now represent increasingly large complex and specialized groupings of settlements and their economic relations then this seems to imply a parallel complexity of the character of private sector interests operative across these regions. The private sector was greatly implicated in post-war mass suburbanization in the US, not least in the marketing and production of housing for what truly became a mass preference. Since this time, it is apparent that developers and housing construction companies have continued to respond to, but also shape and segment, residential preferences in suburban housing markets – to the point that we can begin to question whether a mass collective ideal of suburban living as expressed in residential preferences continues to exist. Some of the most conspicuous developments of the newly post-suburban landscape emerging have been with respect to the lucrative niches of 'vulgaria' (Chaves et al, Chapter 3) in the US and residential mega projects (Heinrichs et al, Chapter 6) and country clubs in Latin America (Roitman and Phelps, Chapter 7).

The state and its interventions represent a critical continuity between suburbia and post-suburbia. The suburbs formed part of a Fordist 'spatial fix' (Walker, 1981) that has itself, and in its unanticipated consequences, become a barrier to further accumulation (Harvey, 1985, p. 122). The emergence of post-suburbia – seen as a rounding-out of traditional suburbs into cities in function but not form – and a new politics associated with it, might be seen as embodying the search for a new 'spatial fix' in which government at all scales is implicated. Here we see continuity between suburbia facilitated by modern state interventions that now generate a host of unanticipated side effects as barriers to accumulation and attempts of a new post-suburban politics to ameliorate them in a present era that Beck terms a second modernity (see Phelps and Wood, 2010).

Beck (1992) concentrates on politicization of some of the biggest and most risky side effects of modernist state interventions – such as environmental pollution and nuclear technologies. Yet the unanticipated effects of state interventions in promoting low-density suburban development can hardly be understated not least given their significant contribution to inducing global climate change and their origin in the systemic properties of automobility (Sheller and Urry, 2000). Thus, one key aspect around which the new post-suburban politics will coalesce concerns the 'retrofitting' of suburbia and the further urbanization of post-suburbia. Not the least in this respect is the politics surrounding infrastructure provision in what Keil and Young in Chapter 4 term the 'inbetween cities' currently being thrown up by contemporary urbanization. Notwithstanding the considerable obstacles – technical and political – to such retrofitting, there is anecdotal evidence from Europe (Phelps et al, 2006) to suggest that the character of some suburbs has been transformed: they may have to if patterns of development in the likes of Pilar, Argentina (Chapter 7) and Khimki in Russia (Chapter 10) are to ultimately to produce both more socially, economically and environmentally-sustainable places.

1.2   Of urbanized regions and 'zombie categories'

For some time now the urbanization process in the United States (US) has produced systems of settlements and associated interaction between them that exceed the mono-centric city-regions or metropolitan areas of modernity to cover much larger heavily urbanized regions. For some these heavily urbanized regions mean that 'traditional concepts and labels – "city", "suburbs", metropolises – are "zombie categories"' (Lang and Knox, 2009, p. 790). As a result we have witnessed a burgeoning terminology describing both the character of these heavily urbanized regions and their newest constituent settlements (Lang, 2003). What becomes clear is that historic cities, their suburbs, outer suburbs, edge cities and the like are specialized locales within wider multi-nodal metropolitan systems (Bogart, 2006; Shearmur et al, 2007; Lang and Knox, 2009).

As a result we need to look to the differences among settlements and their different growth trajectories if we are to speculate on and distinguish post-suburbia. Table 1.1 represents a very simple scheme in which we present a number of scenarios of settlement evolution within the modern city, late modern city-region and, what might be labelled for simplicity's sake, the city-region of a second modernity. In contrast to the relatively predictable linear outward patterns of growth apparent in the modern and late modern periods we stress the highly variable settlement dynamics apparent within a second modernity.

We are less interested in this volume in commenting on the scenarios associated with the modern city, focusing instead on the variable growth dynamics in city-regions of late and second modernity (iii and iv) (or what

Table 1.1   Urban development processes and relationships among settlement types

---

MODERN CITY
   i.   City → Suburb

LATE MODERN CITY REGION
   ii.   City → Suburb → Post-suburb

CITY REGION OF SECOND MODERNITY
   iii.   Post-Suburb → City
   iv.   Growing suburb → Post-Suburb → City
   v.   Stable affluent suburb → Stable affluent suburb
   vi.   Declining suburb → Sub-suburb?
   vii.   City → Suburb

Dear, 2004 and Dear and Dahmann, 2008 consider post-modernity). We are also less concerned with aspects of settlement stasis and decline. Amidst the continued growth within city-regions there is ample evidence of suburban stasis and decline (scenarios v–vii in Table 1.1). Stereotypical notions of suburban homogeneity have contributed to a sense of stability in the residential character of seemingly affluent suburbs. Such a perspective continues to have some salience in the European setting. However, even in Europe rapid growth in the outer suburbs of major city-regions has become apparent as Bontje and Burdack describe in Chapter 8. Suburban stasis has been somewhat undermined in the US where greater variety in suburban social and ethnic complexion and economic performance has been apparent for quite some time (Hanlon et al, 2006; Orfield, 2002). Such decline may take on a rather different form, largely without the same implications for levels of income, in Japan as a result of demographic changes as André Sorensen discusses in Chapter 12. Other scenarios include the pathway by which cities (presumably small former industrial centres) in losing most of their economic function and fiscal capacity might regress into suburbs or dormitory settlements for nearby cities (vii) and, lastly, the somehow sub-suburban futures facing some severely declining industrial suburbs (vi).

1.3   Themes

We can begin by speculating on some of the differences between suburban and post-suburban growth in the late modern city-region – issues we have elaborated on elsewhere (Phelps et al, 2010).

Growth and conservation

Suburbs have rarely been as residentially or industrially mono-functional as often presumed (Muller, 1981; Walker and Lewis, 2001), however, the most notable functional difference centres on the more 'balanced' employment and residential character of post-suburbia. The balancing of economic, residential and other functions was apparent in the US as early as the 1950s and is taken by Teaford (1997, p. 44) to be the signature of post-suburbia. The evolution of suburbs into post-suburbs was also described by Masotti who noted that 'While many of the older, established, and affluent suburbs are able to maintain their "residential only" character ... some of the older, and all of the new "frontier" suburbs have tried to provide for industrial parks, office complexes, major retail (shopping) centers, or some combination of the three' (Masotti, 1973, pp. 16–17). More recently 'the renewed linkage of work and residence' (Fishman, 1987, p. 190) provides the single basic principle of the technoburbs that Fishman sees as signalling the end of the suburban era. What this discussion makes apparent is that there is something of tension between the continued pursuit of growth as signalled in a growth machine politics (Molotch, 1976) licensed by traditional suburban ideology and politics of pursuit of freedom and the desire for small government on the one hand and a rising ideological and political interest in conservation as suburbs mature and additional growth, although recognized, becomes less desirable.

Growth and provision for collective consumption

As we saw, one definition of post-suburbia concentrates on the very difficulty of bounding and defining such new settlement space. As a result, the building of post-suburbia may be considered to display controversies akin to those in what Keil and Young (Chapter 4) refer to as the in-between city. They draw on the work of Sieverts to highlight how the issue of infrastructure of all sorts is central to the politics emerging in our newest settlements which are neither city nor traditional suburb. The broader challenge confronting suburbs of differing complexions resolves itself into one of retrofitting to produce the collectively consumed infrastructure and amenities that we associate with urban places. The moment of transition from suburb to post-suburb is one in which tensions over the continued pursuit of growth versus the provision for collective consumption and production needs that are pervasive to capitalist society (Scott and Roweis, 1977) are brought into sharp relief.

The scales at which growth is governed

One further implication of the difficulty of defining post-suburbia is its 'in-between' complexion in political terms. The likes of edge cities, as Garreau (1991) notes, rarely or imperfectly coincide with existing administrative boundaries. They are not just figuratively but literally in-between in political and governmental terms within the larger urbanized regions of which they are an increasingly important element. Thus in the North American setting, Jonas in Chapter 5 notes, it is the manner in which suburbs are woven into regional structures of governmental relations that is post-suburban. This same broad question of how adequately to understand and represent the governance of some of our newest settlements in metropolitan areas is equally apparent outside of the North American context. It is registered in the 'greyness' of government in the *desakota* extended metropolitan regions of East Asia (McGee, 1991). In Chapter 9 Cochrane deploys the notion of assemblages of power to try to capture the complexity of administrative arrangements that configure the complex suburban nature of settlement space in the South East of England.

1.4   International perspectives and the structure of the book

This book is a product of the desire to widen the geographical scope of discussion of the concept of post-suburbia and its potential relevance internationally when set against established understandings of the term suburbia. The US has long been the dominant source for new concepts and terminology in urban theory – including the interest in post-suburbia. These are often proved to be inescapable analytical reference points outside of the US even where important questions have been posed as to their relevance. Yet the need to examine US concepts is if anything more acute in an era of unprecedented international economic integration in which real estate investment and architectural, planning and commercial management 'models' travel more and more freely. In this connection it is sobering to note as Beauregard (2006) does how the export of American suburbia has only just begun in earnest. This is not to deny national and continental specificity outside of the US, but the aim in this book is to veer neither towards an isomorphic geography of post-suburbia nor towards an 'area studies' focus on idiographic tendencies in suburbanization but to try to consider issues of commonality within difference within the contemporary process of suburbanization in different settings.

The wider geographical coverage aimed for in this book is never-theless partial. First of all we wanted to have greater coverage of inter-national experiences that would complement the coverage of our own United Kingdom (UK) Economic and Social Research Council research.[1] Second, the major regions chosen were then also dictated by a desire to permit some degree of comparison *within* major regions of the globe. Third, the national cases covered in this book were also to an extent the product of chance, notably the additional work that we ourselves were able on conduct on Pilar. We sought to bring together established experts on urbanization processes within nations in the Americas, Europe and East Asia, charging them to explore critically the relevance and meaning of the umbrella term post-suburbia, allowing at the same time for authors to deploy their preferred analytical concepts.

In Part I, the chapters are intended as thematic overviews on the processes of suburbanization and post-suburbanization. Jon Teaford puts the notion of post-suburbia in a longer historical context of urbanization and suburbanization, stressing in the process continuity rather discontinuity. Elisabeth Chaves, Paul Knox and David Bieri have looked particularly at the form of the restless urban landscape in the US which has produced the many different labels that have at one time been prominent in the literature. They focus particularly on the new vulgar niches that have become apparent in the outer suburban residential property markets in the US. Roger Keil and Doug Young's chapter speaks to the politics emerging across systems of settlements in heavily urbanized regions. Following Thomas Sieverts' idea of the *Zwischenstadt*, they focus particularly on questions of infrastructure provision in the in-between settlement spaces within heavily urban-ized regions. Perhaps inevitably, given the dominance of terminology and theory from the US, the chapters have a strong North American flavour. To an extent, this was the intention in order to provide a par-ticular analytical point of departure from which to travel progressively further afield in contributions that speak to the Americas, Europe and then East Asia.

In Part II, chapters begin with a little more critical reflection on the concept of post-suburbia in the US setting provided by Andrew Jonas before departing for South America. Jonas' chapter notably draws attention

---

[1]The research covered the six cases of Croydon (London, UK), Getafe (Madrid, Spain), Espoo (Helsinki, Finland), Tysons Corner (Washington DC, USA), Yizhuang (Beijing, China) and Khimki (Moscow, Russia).

to issues of the geographic scale at which the new suburban politics coalesce, highlighting the potential for regional arrangements to at least partially ameliorate some of the excesses of exclusionary suburban politics. Dirk Heinrichs, Michael Lukas and Henning Nuissl's chapter looks at the case of new suburban developments in Santiago de Chile. While developments such as retail centres and gated residential communities resemble those in North America they are nevertheless a product of some of the peculiarities of Chile. Roitman and Phelps look at the contribution of gated residential communities to the urbanization of Pilar – an outer suburb of the Buenos Aires metropolitan region. They note that these visible elements that might be regarded as post-suburban are part of a socially and spatially fragmented dual suburb that has evolved in the last 30 or so years.

The 'mixed' economies of Europe are the focus of Part III. Clearly three chapters are insufficient to fully capture the range of national experiences in a continental setting that varies markedly north to south and east to west in terms of the nature of the economies involved. Marco Bontje and Joachim Burdack cover cases taken from mainland Europe – including some discussion of the post-socialist nations of east and central Europe. They stress the more central, contained and planned appearance of continental European post-suburban forms. Allan Cochrane's chapter speaks to the peculiar and introverted manifestation of post-suburban elements within the suburban sea that is the urbanized region of the South East of England. Finally, Golubchikov, Phelps and Makhrova cover the Russian transition case in which the 'big bang' of liberalization has neither properly completed land and property markets nor escaped entirely the legacy of the Soviet system of centralized command. The edge city-like rapid growth of Khimki at the edge of Moscow thus is the product of very different political and land development logics from that in the US.

In the final part of the book, the focus is on East Asia where the state is often regarded as playing a more consistently dominant role in all aspects of national development, including the operation of land and property markets, and where a distinctively regional notion of *desakota* exists. We start with Tommy Firman's chapter covering Indonesia which serves both to highlight the potential complexity of *desakota* urbanization and as a reminder that by no means all of the national contexts within East Asia can clearly be subsumed within the developmental state idea. André Sorensen's work whilst reaffirming the relevance of the concept of *desakota* to understanding suburbanization in Japan also presents an intriguing and different meaning of the term post-suburbia, namely the partial abandonment of suburban areas due to suburban population decline. Finally Yong-Sook Lee and HaeRan Shin take up perhaps the best example of the most fully state-led process of population and employment decentralization – that of new town development surrounding Seoul. The new towns surrounding London have sometimes been regarded as some sort of approximation to the likes of edge cities in the US, however, Lee and Shin's study reveals how state-led new town development has been quite impervious to private sector and civic society influence in a way that questions the relevance of North American literature in the developmental state context.

In a final chapter we close with thoughts regarding what the preceding variety of contributions can tell us regarding suburbanization and post-suburbanization. Here we note both some of the limits of the term post-suburbia which inevitably brings with it some sense of the ascendancy of specifically US forms and processes of urbanization but also the potentially different meanings of post-suburbia in different national and continental settings. By the same token, it is clear that, in an era of unprecedented international economic integration including the likes of overseas investment in land acquisition and real estate and an associated mobility of planning, architectural and property 'models', there is a pressing need to consider seriously important elements of commonality alongside difference in international experiences of suburbanization.

Part I
City, Suburb, Post-suburb

2
Suburbia and Post-suburbia: A Brief History

Jon C. Teaford

2.1 Introduction

Suburbs have existed virtually as long as cities. Since ancient times functions and activities that could not exist within the walls or limits of the dense core of the city have gravitated to the periphery. Sprawling livestock yards and brickfields as well as noxious slaughterhouses have been forced to operate on the edge of cities. In the pre-modern era they were joined by the immoral or illegal pursuits of prostitutes or unlicensed hucksters expelled from the walled core. For centuries the very wealthy sought escape from the city to outlying villas where they enjoyed summers in a semi-rural setting. The fringe represented freedom from the city – the ability to do what was not allowed or impossible within the densely-populated core.

The history of suburbia and post-suburbia represents a gradual extension of this freedom to an ever widening range of activities and people. By the dawn of the industrial revolution people no longer perceived the need to cluster behind city walls to escape the dangers of a dispersed rural existence. Consequently, they moved outward. Facilitating this centrifugal flow were new means of transport that expanded each individual's realm. City dwellers could range farther in pursuit of work, leisure, and residence. Over the past three centuries the wealthy have been able to convert part-time suburban villas into full-time homes and have been joined by the middle and working classes who have found lifestyle options in suburbia that were unavailable in the core. Industry has migrated outward to lay claim to the swaths of open space along the fringe. And retailing has followed, lured by the possibility of ample parking. Finally office and research facilities have become increasingly common along the fringe.

The ultimate product is post-suburbia, a world in which nothing is by necessity tied to the historic urban core but virtually all functions and activities are footloose and free to migrate to the open spaces of the periphery. No single centre dominates over a subordinate fringe; the historic central city is no longer so central and the one preeminent fount of metropolitan life. Instead, post-suburbia is an amorphous metropolis of many centres or possibly no centres that has liberated itself from the walled, monocentric past.

2.2   The origins of suburbia

Though suburbs have existed since ancient times, the modern era of suburbanization dawned in eighteenth and early-nineteenth-century Britain. Eschewing the crowded and corrupt urban core, the emerging class of merchants, professionals, and manufacturers began building outlying residences and retiring each evening to these bucolic retreats. Contributing to the attraction of the periphery was the rising concern for wholesome family life among upper-middle-class evangelical Protestants. In the late eighteenth century the evangelical British poet William Cowper wrote, 'God made the country and man made the town' (Fishman, 1987, p. 54). The fields, forests, and fresh air of rural England were God's country whereas the smoky, sinful city was the abode of moral and environmental blight. For businessmen who needed to make their living in the city, the optimal compromise was to remove wives and children to the semi-rural suburban fringe and enjoy an escape from the city each evening and weekend.

This, then, marked the birth of the suburban myth so prominent in the English-speaking world. According to this powerful myth, suburbia was the ideal retreat for the middle-class family, a bourgeois utopia of owner-occupied detached homes with accompanying gardens. In Britain, the United States (US), Canada, and Australia this great suburban dream lured millions of migrants to the metropolitan fringe. Yet many commentators have confused the myth with suburban reality. In fact, in the English-speaking world suburbia was not to be uniformly middle class, residential, or a model of bourgeois morality. Certainly outside the English-speaking world this myth deviated sharply from suburban reality. Throughout the nineteenth and twentieth centuries, however, both defenders and detractors of suburbia repeatedly focused on green lawns and middle-class manses while ignoring the all-too-evident industrial wastes and shack settlements.

Myths of domesticity and sylvan escapism may have fueled much of the suburban migration of the nineteenth century, but improved transportation was vital in facilitating the outward flow. In New York the advent of steam ferry service in 1814 improved the commute across the East River to Brooklyn. By 1823 a developer advertised 'Lots on Brooklyn Heights' which offered 'the nearest country retreat' and 'easiest of access from the center of business'. This suburban subdivision was a place of residence affording 'all the advantages of the country with most of the conveniences of the city' (Jackson, 1985, pp. 31–32). By the 1830s and 1840s the omnibus was similarly improving access from the city core to the suburbs of London as well as Boston and Philadelphia. During the second half of the century horse-drawn tramways further spawned suburban development along transit lines in both Britain and America.

The steam railroad, however, proved the great boon to those seeking liberation from the city. By 1849, 59 commuter trains headed for Boston each day from communities within a fifteen-mile radius, opening new opportunities for suburban settlement. One railroad advertised: 'Somerville, Medford, and Woburn present many delightful and healthy locations for a residence, not only for the gentleman of leisure, but the man of business in the city, as the cars pass through these towns often during the day and evening, affording excellent facilities for the communication with Boston' (Jackson, 1985, p. 37).

Farther west in the fast-growing metropolis of Chicago, the railroads were affording 'business men an excellent opportunity to avail themselves of the beautiful quiet of a country residence without shortening the number of hours usually devoted to their daily avocations' (Ebner, 1982, p. 70). Commenting in 1874 on the rail commuter's preference for a detached home in the suburbs, one observer wrote that it was 'thoroughly established that ninety-nine Chicago families in every hundred will go an hour's ride into the country, or toward the country, rather than live under or over another family, as the average New Yorker or Parisian does' (Chamberlin, 1874, p. 188).

In the London metropolis railroads likewise accelerated the outward flow of population, spawning a multitude of residential suburbs. The gradual adoption of workmen's fares culminating in the Cheap Trains Act of 1883 opened the opportunity for suburban life to a much broader range of Londoners. Whereas in the US rail commuters were primarily upper-middle class, the passengers pouring into London each day comprised workers and clerks as well as managers and professionals.

Yet rail transport not only encouraged residential suburbanization, it also proved essential to the outward flow of industry. Throughout the western world the industrial revolution transformed both the urban core and the suburban fringe. Expansive stockyards and polluting slaughterhouses had traditionally been consigned to the periphery, but in the nineteenth century meat processors developed suburban operations of an unprecedented scale. In 1865 the giant Union Stock Yards opened south of Chicago in suburban Lake Township where it took advantage of the many rail lines converging on the city. Packing houses soon surrounded the yards as did a sea of frame cottages housing workers employed in the plants. Other manufacturers were also gravitating to America's metropolitan periphery. In the Pittsburgh area, steel manufacturers located their sprawling mills along the rail lines in drab working-class communities where smoky palls supplanted the fresh air and sunshine associated with the suburban myth. By 1899, 55 percent of all production jobs in the Pittsburgh metropolitan area were in the suburbs, the central city accounting for a minority of factory employment (Lewis, 1999, p. 149). A decade later a prescient observer commented: 'The time is soon coming when all the large industries will be eliminated from the city, and Pittsburgh proper will become simply the commercial and cultural headquarters of its district' (Muller, 2001, pp. 58–59).

Industrial suburbanization was not confined to the US. In the Montreal area the opening of the expansive Montreal Rolling Mills in the 1860s launched a wave of industrialization in the suburbs of Saint-Henri and Sainte-Cunegonde. Providing housing and jobs for 32,000 working-class residents at the beginning of the twentieth century, the two communities testified to the fact that suburbia was not simply a bourgeois utopia. Writing in 1905, one commentator ranked Saint-Henri as 'the most important of the several suburban cities which form a chain around Montreal city proper' and described it as 'the throbbing heart of one of the largest manufacturing centres in the Dominion of Canada' (Lewis, 2002, p. 124). Meanwhile, in Buenos Aires authorities had moved the metropolis's mammoth livestock and meat packing operations to a new outskirts community dubbed Nueva Chicago. Around the stockyards developed a working-class settlement comparable to that surrounding Nueva Chicago's North American counterpart (Scobie, 1974, p. 19). North of the Paris city limits, the arrival of rail transport in 1843 accelerated industrial development in Saint-Denis. By the close of the century it was a manufacturing hub with a working-class population devoted to socialism. To the south of Paris, Ivry sur Seine likewise emerged as an industrial suburb with glassworks, lumber yards, breweries, distilleries, rubber factories, and warehouses. Like many other communities that would develop around Paris in coming decades, it was both a place of employment and residence.

2.3   Suburbia as a reform alternative

Though poor sanitation, muddy streets, and shack-like housing characterized many of the burgeoning industrial suburbs, by the close of the
nineteenth century suburbanization was becoming an increasingly
popular solution for the ills of the working class. Overcrowded cities
seemed to be sapping the vitality of the western nations, and sta-
tisticians paraded high mortality and low birth rates to demonstrate
that continued urban congestion would spell doom to western society.
British soap manufacturer William Lever founded the model factory
town of Port Sunlight in 1888 which promised a better alternative. At
Bourneville British chocolate manufacturer George Cadbury likewise
offered optional living conditions for the working class amid the fresh
air and green space of suburbia.

Inspired by such model factory communities, commentators increasingly viewed the less-densely-populated metropolitan fringe as the hope
of the future. In 1899 the American statistician Adna Ferrin Weber traced
the growth of nineteenth-century cities, cataloguing the dire ills resulting
from excess concentration of population. At the close of his work, Weber
gave an unqualified endorsement to the 'rise of the suburbs'; suburbia
furnished 'the solid basis of a hope that the evils of city life, so far as
they result from overcrowding may be in large part removed' and
promised 'the advantages of both city and country life' (Weber, 1899,
p. 475). Meanwhile, in 1896 the German Theodor Fritsch published
Die Stadt der Zukunft (*The City of the Future*) which characterized cities as
'cancerous growths of civilization' (Schubert, 2004, p. 10). His solution
was model communities with ample green space where the advantages
of the country would purify city life. In Germany as in the US, crowded
urban tenements appeared to sap the strength of the nation. Green
suburbs or new towns combining city and country were the answer to
the urban dilemma.

No one gained greater fame and a larger audience for the oft-
mentioned goal of combining the advantages of city and country than
the English utopian Ebenezer Howard. In his *Tomorrow: A Peaceful Path
to Real Reform* published in 1898 Howard introduced the ideal of a network of interdependent but self-contained garden cities of limited size
distributed across the countryside. With factories, offices, and stores as
well as residences, the utopian communities would not be commuting
suburbs but towns unto themselves characterized by a perfect mix of
city and country. Howard envisioned a post-monocentric urban world
in which the congested cores of the nineteenth century would yield to

a polycentric future. The 'crowded cities have done their work', Howard wrote, 'but they are in the nature of things entirely unadapted for a society in which the social side of our nature is demanding a larger share of recognition' (Howard, 1965, p. 146). Though eschewing the population sprawl that would characterize twenty-first century post-suburbia, Howard's rejection of the monocentric city as obsolete and his embrace of a diffused polycentric Britain anticipated the post-suburban future.

More prescient about the obsolescence of the monocentric urban world was Howard's British contemporary H.G. Wells. Writing in 1901 of 'the probable diffusion of great cities', Wells predicted that by 2000 'the old "town" and "city" will be, in truth, terms as obsolete as "mail coach"'. Supplanting the monocentric metropolis will be 'urban regions' and 'the London citizen of the year 2000 A.D. may have a choice of nearly all England and Wales south of Nottingham and east of Exeter as his suburb, and...the vast stretch of country from Washington to Albany will be all of it "available" to the active citizen of New York and Philadelphia before that date'. Not only residences but also business and employment would disperse. 'Already for a great number of businesses it is no longer necessary that the office should be in London', Wells noted, 'and only habit, tradition, and minor considerations keep it there'. Moreover, for the working classes, 'their centres of occupation will be distributed, and their freedom to live at some little distance from their work will be increased' (Wells, 1924, pp. 30, 41, 52–53). Thus in 1901 Wells was already describing the megalopolitan, post-suburban world in which the fringe would no longer be subordinate to a magnetic central core. There would no longer be a dominant central city with a dependent periphery, but instead urban regions would sprawl across the nation. Britons and Americans would be as free of the concept of the city as they were of the antiquated transport of the mail coach.

2.4 Twentieth-century suburbia

The transformation that Wells described would take place only gradually over the next century and would occur at a different pace in various parts of the world. In the decades before World War II, the outward flow of residence and manufacturing simply accelerated, continuing the trends already evident in the nineteenth century. Around Detroit many of the new auto plants were located on suburban sites where land for expansion was plentiful. Most notably Henry Ford moved his manufacturing operations as well as his research and administrative centres to suburban Dearborn. 'I don't like to be in the city', Ford explained. 'It pins me in.

I want to breathe. I want to get out' (Barrow, 2004, p. 205). Thousands of others in southeast Michigan shared this feeling, moving into the vast tracts of middle-class suburban bungalows. For those unable to afford a professionally-built house, do-it-yourself construction was an option. In Garden City auto workers could buy 'farmlets' where they could grow some of their own food and build their own frame houses along streets with no pavements, curbs, or sewers. Ford's black auto workers found houses in the suburbs of Ecorse and River Rouge. Meanwhile, auto moguls hired architects to design palatial homes in the privileged suburban enclaves of the Grosse Pointes northeast of Detroit.

In Southern California dispersion was also the rule. In 1924 a business leader predicted: 'The Los Angeles of Tomorrow: From Inglewood to Capistrano, and from Redondo to San Bernardino, industrial communities and centers will be scattered over this southland, each with its bungalows in which will live contented workmen with happy families, and gardens and flowers and lawns' (Viehe, 1981, p. 15). Already Southern California's suburbs seemed to have a place for virtually everyone and everything. Vernon was an industrial haven catering to the interests of manufacturers. Nearby, Bell, Maywood, and Huntington Park were home to manufacturing workers, and East Los Angeles was attracting a disproportionate number of Mexican migrants. Working-class self-builders erected whatever structures they could afford in South Gate and Bell Gardens. Describing their efforts, one sociologist observed: 'Here is a perfectly cubical building about half the size of a one-car garage and covered with tar paper. It is not a chicken coop or a rabbit pen but the home of a family' (Nicolaides, 2002, p. 33). In marked contrast were the movie-star mansions in the world's most famous suburb, Beverly Hills. Just as Detroit's trademark business was moving to the suburbs, so Southern California's famed motion picture industry was finding a home beyond the limits of Los Angeles. Metro-Goldwyn-Mayer and United Artists located their studios in Culver City and Warner Brothers opted for Burbank.

Beyond the US outward migration was also accelerating. During the first decades of the twentieth century working-class newcomers to Toronto joined the ranks of the self-builders, erecting suburban structures that the more affluent deemed shacks. Industrial decentralization encouraged the outward migration. In 1917 Kodak moved its plant to Toronto's far northwestern suburbs and Goodyear built a facility west of the city. Beyond the eastern city limits Ford chose a 17-acre site for its single-storey factory which opened in 1923 (Harris, 1996, pp. 58–59).

In Britain residential suburbanization boomed between the two world wars. With 4.2 million primarily single-family dwellings constructed in England and Wales, the extent of urban land increased nearly 50 percent. A vast, monotonous expanse of semi-detached suburban houses surrounded London, causing the novelist George Orwell to lament: 'Always the same. Long, long rows of little semi-detached houses' (Whitehand and Carr, 1999, p. 484).

The outskirts of Paris were also absorbing the surplus metropolitan population. Whereas the population of the city of Paris remained almost static between 1901 and 1931, the peripheral municipalities more than doubled in number of inhabitants, housing over two million residents by the latter date. Though the western suburbs accommodated many well-to-do residents, the outskirts were home to a large blue-collar contingent who could not afford housing in Paris. In Parisian suburbs as in the blue-collar outskirts of Toronto and Los Angeles, speculators purchased cheap land and sold small lots to workers who then built their own modest structures from whatever materials they could scrape together. Pavements and sewers were unknown. In 1922 a visitor described the typical housing in these settlements as 'a low structure, insufficiently dimensioned...; everything constructed of light materials, infinitely varied and often of the most unexpected sort' (Evenson, 1979, p. 229).

By the onset of World War II much of suburbia was a far cry from the suburban myth of gardens, sunshine, and upper-middle-class family life. Factories as well as families were attracted to the outskirts, shack towns existed not only around Paris but along the suburban periphery in the US and Canada. And the packed mass of semi-detached dwellings engulfing London could not boast of grand lawns or bucolic settings.

Though reality did not conform to myth, suburbanization proceeded at a rapid pace in much of the western world after World War II. In the US millions of families took advantage of the low-interest, long-term mortgages insured by the federal government to purchase a new home in the suburbs. New housing starts peaked in 1950 at 1,952,000, more than twice the prewar high of 1925. Moreover, the housing industry continued to boom throughout the 1950s. Whereas in 1940 only 43.6 percent of American homes were occupied by their owners, by 1960 the figure was 61.9 percent. No one would doubt these figures who visited the sprawling housing subdivision of Levittown outside of New York City. In the former potato fields of Long Island, the firm of Levitt and Sons built 17,447 four-room houses between 1947 and 1951, completing a new house every 15 minutes (Teaford, 2006, pp. 73–75, 82–83). Throughout the nation other private developers were likewise offering the American dream of a home in the suburbs to millions of modest-income buyers who never before had been able to afford a professionally-built detached home.

Most of the building was taking place beyond the central-city boundaries. Consequently, the metropolitan population residing outside American central cities soared from 35 million in 1950 to nearly 76 million in 1970. In 1950 this suburban contingent represented 41.5 percent of America's metropolitan population; 20 years later it constituted 54.2 percent (Teaford, 2008, p. 31). During the 25 years following World War II, the US went, then, from an urban to a suburban nation.

In other English-speaking nations the suburban ideal was also luring residents to a detached house along the metropolitan fringe. In Canada as in the US a rise in the number of automobiles freed metropolitan residents from public transit and allowed them to range farther from the urban core. There were just over 1.1 million automobiles registered in Canada in 1945; this figure almost quadrupled to 4.3 million by 1961. The most noted post-war suburban development in Canada was Don Mills outside of Toronto. Unlike Levittown, Don Mills included many townhouses and apartments among its 8,121 dwelling units, but the Canadian dream like that of the US was a single-family, owner-occupied home in the suburbs (Harris, 2004, pp. 129–130, 138). Reflecting on Canadian housing development during the post-war decades, one authority observed: 'The most sacred belief in Canadian public policy has been the idea that everyone ought to own a suburban home' (McCann, 1999, p. 129).

The same could be said of Australia. The automobile again facilitated the outward movement of metropolitan residents to owner-occupied detached homes. At the close of World War II there was one motor vehicle for every 8.7 Australians; by 1968 this ratio had risen to one for every 2.8 people. In the Sydney area the share of homes occupied by owners soared from 40 percent in 1947 to 70 percent in 1966; in Melbourne the rise was from 46 percent to 74 percent (Front and Dingle, 1995, pp. 31, 34). By the mid-1960s this fulfillment of the Australian dream led one observer to proclaim Australia 'the first suburban nation' (Davison, 1995, p. 40).

With its long history of suburbanization and miles of interwar suburban homes, Great Britain perhaps better deserved this title. But during the post-war era British authorities attempted to control the centrifugal predilections of their people and channel dispersion into government-sponsored new towns. The New Towns Act of 1946 provided for 11 new towns vaguely modelled after the ideas of Ebenezer Howard. Eight of these were intended to draw people out of congested and bomb-devastated London to planned suburban communities where Britons could enjoy the green space and modern amenities of housing along the metropolitan fringe (Clapson, 1998).

On the European continent outward migration was also evident. Sweden and Finland experimented with new towns following the British example. Finland's Tapiola constructed in the 1950s won international praise as a model suburban new town. To house the millions of people who continued to migrate to the outskirts of Paris, the French opted to build massive, multi-storey apartment complexes, the *grands ensembles*, that were the very opposite of the American dream of a suburban detached, owner-occupied home. Yet French aspirations may have been closer to the American dream than French planners were willing to admit. A 1964 survey asked Paris area residents, 'Would you prefer to live in an apartment building not too far from the centre of greater Paris, or in a house far from the centre?' Sixty-eight percent opted for the house, leading to the conclusion that Paris area residents definitely preferred 'a city a l'americaine' (Evenson, 1979, p. 251). By the second half of the 1960s, the British option of new towns with a mix of housing types had replaced the much-criticized *grands ensembles* as the French government's answer to the population explosion along the Parisian periphery.

2.5   The suburbanization of business

Accompanying the ubiquitous outward migration of population was a continued movement of manufacturing to the suburbs. As single-level assembly-line production made the multi-level mill building increasingly obsolete, manufacturers sought the open spaces of suburbia for their expansive plants. The growing importance of truck transport also necessitated a location near intercity highways and preferably away from inner-city traffic congestion. In the US auto factories continued to proliferate in the suburbs around Detroit, and sprawling aircraft plants located in suburban Long Island and in the outlying expanses of Southern California. Likewise in the Melbourne and Toronto areas ground-hugging behemoths sprawled across suburban spaces, proving that Australia and Canada were not far behind the United States in the suburbanization of employment.

Yet nowhere were the centrifugal forces so great as in the US, and the result was a city turned inside out. From the 1950s to the close of the century, the outward migration so evident since the early nineteenth century accelerated and affected every aspect of American life. Virtually everything moved to the suburbs, making the periphery central to American life and the urban centre peripheral. The suburbs were no longer sub to the urb. During the second half of the twentieth century the US created post-suburbia, a pattern of work, settlement, and leisure that defied older monocentric urban models and demanded a reconceptualization of metropolitan life.

Especially significant was the movement of retailing from the centre to the fringe. During the late nineteenth and first half of the twentieth centuries the downtown department store was the shopping mecca for Americans. Its unequaled range of merchandise drew shoppers to the core and made it the unparalleled hub for American consumption. The city's streetcar lines converged at the doors of the major department stores ensuring the retailing preeminence of a monocentric downtown.

In the 1950s and 1960s, however, the pattern of American retailing shifted markedly with serious consequences for the central business district. Some downtown stores had opened outlying branches before World War II, but the proliferation of auto-oriented suburban shopping centres during the post-war decades produced a lasting shift in American shopping habits. The best of these new centres offered everything that one could find downtown plus ample parking. For example, in 1954 Detroit's largest department store, J.L. Hudson Company, financed construction of Northland Shopping Center in the Detroit suburb of Southfield. Not only did the new centre contain 100 stores along handsomely designed pedestrian malls and a Hudson's branch, it boasted of free parking for 10,000 cars. No longer would suburbanites in Southfield and surrounding communities have to make the long trek to the Detroit central business district and pay a parking fee in a crowded downtown garage. Instead, they could shop conveniently and close to home.

Northland was an open-air centre, but its architect the Austrian immigrant Victor Gruen soon transformed American retailing by designing a fully-enclosed mall. Opened in 1956, Gruen's Southdale Mall in Edina, Minnesota, immediately west of Minneapolis, could claim 75 stores on two levels in climate-controlled comfort. Though located in frigid Minnesota, it offered a three-storey garden court with tropical plants, a 21-foot cage for 80 canaries, and a sidewalk café (Teaford, 2006, p. 94). Nothing like this existed downtown, and it immediately became an attraction for shoppers and sightseers alike.

Gruen and his fellow shopping mall developers realized that they were fashioning new centres for American life. Writing of his creations,

Gruen compared them to 'the ancient Greek Agora, the Medieval Market Place and our own Town Squares' (Gruen and Smith, 1960, p. 24). Mall magnate James Rouse commented that 'in the development of major regional shopping centers, we are really building new, well planned central business districts' (Bloom, 2004, p. 110). The developers of Long Island's Roosevelt Field shopping centre agreed. With a major branch of Macy's department store, 77 other retailers, and 11,000 parking spaces, it seemed to be a new downtown along the suburban fringe where according to conventional wisdom downtown was not supposed to be. Realizing that their new hub was neither traditionally urban nor suburban, they coined the term 'co-urban' to describe the new world they were inventing (Teaford, 1997, p. 46). Already in 1956 some Americans recognized that the old concepts and nomenclature of city and suburb no longer were adequate. An unfamiliar co-urban world was emerging in Long Island and elsewhere in the US.

The declining figures for downtown retailing testified to this change. Highway planners laid out massive centripetal expressway systems converging on downtown, thereby replicating and reinforcing the centripetal public transit system that had previously ensured the preeminence of the central business district. Moreover, city leaders cleared blocks of decaying downtown structures to build new parking garages for auto-borne shoppers. Yet none of this stemmed the outward flow of retailing dollars. Between 1958 and 1963 retail sales in current dollars fell 18.6 percent in downtown Baltimore but rose 17.9 percent in the metropolitan region as a whole; the drop in downtown St. Louis was 17.7 percent compared to an overall rise in the metropolitan area of 17.4 percent. In 1957 a woman shopper who had recently moved to the decentralized Los Angeles area summed up the emerging reality when she admitted: 'I've never been downtown. I'll probably never go' (Teaford, 2006, pp. 91, 99).

Retailers, however, were not the only migrants to the fringe. Corporate offices and research facilities also found the open spaces of suburbia an attractive alternative to the congestion of the central business district. In 1954 General Foods left Manhattan for a new headquarters on a 46-acre site in New York City's northern suburbs. The site selection committee explained the move when it characterized the urban core as suffering from the 'discomforts caused by dirt, dust, noise, and the ever increasing problem of traffic congestion'. By comparison, the company's president said of the new site: 'We shall...find ourselves working in a parklike setting and a more peaceful atmosphere with reduced nerve strain on everyone' (Mozingo, 2000, pp. 29–30). Gradually other corporations opted for the bucolic peace of outlying campus headquarters. When in 1956/1957 Connecticut General Life Insurance left downtown Hartford, Connecticut, for 280 acres in suburban Bloomfield, the company extolled not only the calming natural beauty of the new location but the ample space for parking lots. For a company employing a white-collar workforce living in suburbia and commuting by automobile, an outlying location seemed far preferable to one in the crowded core. Meanwhile, the Stanford Industrial Park in suburban Palo Alto south of San Francisco was attracting research facilities and most notably in 1957 the corporate headquarters of Hewlett-Packard. This suburban site became the heart of the Silicon Valley, the most famous high-tech region of the late twentieth century. The Silicon Valley defied the contentions of urbanphile traditionalists that cities were necessary to creativity and suburbia was a mindless wasteland. An amorphous, centreless string of communities stretching south from San Francisco was nurturing the future world.

The movement of the centre to the periphery became even more pronounced during the 1970s and 1980s. From 1967 to 1977 downtown retail sales adjusted for inflation dropped 48 percent in Baltimore and 44 percent in St. Louis. In 1967 suburban emporiums contributed 54 percent of nationwide department store sales; by 1976 this figure was up to 78 percent (Teaford, 1990, p. 208). In 1970 a prescient marketing report on the suburbanization of American retailing concluded correctly: 'By the end of the decade the suburbs will be central and the central cities peripheral' (*The Suburbanization of Retail Trade*, 1970, p. 10). Across the nation huge suburban malls were the new shopping downtowns. Cumberland Mall outside of Atlanta opened in 1973 with four major department store anchors; by 1983 it boasted of double the sales figures for downtown Atlanta. Woodfield Mall in Schaumburg, Illinois, northwest of Chicago produced annual sales figures more than equal to the combined totals of the central business districts of St. Louis, Kansas City, and Omaha (Teaford, 2006, p. 194).

Yet by the 1980s the suburban malls themselves faced new competition from sprawling 'big box' stores that offered huge inventories and low prices. They also boasted of convenient locations and mammoth parking lots. The most notable was Wal-Mart, the world's largest retailer with 4,190 stores in 2000. In a reversal of traditional patterns, Wal-Mart had first prospered in small towns, then moved into the suburban market, and finally pioneered urban venues. By 2003 it still had not penetrated Chicago, Detroit, and New York City. In the early twentieth century the urban core was the only place to find the world's largest retailers; by the dawn of the twenty-first century it was the last place for them to locate.

Many offices remained in traditional downtowns, but the proportion continued to decline. In 1969 only 11 percent of the nation's 500 largest corporations had head offices in the suburbs; by 1994, 47 percent had opted for outlying locations. The number of these giant corporations headquartered in Manhattan fell from 138 in 1968 to 29 in 1994. By the latter date 64 percent of the headquarters in the New York metropolitan area were in the suburbs (Muller, 1997, pp. 52–53). Employment figures also reflected the outward flow. In 1996 in the 100 largest American metropolitan areas, only 22 percent of the employed worked within three miles of the city centre. In the highly decentralized Detroit metropolitan area the figure was only 5 percent with 78 percent working more than ten miles from the core (Glaeser et al, 2001, pp. 1–2, 5).

Though the automobile contributed to this centrifugal flow, some transit-oriented suburban business zones also attracted jobs and headquarters. Along the Rosslyn-Ballston corridor of Arlington County, Virginia, the opening of a rapid transit line to Washington, D.C., sparked massive commercial development around each of the stations. In 1985 Rosslyn-Ballston had a daytime workplace population of 51,600, far in excess of its resident population of 23,900. By the early 1990s a 26-storey hotel-apartment tower and 12-storey office block were landmarks at the last stop on the transit line (Teaford, 2006, p. 196; Leach, 2004).

2.6   Recognition of post-suburbia

During the last decade of the twentieth century an increasing number of observers recognized this changing world and grappled with the problem of defining and naming it. Every commentator seemed to have their own label for the new phenomenon. Suburban downtown, technoburb, outer city, urban village, and post-suburbia were all suggested, and in the early 1990s 'edge city' gained popularity as a result of an influential book by journalist Joel Garreau. In his 1991 book Garreau defined edge cities as suburban business centres with a minimum of five million square feet of leasable office area, at least 600,000 square feet of retail space, and more employees than residents. He specifically identified 119 edge cities across the nation, landmarks of a fundamental change in American life. 'Americans are creating the biggest change in a hundred years in how we build cities', Garreau claimed. Metropolitan areas were developing 'multiple urban cores' which were 'new hearths of our civilization' (Garreau, 1991, p. 3).

In 2003 Robert Lang added a new option to the discourse when he suggested that the new hearth of civilization was actually the edge-less city, 'a form of sprawling office development that does not have the density or cohesiveness of edge cities' (Lang, 2003, p. 1). Most office space was not in edge cities but spread across sprawling amorphous swaths of business and residence. Metropolitan America was not increasingly polycentric; instead it was becoming noncentric.

In 1987 historian Robert Fishman perhaps best described the new reality when he rejected the notions of urban and suburban and claimed the American metropolis was 'defined by the locations [Americans] can conveniently reach in their cars'. Fishman claimed: 'The true center of this new city is not in some downtown business district but in each residential unit. From that central starting point, the members of the household create their own city from the multitude of destinations that are within suitable driving distance' (Fishman, 1987, p. 185). The American metropolis was certainly not monocentric; nor was it simply polycentric or noncentric. Rather it was millicentric with every resident defining their own hub and periphery, their personal metropolitan sphere.

In any case, virtually everyone agreed that the urban core was no longer central and inherited notions of urban and suburban were obsolete. First the railroad, then tramways and other public transit, and finally the automobile had freed Americans from the compact city, allowing them to move outward and claim breathing space. Residents and manufacturers were the first to take advantage of this liberation from the core, but retailing and offices followed their lead during the second half of the twentieth century. In the post-suburban era of the early twenty-first century, traditional notions of urban and suburban no longer were relevant. Americans had fashioned something different, and observers bound to past concepts struggled to grasp this strange, but very present, new world.

Though the US pioneered post-suburbia, elsewhere signs of the same phenomenon were increasingly evident. Garreau identified four full-fledged and five emerging edge cities around Toronto. And he reported that 53 percent of the office space in the Toronto area was outside the central business district (Garreau, 1991, pp. 437, 439). Moreover, Canada's West Edmonton Mall in Edmonton, Alberta, claimed to be the world's largest shopping centre with the world's largest parking lot. With over 800 stores, 110 eating establishments, 21 movie theatres, a chapel, and parking for over 20,000 automobiles, it surpassed anything in the US. In addition, it boasted of the world's largest indoor amusement park and world's largest indoor wave pool, making it a focus for recreation in the Alberta capital ('West Edmonton Mall', n.d.).

Purportedly the world's first suburban nation, Australia was also recognizing a post-suburban future. In November 2005, scholars held a 'Post-Suburban Sydney: City in Transformation' conference to discuss the emerging new world. 'Without wanting to transpose American models onto Australian realities too hastily', one of the participants commented, 'I would none the less suggest that in most outer suburban areas of Sydney today, some of these [post-suburban] trends are readily recognised'. According to this observer, 'Housing estates, neighborhoods and communities sit next to commercial and shopping spaces, simultaneously separate from and yet linked to nearby agglomerations of business and technology parks, offices, and other industrial activities, with all dispersed yet interconnected by the travel paths of private automobiles'. Describing the standard post-suburban scenario, she concluded: 'Within these employment, residential, and shopping patterns, the central city becomes increasingly peripheral to the day-to-day lives of many people' (Allon, 2005).

Meanwhile, in Europe one could discover some of the emerging landmarks of post-suburbia. Despite government action to limit the development of suburban shopping malls, Britain could claim some outlying retailing meccas that rivaled the best in the US. The malling of Britain began with the opening of Brent Cross north of London in 1976, and by 2000 the birthplace of suburbia was enjoying such spectacular megamalls as the 1.5 million-square-foot Trafford Centre near Manchester. It boasted a dome larger than that of St. Paul's Cathedral, a hotel, a 20-screen movie theatre complex, and an indoor sports facility. Moreover, some of these out-of-town centres generated surrounding office development, leading one observer to claim that 'it is demonstrable that many of Britain's existing regional shopping centres...clearly do possess all the basic features of Garreau's five-part definition' of an edge city (Lowe, 2000, pp. 261, 272).

During the first years of the twenty-first century, Spain, however, could claim Europe's largest suburban shopping mall. Located 23 kilometres southeast of the historic centre of Madrid, Xanadu mall offered 220 shops, 30 restaurants, 8,000 parking spaces, and leisure facilities surpassing anything found in the malls of the US. Most notably it sheltered an indoor snow park complete with a 240-metre downhill ski slope. With 25 to 30 million visitors each year, Xanadu could hardly be regarded as being on the outskirts of life in the Madrid area (Borsdorf, 2004, p. 143). In this case, as in post-suburban America, the periphery was central.

Even more significant to European retailing was the strong centrifugal pull of the suburban hypermarket. At the beginning of the twenty-first century the second largest retailer in the world, surpassed only by Wal-Mart, was the French hypermarket chain Carrefour. Paralleling the development of the American giant, Carrefour pioneered the big-box formula of large inventories offered at low prices. With ample free parking Carrefour's one-stop shopping was accessible to the auto-borne consumer. Building its first hypermarket in 1963 at a suburban site 30 kilometres south of Paris, Carrefour gradually expanded its operations throughout most of Europe, Latin America, and East Asia. In 2002 it opened its first Romanian hypermarket with a sales area of 10,500 square metres (113,021 square feet) and 2,000 parking spaces, and by 2008 it had inaugurated its 113th hypermarket in Brazil, opening a big-box outlet in the heart of the once-remote Amazon region. That same year it launched its 15th store in Malaysia, an outlet in the suburb of Johor Bahru with a sales area of 7,222 square metres (77,737 square feet) and parking space for 2,083 automobiles (Carrefour SA, n.d.). By 2008 the sun never set on the suburban big-box store as consumers throughout the world opted for retailing outside the traditional urban core.

The outward movement of office space was also evident in Europe. As early as the 1960s and 1970s the borough of Croydon on the south side of metropolitan London developed as an office centre complete with glass-encased high-rise structures reminiscent of the most modern American cities. In part this was owing to government policy encouraging the dispersion of office development to relieve pressure on the urban core. During the years 1963–1973, 30 percent of office jobs leaving central London migrated to Croydon. In 1969 the borough council boasted: 'Vast office blocks have made a new skyline, their towering elevations dwarfing older buildings...enough has already been accomplished to show that this is truly becoming a city of the present and also of the future' (Phelps et al, 2006, pp. 177–179). By the beginning of the twenty-first century this outlying office node was already such a venerable facet of the metropolitan landscape that it needed rejuvenation. Croydon 2020, a scheme for reviving the aging hub, included a new shopping mall of over one million square feet and an office tower of more than 40 storeys (Croydon Business, n.d.). The borough council's action plan claimed: 'By 2021 Central Croydon will be firmly established as London's third city centre and will be the main centre in the South East south of the Thames for shopping, business, education, leisure and entertainment' (Croydon Council, n.d.).

In the Paris area La Defense was another example of the outward movement of office space. Developed in the 1960s on a site in the inner ring of western suburbs, La Defense was intended to accommodate high-rise commercial development that otherwise might mar the landscape and skyline of the city of Paris. At the beginning of the twenty-first century it met all of Garreau's requirements for an edge city. It boasted of being Europe's largest business centre where 150,000 people worked and 20,000 people lived. It had 3.3 million square metres (35.5 million square feet) of office space, a massive shopping centre, Les Quatre Temps, and an ample supply of major hotels and restaurants ('Everything about La Defense', n.d.). Like Croydon, however, this pioneering effort at outward office relocation was showing its age, necessitating plans for renewal.

Many of Europe's new towns also manifested signs of emerging post-suburbia. Ebenezer Howard had dreamed of self-sufficient communities correcting the congested monocentric pattern of the late nineteenth century, and the post-war new towns vaguely based on his ideal partially realized this goal of dispersed development. The five government-sponsored new towns created around Paris in the late 1960s and 1970s incorporated not only housing but places of employment. By the 1990s one of them Noisy-le-Grand conceived of itself as sufficiently post-suburban to join with Croydon and a number of other fringe municipalities across Europe to form the Edge Cities Network. Perceiving themselves to have something in common with Garreau's model, these communities all coped with emerging post-suburban realities. A local official expressed Noisy-le-Grand's aspirations to transcend suburbia and become post-suburban when he commented: 'We do not want to be a dormitory town for Paris...We want to put in place all the services and employment structures necessary for a balanced life in Noisy' (Phelps et al, 2006, p. 127).

Another member of the Edge Cities Network was the Finnish city of Espoo, the site of the famed new town of Tapiola. In 1950 Espoo had only 23,000 residents and was hardly a rival of adjacent Helsinki, the nation's traditional urban hub. By 2007, however, it boasted an estimated population of 235,000, making it the second largest city in Finland, surpassed only by the capital. Moreover, it was the headquarters of the internationally prominent high-technology Nokia Corporation as well as the nation's University of Technology and the Technical Research Centre of Finland. With 107,000 jobs, shopping malls, hypermarkets, and a museum of modern art which claimed to be the largest art museum in Finland, Espoo seemed to embody the essence of post-suburbia (Espoo, 2008, pp. 10, 15).

The promotional literature for the Danish member of the Edge Cities Network, Ballerup, summed up the growing post-suburban perception of some European communities. Rather than conceiving of itself as simply a suburb of Copenhagen, Ballerup boasted that in the past 50 years it had 'developed from a village enclave into a typical suburb and further into a modern urban community with every conceivable facility'. With 39,000 jobs, the community of 47,000 residents was not simply a dormitory. Instead, it was at the heart of 'the country's largest concentration of companies in research, administration and high technology, earning the area its obvious name "Denmark's Silicon Valley"'. With all this Ballerup was now 'a player in global society' (Ballerup Commune, n.d., pp. 4, 12, 14). Copenhagen may have been the centre of traditional Denmark; Ballerup believed it was the cutting edge of the high-tech global future.

2.7   Conclusion

This emerging European post-suburbia is not identical to that of America, but then there actually is no uniformity in the US itself. Instead, in the US, Canada, Australia, and Europe there are signs of change that add up in varying degrees to a new world in which the monocentric city has yielded to a more diffuse pattern of living. With changing transportation options and lifestyles, the urban core no longer exercises the same magnetic attraction in the day-to-day lives of metropolitan residents.

The resulting post-suburban cityscape is simply suburbanization carried to the extreme, the end product of two centuries of continuous deconcentration of metropolitan population. Continuity, rather than discontinuity, characterized the incremental shift from suburbia to post-suburbia. During the nineteenth and twentieth centuries people gradually liberated themselves from the necessity of living in huddled masses. Manufacturers seeking more space for their businesses, bourgeois families yearning for the privacy and relative peace of an outlying home, retailers hoping to better attract auto-borne customers, and offices opting for locations nearer the homes of their employees and clients, all contributed to the creation of a new metropolitan landscape. Urban residents migrated outward and adopted a mobile lifestyle, moving in a variety of directions for their shopping, leisure, and work. Footloose humanity travelling to a multitude of destinations within the metropolitan agglomeration made the concept of core and periphery increasingly obsolete. Suburbia segued into post-suburbia and fashioned a new metropolitan world.

3

The Restless Landscape of Metroburbia

Elisabeth Chaves, Paul Knox and David Bieri

3.1   Introduction

The metropolitan form in the United States (US), a product of egalitarian liberalism, the New Deal, the collapse of the welfare state, and then the rise of neoliberalism, is a landscape of political and economic change that manifests itself in physical and social landscapes. In turn, these landscapes naturalize these political-economic structures. The challenges of characterizing this changing metropolitan form have prompted a great number of neologisms, including exurbia, edge city, edgeless city, exopolis, boomburb, cosmoburb, nerdistan, technoburb, generica, satellite sprawl, mallcondoville, as well as post-suburbia and metroburbia. The term 'metroburbia' emerged in Internet and media usage around 2005 to capture an important dimension of the New Metropolis: the intermixing of office employment and high-end retailing, with residential settings in suburban and exurban areas, along with established dormitory towns and small cities within a metropolitan area that has acquired many of the amenities of a large city. In short, it represents a fragmented and multi-nodal mixture of employment and residential settings, with a fusion of suburban, exurban, and central-city characteristics.

   Post-suburbia and metroburbia can be used almost interchangeably to describe these evolving landscapes, although the latter may better emphasize the blending or blurring of the traditional urban and suburban settings within the US. While post-suburbia signals a change in form or an end to or movement beyond a previous form, metroburbia describes post-suburbia as a polycentric hybrid that in many ways erases the difference between traditional or 'zombie' categories of city and suburb, urban and rural (Beck et al, 2003). Metroburbia functions as a designator of new forms and new processes. Not only has the physical landscape changed but so have the political, economic, and social landscapes.

Within the multiple urban forms of metroburbia, a new moral geography has emerged. It is the outcome of a serial process of enchantment, disenchantment, and then attempted re-enchantment worked upon the suburban and now metroburban landscape. Each phase has been shaped to some degree by intellectuals, designers, developers, builders and realtors, as well as by the aspirations of households and the resources, economic climate and technologies of the time. The cumulative legacy of this process is central to the condition of contemporary metroburban America. Its conservative result is a new morality that entails an emphasis on privatism, exercised through individual spending and acquired lifestyles, and a de-emphasis on social commitment. Its physical and cultural landscape is largely one of excess and affect, what Knox has called 'vulgaria', while its social landscape is one of growing inequality.

Metroburbia's new morality manifests itself most clearly in its wealthier residential landscapes where vulgaria is so widespread that it has naturalized the neoliberal ideology of competitive consumption and disengagement from notions of social justice and civil society that have been fostered within private, master-planned communities. Physically designed and tightly regulated through homeowners' associations to provide privacy, autonomy, stability, security, and partition, private, master-planned communities have propagated a kind of moral minimalism in their residents: Bound only by their contracted commitment to lead a private life, most residents have little social contact with neighbours, virtually no social interaction beyond their workplace, and, as a result, few bonds of mutual responsibility. Most are broadly and insouciantly indifferent to issues that go beyond their own property and lifestyle.

Vulgaria has colonized suburban settings within metropolitan regions where startling increases in household income have differentiated its residents from their neighbours (see Map 3.1). For example, in the Washington, D.C. metro region, the median income for the top-quintile tracts reached $103,603 in 2000. Meanwhile, the median income for the D.C. metro region as a whole was just $58,750 (2000 Census, tract-level data). Vulgaria's settings often are not contiguous, which only amplifies the sense of enclaving of their residents.

Additionally, their secession reduces their ties to traditional notions of community and place. It allows a certain indifference to or ignorance of the less affluent, resulting in, for example, a situation where the country's most affluent county in terms of median household income, Loudoun County, Virginia, was also home to a small community still

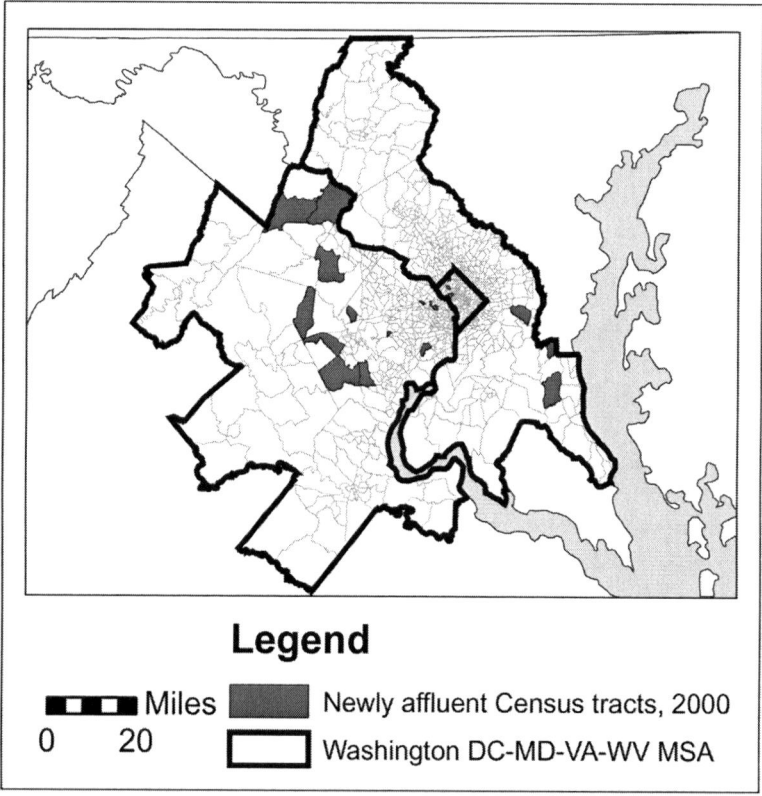

Map 3.1   The location of new affluence in the greater Washington DC MSA

without indoor plumbing in 2006 (Gardner, 2006). Understanding the new moral geography of vulgaria requires an investigation into the political, physical, and social environments that shape it. What emerges is a restless landscape of increasing inequality.

3.2   The structuring of metroburbia

In the US, the median size of a single-family home increased from 1,525 sq. ft. in 1973 to 2,135 sq. ft. in 2009, marginally below its historic peak of 2,277 sq. ft. in 2007 (US Census Bureau, 2010). Moreover, according to the US Census Bureau, the number of homes over 3,000 square feet doubled between 1978 and 2009, comprising almost a quarter of the new housing supply in 2009. A simple economic analysis of this trend may conclude that a demand for larger homes has appeared over time, and builders have met that demand with a supply of increasingly bigger homes. However, such an analysis takes preferences as given and does not investigate why or from where that demand arose. The work of Pierre Bourdieu provides an alternative analysis that argues for an embedded understanding of economic practices:

> Against the ahistorical vision of economics, we must, then, reconstitute, on the one hand, the genesis of the economic dispositions of economic agents and, especially, of their tastes, needs, propensities or aptitudes (for calculation, saving or work itself) and, on the other, the genesis of the economic field itself, that is to say, we must trace the history of the process of differentiation and autonomization which leads to the constitution of this specific game: the economic field as a cosmos obeying its own laws and thereby conferring a (limited) validity on the radical autonomization which pure theory effects by constituting the economic sphere as a separate world (Bourdieu, 2005, pp. 5–6).

Bourdieu's analysis of the state of housing in 1970s France traced the historical development of the creation of both the demand for and the supply of housing as many more people became homeowners, arguing that this movement toward increased home ownership was not independent of the social, political and cultural conditions that structured it. 'Housing policy' is produced by what he calls a 'mobilized, organized fraction of the "opinion-makers"', comprised of state officials as well as journalists, publicists, professional organizations, trade unions, and consumer groups, which in turn shapes supply and demand (Bourdieu, 2005). Since the state in France plays what is perceived to be a more visible and direct role than in the US, Bourdieu's analysis applied here may give too much emphasis to the state. However, the indirect effects of governmental policy, such as the mortgage interest deduction, or the state's ideological commitment to an 'ownership society', both discussed below, counter the commonly accepted version of the state's more absent role under neoliberalism. So, perhaps Bourdieu's understanding of the state's contribution to the construction of the housing market can be similarly applied here.

> In effect, the state – and those who are able to impose their views through it – contributes very substantially to *producing the state of the housing market*, doing this largely through all the forms of regulation and financial assistance aimed at promoting particular ways

of bringing tastes to fruition in terms of housing, through assistance to builders or private individuals, such as loans, tax exemptions, cheap credit, etc. ... In short, the market in single-family houses is (as all markets no doubt are to varying degrees) the product of a *twofold social construction* to which the state contributes crucially: the construction of demand, through the production of individual dispositions and, more precisely, of systems of individual preferences – most importantly regarding ownership or renting – and also through the allotting of the necessary resources, that is to say, state assistance for building or for housing, as defined in laws and regulations whose genesis can also be described; the construction of supply, through policy of the state (or the banks) in respect of credit to building companies, which contributes, together with the nature of the means of production used, to defining conditions of access to the market and, more precisely, a company's position within the structure of the – highly dispersed – field of house builders, and hence, the structural constraints applying to the decisions made by each of them with regard to production and advertising. And one has only to take the analysis a step further to discover that demand is only specified and defined fully in relation to a particular state of supply and also of social (and, particularly, legal) conditions (building regulations, planning permissions, etc.) which allow it to be satisfied (Bourdieu, 2005, pp. 15–16).

Bourdieu traced the structuring of the French landscape from the 1970s under neoliberalism and highlighted the intertwined and mutually constitutive forces of policy, supply, and demand. As renters in France became homeowners, they bought industrially-produced homes that symbolically, if not physically, resembled the mason-built homes of the French ideal. Further, they found themselves saddled with mortgages, that although often state-subsidized, still imposed heavy financial burdens. Poor construction increased these burdens, as the new owners' often quickly- and shoddily-built dream homes required repairs that had to be squeezed into their meager spare hours reduced by long commutes as suburbs were situated farther and farther from urban centres (Bourdieu, 2005). Yet they were homeowners, and the meritorious associations attached to ownership by the state, the building industry, the banks, and cultural attitudes assuaged the downsides to ownership by some degree. However, they were not the only ones that experienced the shortcomings of ownership.

[E]ven if it [the promotion of home ownership] fostered a profound transformation of the social order, and one profoundly in keeping with the desires of its promoters, liberal policy has undoubtedly not brought its promoters the political benefits they expected. The family unit, centred on the upbringing of the children, which is seen as a path of individual social ascent, is now the site of a kind of collective egoism that finds its legitimation in a cult of domestic life permanently celebrated by all who live directly or indirectly by the production and circulation of domestic objects (Bourdieu, 2005, p. 191).

The resultant demand and supply of housing, in a situation such as 1970s France, also then work upon the field that constructed them, creating a 'sociospatial dialectic' (Soja, 1980). As Knox has argued elsewhere, '[t]he central premise is that the built environment is both the product of, and the mediator between, social relations' (1991, p. 182). In other words, one cannot argue only that neoliberalism created a demand for ownership in France or a demand for increasingly ostentatious houses in the US. One must also consider how distinctive cultural values of home ownership predating neoliberalism contribute to this trend (Ley, 1985). Further, one should reflect on how previous political and social ideologies, such as those of the welfare state, contributed to landscapes of suburban sprawl as federal highway projects and federally-guaranteed mortgages enabled residential living more and more distanced from urban centres, perhaps setting the stage for the mythical appropriation of community realized in the master-planned, gated communities of neoliberalism. It is difficult to argue cause-and-effect, especially considering the widely differentiated forms of metroburbia, but a sociospatial dialectic framed around growing inequality requires attention. One prominent feature of the new urban landscape that can be examined is housing, which contains many of the contradictions of neoliberalism and which displays much of its attendant inequalities.

A house is highly symbolically charged (Bourdieu, 2005). The meanings that consumers associate with home ownership are culturally historic as well as fostered by the state and realized and manipulated by the actors who supply the dwelling, including the developers, builders, marketing professionals, financial services providers, and real estate agents. As a major life choice and substantial component of one's material wealth, a home

> expresses or betrays, in a more decisive way than many other goods, the social being of its owners, the extent of their 'means', as we say; but it also reveals their taste, the classification system they deploy in their acts of appropriation and which, in assuming objective form in

visible goods, provides a purchase for the symbolic appropriations of others, who are thereby enabled to situate the owners in social space by situating them within the space of tastes (Bourdieu, 2005, p. 19).

The provision of housing is as much a process of enchantment as it is a process of supplying an essential need. Moreover, when a home has far exceeded the basic requirements of shelter, containing more space than one reasonably requires, or amenities closer to gadgetry than necessity, the symbolic construction of the home becomes as important, if not more important, than its physical construction. Further, the demand for supersized homes is as much a culturally driven choice as an economic one. Housing consumption meets the need for shelter but for those who can afford more, it also meets more intangible desires. The structuring of the housing market cannot be understood unless its economic and cultural foundations are both taken into account.

> [T]he economy in all its spheres, from production and consumption to distribution, regulation and circulation, has to be seen as an act of many goals, from meeting material needs and making a profit or earning a living, through to seeking symbolic satisfaction, pleasure, and power (Amin and Thrift, 2007, p. 145).

However, while larger homes have grown more prevalent, and an industry associated more with marketing than with building and selling them has emerged, they remain affordable only to a segment of the population. For those who cannot afford homes of 3,000 sq. ft. and upwards, the symbolism of home ownership either must be deployed in different ways or more people must be made to believe that such a home is within their reach. The latter became prevalent in the last decade with a booming sub-prime mortgage market that offered no interest mortgage payments (for a time) and/or no money down (in the form of multiple mortgages) that drove home prices higher and put homeowners into houses they could not afford under traditional mortgages. Development rushed forward to meet this demand for larger homes that meant more profits. Housing starts for homes over 3,000 sq. ft. were 23 percent of all new construction at the peak of the housing bubble in mid-2006, and still rose to 26 percent by 2008, compared to only 13 percent in 1995. While over the same time period, the average lot size remained roughly stable at 15,500 sq. ft. The home became not only an asset but also an investment strategy. The state encouraged ownership and held out the home as a site of stability and security (Béland, 2007).

3.3   The policy landscapes of metroburbia

While under neoliberalism the state has 'rolled back' or 'withdrawn' from certain activities in the social and economic spheres, the state has also 'rolled out' new forms of activity (Peck and Tickell, 2002). Roll-back neoliberalization has meant the deregulation of finance and industry, the demise of public housing programmes, the privatization of public space, cutbacks in redistributive welfare programmes like food stamps, the shedding of many of the traditional roles of federal and local governments as mediators and regulators, curbs on the power and influence of public institutions like the labour unions and the US Department of Housing and Urban Development, and a reduction of investment in the physical infrastructure of roads, bridges, and public utilities. Roll-out neoliberalization has meant 'right-to-work' legislation, the establishment of public-private partnerships, the development of workfare requirements, the assertion of private property rights, the encouragement of inner-city gentrification, the creation of free-trade zones, enterprise zones, and other deregulated spaces, the assertion of the principle of 'highest and best use' for land-use planning decisions, and the privatization of government services (Peck and Tickell, 2002).

The changed nature of the state can also be thought of in terms of a move from discipline to control (Dodson, 2006). The centralized state as a visible site of disciplinary authority has been replaced by more decentralized, and therefore dispersed and less visible, multiple-sites of control. The fragmented geographies of metroburbia mirror the diffuse form of the state. Metroburbia can then be understood as the spatial expression of neoliberalism, an ideology that emphasizes individual ownership and responsibility and disembeds the economy from society. While the economy, and importantly here, housing supply, is falsely perceived as the aggregated outcome of individual decision-making, 'the production, articulation and implementation of housing policy...continues to be the domain of the state, irrespective of whether the policy specifies a social or a market mode of action' (Dodson, 2006, p. 227).

One manner in which the state intervenes in the demand and supply of housing is through the promotion of home ownership. Historically, the promotion of home ownership was tied to the notion of living the 'American Dream', coined in 1931 by James Truslow Adams in his book, *The Epic of America* (Adams, 1931). Real estate professionals latched onto the symbolic associations of individual betterment and prosperity through hard work, translating them into a normative ideal of home ownership as a sign of achievement of the American Dream by the middle class (Hornstein, 2005). Making the promotion of home ownership explicit, realtors joined with government agencies and civic groups to create the Own-Your-Own-Home campaign from about 1915 through the 1920s. One pamphlet in 1922 went so far as to declare that home ownership would put the 'MAN back into MANHOOD' (Eaves, 2007).

During the Depression, the National Association of Real Estate Boards, the realtors' professional organization founded in 1908, worked closely with President Herbert Hoover's White House Conference on Home Building and Home Ownership. They secured support for a tax reduction on real estate and endorsement for a federal mortgage discount bank to facilitate long-term mortgages. President Franklin Delano Roosevelt carried these initiatives forward through the New Deal, creating the Federal Housing Administration (FHA) in 1934 that provided federal insurance for mortgages. In effect, home ownership was subsidized by the state. Fordist-style home production, suburban development, federal roads projects, and accessible mortgages for veterans returning from World War II made the 1950s the decade of the greatest-ever growth in suburban population.

Disenchantment with the Keynesian welfare state beginning in the 1970s shifted the country's political and economic ideology away from egalitarian liberalism, where access for all to the American Dream was fostered by the state, to neoliberalism, where the American Dream would be provided through the market. A process of deregulation and withdrawal under President Reagan appeared to remove the government from intervention in decisions best left to individual market actors. However, as argued above, '[t]he state continues to define the reality and dimensions of its own practices even if those practices may change' (Dodson, 2006, p. 227). In other words, under neoliberalism, the state continues to promote ownership but in a different manner. By encouraging ownership, its counterpart being individual or private responsibility, the state can absolve itself of the provision of public services. Although, notably, state subsidies for home ownership have not disappeared, one of neoliberalism's contradictions.

Late into President George W. Bush's first term, he began to use the phrase the 'ownership society' with increasing frequency (Béland, 2007). His promotion of ownership took on evangelical qualities as he argued that 'there's no greater American value than owning something, owning your own home and having the opportunity to do so' (Eaves, 2007), that '[w]hen families move into a home of their own, they gain independence and confidence, and their faith in the future grows', and that '[i]n changing times, it helps if you own something' (Béland, 2007, p. 98). Home ownership in 2003 had already reached 68.3 percent in the US, before reaching a record 69.1 percent in early 2005. Since the peak of the housing bubble in 2006, home ownership has declined marginally, retreating to 'only' 66.9 percent in 2010 according to the US Census Bureau's Housing Vacancy Survey. Comparatively, just 34 percent of the Swiss, 42 percent of Germans and 54 percent of the French own their own homes (OECD, 2007). In fact, since the 1950s, home ownership in the US has remained fairly constant within a fixed band of 63 to 69 percent (Glaeser and Shapiro, 2002). It is hard to comprehend then why ownership needs to be improved. What makes more sense is that the promotion of ownership excuses the state from any sort of social role.

The 'ownership society' became the foil to 'big government', allowing the government to remove itself further from social policies that would protect the many rather than the few. The 'ownership society' was a smart move for the Republicans because it melded so well with past iterations of the promotion of ownership even under Democrats, albeit in a different form. Additionally, as Grover Norquist, a president of Americans for Tax Reform, argued 'You can't have a hate-and-envy class if 80 per cent of the public owns stock. That makes it impossible for Democrats to govern. It spells the end of their world' (Béland, 2007, p. 96 citing Julie Kosterlitz). Interestingly, neoliberalism's and President Bush's promotion of ownership has resulted more in a redistribution of income than an increase in ownership across the board, only it has been an upward rather than downward redistribution. 'Redistributive effects and increasing social inequality have in fact been such a persistent feature of neoliberalization as to be regarded as structural to the whole project' (Harvey, 2005, p. 16).

A prime example of a policy contributing to the production of vulgar landscapes are the substantial housing-related income tax benefits in the US. With some 40 million American households each claiming an average of $9,500 in mortgage interest deductions (MID) and almost $3,000 in property tax deductions in 2003, the subsidy of homeownership is indeed one of the most prominent features of the American tax code altogether (Gyourko and Sinai, 2003). Beyond the large spatial disparities with regard to their geographic incident, these subsidies also represent one of neoliberalism's many contradictions, the provision of 'hidden welfare' (Béland, 2007, p. 96 citing Christopher

Howard). Argued as a strategy of promoting home ownership, the MID instead protects the wealthy through substantial tax benefits on large homes.

The corporate welfare programmes that now exist in the US at federal, state, and local levels amount to a vast redirection of public moneys for corporate benefit (directly as in the case of subsidies to agribusiness and indirectly as in the case of the military-industrial sector), in much the same way that the mortgage interest rate tax deduction operates in the US as a subsidy to upper-income homeowners and the construction industry (Harvey, 2005, p. 165).

The National Housing Institute refers to the MID as the 'mansion subsidy' (Dreier, 1996). Among homeowners, only about half claim the deduction, and in 2006, the deduction was expected to cost the government $76 billion, with a little over half that benefit taken by just 12 percent of taxpayers, all with incomes of $100,000 or more (Lowenstein, 2006). The president's fiscal year 2010 budget estimates that the MID will cost the government about $131 billion, dwarfing the Department of Housing and Urban Development's budget of $48 billion (Toder et al, 2010). Further, contradictory to the 'owner-ship society', the MID actually does not encourage home ownership but rather encourages the purchase of larger homes, as 'the deduction serves mainly to increase housing consumption and to change the progressiveness of the tax code' (Glaeser and Shapiro, 2002, p. 4).

There have been several unsuccessful attempts to reduce or eliminate the MID, all being fiercely opposed by the real estate and construction industries. In 2007, Congressman John Dingell put forward legislation that would have eliminated the MID for homes over 3,000 square feet (Harney, 2007). He has since reworked his proposal to allow for a reduced deduction beginning for homes over 3,000 square feet, that diminishes in inverse proportion to home size and is eliminated completely for homes over 4,000 square feet (Dingell, 2008). Recently, President Obama also put forth a proposal to reduce the MID for wealthy homeowners (Christie, 2009). Only time will tell if the change will finally be made. At the same time, however, the Obama Administration announced a plan in February 2010 to direct $1.5 billion in taxpayer money to the five states hardest hit by the housing crisis to help them develop new programmes for addressing the housing crisis in their communities. It is perhaps not surprising that these very same states – California, Nevada, Arizona, Michigan and Florida – are among the largest net recipients of MID-related tax benefits and have seen the largest house price increases before the crisis.

> There are, no doubt, few markets that are not only so *truly constructed by the state*, particularly through the financial assistance given to private individuals, which varies in quantity and in the forms in which it is granted, favoring particular social categories, and consequently, particular fractions of builders to differing degrees (Bourdieu, 2005, p. 90).

The MID and other government-subsidies of home consumption through insured mortgages and the first-time homebuyer tax credit underscore Bourdieu's assertion.

Although home ownership has increased slightly over the past few decades from 61.9 percent in 1960 to 67.5 percent in 2009 and home size has substantially increased as shown above, home equity has remained stagnant (US Census Bureau, 2010b). Additionally, home-ownership rates have remained low among the lowest-fifth in terms of median income and among minorities (Carasso et al, 2005).

The ballooning of the subprime market in the last decade made home ownership more accessible but also adversely affected low-income buyers, sometimes resulting in negative amortizations where homeowners owe more than their homes are worth. In western parts of the country, the housing boom caused sleepy exurbs to morph into bustling communities almost overnight. For example, Surprise, Arizona, a small exurb of Phoenix with a population of about 500 in 1960, grew to a small metropolis of 100,000, with most of that growth occurring in the last decade. The exurb added more than 7,000 homes in 2005 alone. The bursting of the housing bubble and the following economic crisis have caused numerous foreclosures across the country. In Nevada, the foreclosure rate in late 2009 one in 23 homes, almost six times the average in the US (Inglis and Thompson, 2009). The 'ownership society' is now a rude joke to many who find themselves forced out of their homes.

3.4   The physical landscapes of metroburbia

Developers or 'place entrepreneurs' have profited under neoliberalism as the drive for conspicuous consumption and living large increased their profit margins. Not only did the size of the homes being built grow but so did the size of the developers' firms as a convergence effect resulted in the top ten builders capturing just over 25 percent of the national market in 2006. One reason for this consolidation is the availability and cost of land. Larger firms, many publicly-owned, are better able to acquire large parcels of land and navigate the bureaucratic and regulatory structures of local governments (Power, 2004b). Between 1990 and 2005, there was a 2,284 percent increase in lots controlled by 12 public builders (Butterfield, 2008a). As a corollary, smaller builders that cannot compete on such a scale must try to profit from higher-end floor plans (Power, 2004b). The large builders experienced record profits in the last decade with the top ten builders experiencing a growth in revenue from $21.6 billion in 1998 to $92.9 billion in 2005, as their market share grew from 9.40 percent to 20.97 percent in the same period (Butterfield, 2008a).

Another change to the building industry has involved the construction process itself. Deploying new technologies and refined production methods, big builders are able to reduce costs and push smaller and mid-sized firms further out of the market. Prefabrication means less is built on-site and more home components are mass-produced in factories. As one builder, Centex CEO Tim Eller, remarked, 'building homes is a manufacturing process' (Butterfield, 2008b). Using consumer segmentation techniques, builders can also create floor plans to meet every foreseeable demand, diminishing the need for customization of floor plans and features. This also allows firms to reduce their product variation to save money and remove complexity. For example, Pulte Homes reduced its floor plans from 2,200 to 600 (Kerwin, 2005). Moreover, the developers themselves do little real building, nearly all the physical work is contracted or subcontracted to electrical, framing, roofing, painting, masonry, and plumbing companies, many of which follow the big firms in itinerant fashion from development to development. These contractors do the actual building in accordance with the big firms' signature designs and management guidelines.

To disguise their efficiency-driven standards, the developers must increasingly enchant their products through marketing and branding. Through options and varied amenities, poetic naming and design, and community facilities, ranging from clubhouses to equine stables to conservation projects, developers can extend the '"Paradise Spell" of relentless individual aspiration and restless consumption' (Knox, 2008, p. 76). In Loudoun County, Virginia, one group of developers went so far as to create a 905-acre gated community, Creighton Farms, with a

Jack Nicklaus-designed golf course, home prices from the low $2 millions, and concierge service from the Ritz-Carlton Hotel Company.

Moreover, the building firms' process of enchantment retains traditional mythic meanings of home ownership and, within those broad parameters, appears to respect a heterogeneity of preference.

> Since the big industrial firms have never truly chosen the path of subversion and outright modernism, they are particularly noteworthy for the scale of the symbolic campaigns of transfiguration mounted by their commercial departments (particularly their advertising departments, but also their sales forces) in order to make good the potential gap between the product as actually supplied and perceived and the expectation of that product, and to convince clients that the product on offer is made for them and they are made for that product (Bourdieu, 2005, p. 54).

In periods of housing booms, like the recent one, when affluent home buyers consume the larger and more luxurious homes on offer, a moral landscape emerges that both echoes and reproduces the aesthetic, cultural, political, and economic values of a relatively small but culturally dominant class fraction.

As a result, the other major change in the housing supply, as mentioned above, has been sized. In 2005, the American Housing Survey found nearly 3.9 million homes in the US with 4,000 or more square feet of space, an increase of 35 percent since 2001. The big developers have led this trend. Centex Homes trademarked the phrases 'The Most Home for Your Money' and 'Big Homes, Little Prices', while Toll Brothers' best seller in 2005 was their 4,800 sq. ft. Hampton model. In response, some communities have sought to enact 'anti-McMansion' ordinances, usually applied to reconstruction of tear-downs that dwarf their neighbours. This move has continued despite the economic downturn when hampering any construction might be seen as a further blow to the building industry. For example, in 2008, Montgomery County, Maryland, enacted legislation to reduce home size by 14 percent on small lots and by 20 percent on half-acre lots. However, owners would still be able to build homes as big as 4,500 square feet on lots as large as 6,000 square feet (Marimow and Spivack, 2008). Similar ordinances have been enacted across the country, many in wealthier areas, such as Montgomery County, and even in parts of the country best associated with 'bling' lifestyles such as the City of Los Angeles and nearby Beverly Hills and Santa Monica.

The building industry has sustained some heavy hits due to the economic downturn. As of 2008, Pulte Homes had cut over 55 percent of its full-time workforce from its peak size (Butterfield, 2008b). In fact, more than half of the building firms have laid off employees since the downturn, reversing the trend of giant developers as companies with more than 50 people has shrunk to just 14 percent (Cushman, 2009). Almost all of the top ten builders experienced revenue losses over 20 percent from 2006 to 2007, some with losses around 40 percent. The revenue of the top ten builders crashed from a high of about $92 billion in 2005 to around $23 billion in 2009 according to Builder-Online. Analysts compare the current housing conditions to those of the 1930s, with housing starts in 2009 continuing to achieve record lows as spending on improvements to existing homes has exceeded new construction value (Crutsinger, 2009).

A scaling back of the size of builders and perhaps also homes may continue in the foreseeable future. Luxury has also taken a hit. For example, Creighton Farms, mentioned above, recently announced that the Ritz-Carlton hotel company would no longer be associated with the project, sad news for owners of the mostly unbuilt lots that hoped the company's presence would ensure some of the community's value. The original developers have since sold Creighton Farms, and a new developer plans to move ahead with a 'slightly less opulent' community (Kravitz, 2009).

Also in Loudoun County, Virginia, a jury awarded a family $4.75 million in a mold case, among the largest awards of its type in the state. The family had purchased a $900,000 home in 2005 from the Drees Co., a top 30 builder based in Kentucky, according to Builder Online. Complete with a wrought iron staircase, Brazilian cherry flooring, high ceilings, three fireplaces, and a major case of mold, the homeowners were forced to move from their dream home due to illness. The family's attorney argued that the builder had failed to supervise its subcontractors and had been indifferent to water intrusion during construction. The home is still owned by the family who believe it will cost $400,000 to ameliorate the mold problem (Mummolo, 2009). It therefore sits empty, not unlike other luxury homes that have failed to find a buyer as the realities of their overindulged size, pastiche styles, and sometimes poor construction can no longer be hidden behind mantras of 'more is more'. Currently, one in nine homes sits vacant in the US (El Nasser, 2009).

3.5   The social landscapes of metroburbia

In John Kenneth Galbraith's affluent society of the late 1950s, the rich were reluctant to be showy with their wealth. For Galbraith, the explanation was that luxury spending had become commonplace or vulgar. 'Lush expenditure could be afforded by so many that it ceased to be useful as a mark of distinction' (Galbraith, 1958, p. 92). If too many could afford a conspicuous level of material consumption, then showing one's wealth no longer signified distinction. The problem with affluence was that it had become too available. Fifty years have passed since Galbraith considered vulgarity passé or inutile. Arguably, in the past quarter century, vulgar affluence has made a comeback. This is readily seen in the landscapes of metroburbia where homes are tract mansions and starter castles of 4,000 square feet and upward, featuring two-storey entrance halls, great rooms, three- or four-car garages, huge kitchens, spa-sized bathrooms, his-and-hers room-sized master closets, media rooms, fitness centres, home offices, high-tech security systems, and perhaps even an au pair suite. Vulgaria's exterior residential styling deploys any kind of hybridized neotraditional motif as long as the street frontage is impressive, with high gabled roofs, unusually shaped windows, and architectural features such as turrets, bays, and porte-cocheres. The overall effect is an outlandish brashness of contrived spectacle, serial repetition, and over-the-top pretension. It is nouveau riche tackiness on an unprecedented scale.

If vulgarity disappeared because more people could afford to be vulgar, then perhaps its resurgence indicates that ostentatious living has once again become the privilege of the few. But while income inequality has dramatically increased in recent years, this greater division between the 'haves' and 'have nots' cannot fully explain, for example, the prevalence of McMansions in the built environment. So, then, why is flaunting one's wealth acceptable? To answer that we must consider what has accompanied the return of vulgarity: a neoliberal ideology that encourages material consumption among all and holds out conspicuous consumption as an ideal to be attained rather than resented. Further, if you do not have the financial wherewithal to afford a luxurious lifestyle, you can always charge it. A rise in consumer debt and a sharp reduction in savings has also accompanied this vulgar (re)turn.

The social landscapes of metroburbia have witnessed the birth of a new utopian form, the 'privatopia' (McKenzie, 1994). The lacuna created by the withdrawal of the state has been to some degree filled by homeowners associations (HOAs), resulting in a politics of privatism. Master-planned and often gated communities provide their own governance and their own 'public' services, ranging from schools to security. As '[n]eoliberalization has unquestionably rolled back the bounds of commodification and greatly extended the reach of legal contracts' (Harvey, 2005, p. 166), homeowners now accept covenants, controls, and restrictions that govern whether or not their back gate has worn their grass down too much. Functioning as parapolitical structures, the number of HOAs in the US has grown to almost 300,000, compared with fewer than 500 in the early 1960s and around 20,000 in the mid-1970s, according to the Community Associations Institute.

Community has been replaced with an avoidance of an exposure to 'otherness' (Sennett, 1990). Now a key sales feature, 'community' can be purchased rather than fostered. However, the enclaving of homogenous groups in gated-developments has not produced the positive effects of community. Rather, according to a national survey of residents of HOAs, although most respondents felt their developments were 'friendly', only 8 percent felt they were 'neighbourly and tight-knit', while 28 percent felt their neighbourhood was 'distant or private' in feeling (Blakely and Snyder, 1997).

At the same time, the distance between those 'forted up' and those outside these communities has increased. For example, in 1975, the most affluent 20 percent of American households accounted for just over 43 percent of aggregate household incomes, while the top 5 percent accounted for just over 16 percent. By 2005, the numbers were 50.4 percent and 22.2 percent, respectively. The average income of the top 20 percent increased from $96,189 in 1995 to $159,583 in 2005, in constant (2005) dollars. The average income of the top 5 percent rose from $145,968 to $281,155 (Knox, 2008).

Many Americans are unable to afford a home, let alone one in a gated community. In 2003, a study by the California Association of Realtors found that 70 percent of all home sales in the state were to repeat home buyers with incomes averaging $100,000 (Power, 2004a). Despite similar statistics across the country, little attention has been paid to the creation of affordable housing. Rather, in cities like Miami, Florida, existing affordable housing was torn down during the housing boom to make more room for luxury condos. Similarly, in the Washington, D.C. metro region, the share of affordable housing did not keep pace with the building boom and hovered around roughly 1 percent during the last decade (US Census Bureau, 2009). Further, the subprime mortgage market took advantage of lower-income buyers. Some activity in the area reached criminal levels. For example, one woman in Greenbelt, Maryland, scammed $16 million from homeowners and mortgage lenders from 2004 to 2007 (Cauvin, 2009a). A former stripper, the woman having since pled guilty to fraud, faces ten to 12 years in prison. During the heyday of her scheme, she spent

$800,000 on her wedding in 2006, with Patti LaBelle entertaining her guests, perhaps an exaggerated example of vulgaria's reach. In a similar story, a woman pled guilty to money laundering in Greenbelt, Maryland for her role in a $70 million mortgage fraud Ponzi scheme. Her employer, Metro Dream Homes, defrauded at least 1,000 people who invested money with the company in exchange for the promise that their mortgage would be paid down in five to seven years. In addition, the defendant admitted lying about her income to qualify for the purchase of a $200,000 Bentley. Two senior executives at Metro Dream Homes purchased Bentleys on a single day (Cauvin, 2009b).

In the midst of the economic crisis, it is reasonable to think that affordable housing would reemerge as a priority, especially with the recent rash of foreclosures. However, just the opposite is occurring. With homes sitting vacant on the market, communities are reluctant to make affordable housing a priority, fearing that it will only contribute to an increased over-saturation of supply. Prince William County in the D.C. metro region recently updated the housing chapter of its comprehensive plan, eliminating references to the county's need for more affordable housing (Mack, 2009). Similarly, Fairfax County, Virginia is considering scaling-back a popular affordable housing programme in an effort to reduce the county's budget (Somashekhar, 2009). By March 2009, foreclosure rates in parts of the D.C. metro region, particularly, in Northern Virginia, reached some of the highest levels in the nation with highs of 67 in 10,000, compared to 55, 81 or 156 in 10,000 in Florida, California or Nevada, respectively.

3.6   Conclusion

The roles of suburbia, now metroburbia, have been recast several times, as reflected in significant changes in the 'structures of building provision'. The suburbs have been reconceived from intellectual utopias to bourgeois utopias to degenerative utopias to conservative utopias each with a distinctive physical form and moral landscape. The re-enchanted conservative utopia of metroburbia offers the affluent upper-middle classes 'islands' of privacy, autonomy, stability, security and partition. What is enchanting about conservative utopia is not its appeal to social life but to exclusionary impulses and above all their self-identity as consumers.

While this ideal may only be attainable by a minority, it provides a landscape that consists not only of the built environment but also of an ensemble of material and social practices and symbolic representations that resonate across American society. Placemaking is an inherently elite practice, determined by those in control of resources. McMansions may only be affordable to the few, but they have a wider impact on the many. Situated within gated communities, their contribution to the landscapes of vulgaria along with the 'schlock-and-awe' urbanism embodied by other megastructures, such as megamalls and megachurches, amounts to a new moral geography that both echoes and tends to reproduce society's core values and performs vital functions of social regulation.

If suburbia ideally signified arcadian settings, community, and civic mindedness, post-suburbia, as seen in the metroburban form, reflects privacy and status. With private master-planned developments exempt from most municipal land-use planning regulations, an increasing amount of new residential fabric is likely to be framed within such developments, intensifying the arena of competitive consumption at the leading edge of metroburbia, deepening the sociospatial divisions within metropolitan regions as a whole, and seriously impeding any attempt at regional and metropolitan-wide planning. Whether the current economic crisis will restructure once more the metropolitan form remains to be seen. New construction continues to stall, and many Americans can no longer participate in conspicuous consumption to the degree that they could before. However, it seems unlikely that a short-term economic recession alone will alter the course of post-suburban development or the increasing separation of public and private life.

4
Post-suburbia and City-region Politics

Roger Keil and Douglas Young

4.1   Introduction

Robert Beauregard (2006) has noted that the suburbanization and fragmentation of cities effectively produced the metropolitan problematique. Since at least the Second World War, cities in North America and Europe, later also in other parts of the world, were physically extending into the surrounding regions, metabolically connecting into material streams way beyond that region, and economically into the national, and later international and world economies that constituted the roles played by each city-region in the international division of labour. A number of governance problems emerging from this extension have been widely researched. Since the 1950s, metropolitan regions or conurbations were the subject of a broad debate in geography, planning and political studies. While the community power literature continued to focus predominantly on the central city, metropolitan integration of services and consolidation became an important field of study. In the 1990s, the literature on the new regionalism added a considerable body of work. Scholars and practitioners working in this context commonly assume that city-region politics is mainly about the reconciliation of the metropolitan paradox: suburbanization leads to fundamentally different politics, socio-economics, socio-cultures, and socio-ecologies in the centres as opposed to the peripheries of cities, and the ensuing gulf between cities and suburbs needs to be addressed through territorial, functional or institutional policies and arrangements that narrow the gulf in socially just and environmentally sustainable ways (e.g. Dreier et al, 2001). Brenner (2002) and others (Boudreau et al, 2007) have critiqued this view of the regionalist problematic and introduced a broader notion of rescaling at the heart of the processes that characterize metropolitan expansion and contraction. Following in this line of argument, we advance the argument that current forms of post-suburban development are engaged in a complex, multi-rhythmic dance with the governance of city-region politics.

Painter (2008, pp. 343–345) distinguishes four strands of new regionalism literatures: 1. Research on economic geographies of industrial agglomeration, untraded interdependencies, clustering etc.; 2. Work on 'soft' institutional supports for regional development; 3. Investigations on the 'hard' institutions particularly of the state and 4. a mostly North American debate on the regional governance of expanding metropolitan regions. Painter discovers here a tendency to re-bind the (economically) unbound regions through political process and institution in talk of 'regional spaces' (the economic) and 'spaces of regionalism' (the political attempts/realities of constructing regionalism) (Jones and MacLeod, 2004, p. 435). There is a continuous tension here between notions of territorial boundedness and scales on one hand and more relational, scalar ideas of regional space. It is, in fact, from this ongoing tension that the need for political regulation of space emerges in the first place (MacLeod and Jones, 2007).

The uneven geography of emerging political spaces challenges existing schemes for both state intervention and activism at multiple scales. The extent to which one can speak of the emergence of a collective actor at the city-regional scale depends on the degree of consensus in each city-region about such diverging goals as – typically elite-driven – projects of international competitiveness, cultural and 'creative' strategies and megaprojects on one hand and social coherence on the other. As citizens object to further compromises to their living environments, they cross traditional urban/suburban, ethnic, racial and class divides. Ongoing social and technical infrastructure issues such as the control of sprawl, transportation gridlock, and the provision of water and sewerage services stretch the regional imagination and policy-making capacities of politicians, experts, corporations and activists across the urban region. Public health concerns are regionalized as cities are more vulnerable to global threats of pandemic disease and classical spatio-institutional arrangements for human security are tested. This happens in the context of the 'new normal' accentuating challenges in policy sectors such as public health, infrastructure, open space and human security (Ali and Keil, 2006).

Metropolitan governance has received increasing attention in the era of post-suburbia as cities spill over their traditional political and bioregional boundaries and as the cores of growing urban regions have become amorphous 'in-between cities' (Sieverts, 2003) without clear morphological and density delineations typical of the older separations of suburbs and inner cities (Teaford, 1997; Wu and Phelps, 2008). Post-suburbia relates to other conceptual approaches, among them exopolis (Soja, 1989), Edge Cities (Garreau, 1991; Teaford, 1997), Outer Cities (Herrington, 1984), Metroburbia (Knox, 2008), FlexSpace (Lehrer, 1994) and the Inverted Metropolis (Bloch, 1994). The new phase of post-suburbia is characterized by a 'composite picture' not least because of its global origins and divergences which include contradictory demographic development in older and newer suburbs; mixing of land uses, less predictable geographic form; new politics; new work-residence relations; and discordant mix of land uses (Wu and Phelps, 2008, pp. 465–467). For our purposes here, we use Sieverts' term 'in-between city' to denote aspects of this development.

We argue that in today's city-regional political socio-spatiality, politics will have to be found 'in-between' the old lines of demarcation. Following Tom Sieverts' (2003) advice to look at the 'in-between' cities that are neither old downtown nor new suburb but complex urban landscapes of mixed density, use and urbanity, we reveal the political vacuum that is at the heart of the urban region today. Political problems in today's metropolitan in-between city are co-generated by the failure of conventional political spaces and processes to capture the connectivities threaded through those places that are in-between the centre and exurbia. Using the examples of the Frankfurt and Toronto regions, we will show that attempts to regulate the space and governance of metropolitan expansion have produced their own sets of dynamic problems, which feed into the ways in which post-suburban spaces are developing. We will argue that it is critical to the understanding of city-region government in both cities to focus on the role of post-suburban 'in-between cities' (Sieverts, 2003) that explode the traditional, dichotomous notion of city and suburb and to find more integrated ways of politicizing regional or metropolitan problematiques of post-suburbia. A new politics for this in-betweenness now needs to be found as these spaces take over important functions in the overall regulation of the city. In the Toronto case, we concentrate on the specific vulnerabilities of areas that have been produced as marginal spaces since the 1970s. Housing and transportation issues there have been prisms and bottlenecks of infrastructure problems faced in the region overall. In the Frankfurt case, we look at how the city-region has begun to integrate by internalizing the demands of globalization that have been projected on the 'in-between spaces' of the region.

4.2 Urban politics and the void in-between: From polarity to hybridity

Urban politics is usually considered in two distinct locations: the *city* (understood in many ways in quite conventional centralist ways) and in the *suburb* (understood as spatially peripheral and politically at odds with the central city). At the metropolitan scale, the two types of urban politics are discussed in relation to one another. Institutions and processes of metropolitan politics reflect a rift and perpetual conflict around the issues that separate city and suburbs. In many ways, while the rhetoric of consensual regionalism has been pervasive in much of post-WW2 metropolitan policy-making, the reality has been less than that. Rather, typically, place entrepreneurs and local politicians have defended the interests of their particular jurisdictions against those of other jurisdictions. In a nutshell, these interests would have included attracting development, business and growth while lowering the service commitments of local government in any particular place and external-izing social, cultural and environmental cost to other places near or far (Logan and Molotch, 1987). At the heart of the urban region's 'struc-tured coherence' (Harvey, 1989a) is a definition of boundaries (how far out will public transit go? How will this land be zoned?), the techno-logical mix (will highways or tramways be built? Will our high rise housing be 'green'?), the socio-ecological relationships (will water be privatized?) and similar issues that belong to the quotidian and long-term planning and service concerns of municipal and regional gov-ernance. Tom Sieverts (2003) recognizes the particular need for politics and planning to deal with the specific voids and silences that are pro-duced through and by the emergence of the in-between city. He notes explicitly that decision-makers need to counteract the isolating ten-dencies of the *Zwischenstadt* (p. 71) and takes the 'anaesthetic' environ-ment of the *Zwischenstadt* as the starting point for a new politics and planning ethos. He notes that the in-between city is:

> the result of countless rational singular decisions from different times which produce a seemingly irrational result. Historical traces that appear to stem from preindustrial times sit besides monuments of old industry and are increasingly dominated by the large containers of the globally operating economy: in-between, there are 'soft' little

defined interim uses in small scale and, of course, the vast, uniform single family home areas (Sieverts, 2007, p. 8).

Sieverts goes on to outline the many contradictions that beset the *Zwischenstadt* and notes the particular problem of having a very structured environment where rapid social change occurs (the in-between city is built up and resistant to change but populations will get poorer and older and transportation will be more expensive). The fractal and fragmented character of the *Zwischenstadt* poses challenges to planning but it also offers inevitable opportunities as the in-between city is more and more an image of the society in which we live. Public and private infrastructures will reflect societal contradictions: automobile traffic and transit, gated communities and tower blocks will be part of a general and overall spectrum of metropolitan solutions to transportation and housing. Sieverts asks whether those contradictions will stand in anarchic chaos or whether they will allow for a regional federalism of spatial distribution? (Sieverts, 2007, pp. 11–12).

In-betweenness is a metaphor which signifies that no fixed boundaries may exist to separate collective and individual identities in 'essential' or 'natural' ways. Sieverts confirms that 'cultural plurality is a positive characteristic of the *Zwischenstadt*' (2003, p. 52). Hybridity and creolization are important concepts through which to understand the post-colonial world in which many communities find themselves today (Bhabha, 1994; Goonewardena and Kipfer, 2004). Bhabha, for example, takes 'the cultural and historical hybridity of the post-colonial world...as the paradigmatic place of departure' for looking at our world today (1994, p. 21). It is in these less than determined spaces 'in-between' where urbanizing societies also develop the social spaces in which hybridity is cultivated through a mix of (exclusionary) state or corporate practices and (liberating or accommodating) popular activities. In a related argument, Yiftachel speaks of 'gray cities', places 'positioned between the "whiteness" of legality/approval/safety, and the "blackness" of eviction/destruction/death' (2009, p. 89). While conditions in Frankfurt's or Toronto's in-between city don't compare easily with those found in Palestine, which serves as Yiftachel's area of study, hybridity of this kind is potentially deadly, not a safe space, a space of vulnerability, invisibility and powerlessness. Yiftachel notes that '[g]ray spaces contain a multitude of groups, bodies, housing, lands, economies and discourses, lying literally 'in the shadow' of the formal, planned city, polity and economy' (2009, p. 89). We can also evoke here the complex of issues that Ananya Roy has recently summarized under the title 'exurbanity and extraterritoriality' which point towards some form of hybridity between urban and national spaces where identities are formed in complex layered interactions (2009, pp. 827–828).

We add to this line of arguments a new twist, which we take specifically from the more recent literature that attempts to explain the politics of peripherality and marginality in Europe and the United States. Our argument here is that the relationships between spatial centre and periphery and social core and margin – broadly defined – are somewhat *path dependent, place-specific and dependent on a specific logic of policy, planning and politics in situ*. Our starting point for this discussion is the 'comparative sociology of advanced marginality' offered by Loïc Wacquant (2008). In his work on the American ghetto and the French banlieue, Wacquant observes that 'the declining urban periphery of France and the African-American ghetto constitute two disparate sociospatial formations, produced by different institutional logics of segregation and aggregation, which result in sharply higher levels of blight, isolation and hardship in America's dark ghetto' (2008, p. 5). While the American ghetto is a product of 'a gamut of racially skewed and market-oriented state policies that have aggravated, packed and trapped poor blacks at the bottom of the spatial order of the polarized city', marginalization in the French banlieue (the Red Belt) 'is primarily the product of a class logic, in part redoubled by ethnographic origin and in part *attenuated* by state action' (2008, p. 5). Whereas the state seems all but absent in the American ghetto (if one disregards the penal state), 'the French urban periphery is typified on the contrary by a fundamentally *heterogeneous* population according to ethnonational provenance (and, secondarily, class position), whose isolation is mitigated by the strong presence of public institutions catering to social needs' (2008, p. 5). While the state is absent in the ghetto, it seems, it is all over the banlieue by contrast. In our analysis of the in-between city and its politics in Toronto and Frankfurt, we start from the assumption that the situation we encounter there is very much a mix of the two extremes. In fact, where Wacquant (2008) sees a fundamental difference between the ghetto in the United States, which is a space vacated by the state, and the French banlieue, a space entirely occupied and produced by state action, we would point to the in-between city we study as a mixed product of both, state presence and state retreat, but clearly also of popular action (see Young and Keil, 2011 for an extended version of this argument). The in-between city in Toronto is a combination of obsolescence and overburdening through the (local) state.

In posing this hypothesis, we take Wacquant's work partly literally, and partly figuratively. We take it *literally* in two ways: First, we acknowledge that the in-between city is a product of very decisive state action as infrastructures of housing and transportation have been laid out through the area in planned and sometimes authoritarian ways. These actions have unfolded over the past 60 years as a mix of, at first, Fordist-Keynesian and, later, post-Fordist state interventions. But we also note that the in-between city is a place of rampant market activity as developers and place entrepreneurs at various scales have imprinted their profit interests on the landscape. Secondly, we note that the production of marginality (and hence, in the Lefebvrian sense also centrality) in a period of advanced neoliberalization is a somewhat predictable set of processes which can be studied along a register of welfare state retreat/destruction, market-oriented policy, etc. which are somewhat similar in advanced capitalist countries but also different as argued here. In this sense, Canada/ Toronto and Germany/Frankfurt are located in the mid-range of a scale in which France/Paris and USA/Chicago are extremes. This has to do with the traditionally mixed social and capitalist economy in Toronto and the particular corporate global city political economy in Frankfurt.

But we also take Wacquant's argument *figuratively* in the sense that no place of marginality is on its own but that we can learn a lot by looking at 'the *function* it performs for the broader metropolitan system' (2008, p. 11) of whose contradictions it is a product. When we look at marginal spaces in the in-between city, then, we are particularly interested in their connectivity or disconnectivity and resulting vulnerabilities for the populations there. We are more interested in the politics that have both constructed and avoided, overlooked and forgotten (intentionally or not) those spaces in-between. We are also interested in how the ghettoized, marginalized spaces and institutions of the in-between city relate to other spaces in their *spatial* proximity which define them by their *social* difference from them. This will lead us to concluding that the production of marginality in the in-between city is a function of complex interrelationships with the old centre (downtown) and the new centres in the outer periphery, the glamour zones of the Toronto and Frankfurt regions' blubber belts.

In an era of splintering urbanism (Graham and Marvin, 2001) the in-between areas we study both have too much and too little infrastructure. There are spaces that are hyperconnected, fast and expensive in close proximity to spaces that are not connected, slow and cheap. We need to take into account the politics that produced such contradictions and the ways in which infrastructures have been designed with the result that residents and users either 'get stuck' in marginality (housing or transit as an example) or they get connected to other prime networked spaces (easy to get from Toronto's suburb Vaughan by car to the international airport, for example).

Lastly, immigration is absolutely central to the structuring of space in the in-between city and increasingly its politics. This creates its own hybridities and mixities that express themselves politically. Four ways are mentioned here: 1. The increasing concentration of racialized immigrants in tower housing in the old suburbs in Toronto and the emergence of enclaves of foreigners in less desirable areas of the Frankfurt region; 2. The rapid increase of immigration from South Asia, East Asia and other new centres of migration to the single family home suburbs surrounding the Toronto neighbourhoods characterized by tower housing; this finds its equivalent in the concentration of Turkish home ownership in places like Raunheim under the flight path of the Frankfurt airport; 3. The concentration of students from immigrant families at educational organizations and in apprenticing shops in the suburbs; and 4. The concentration of immigrant labour in the low-wage service sectors and industrial manufacturing in the in-between city.

4.3   In-between politics in Toronto

Sixty years of state and market activity have generated a contradictory landscape of connectivity and disconnectivity (see Boudreau et al, 2009 for an overview of Toronto regional politics). Transportation and housing have been particularly important networks of infrastructure in the socio-spatial shaping of Toronto's in-between city. The proximity and overlay of fast and hyper-connected with slow (or stuck) and disconnected is often startling. For example, the premium Highway 407, originally built by the Province of Ontario but subsequently sold to a multi-national private consortium, offers fast east-west travel to toll-paying drivers. A few kilometres to the south the publicly-owned non-tolled Highway 401 runs roughly parallel to 407 but, as the busiest highway in Canada, promises rush hour congestion. Ironically, while both highways provide travel routes through the in-between city, they create quite significant barriers to any non-automobilized north-south travel within the study area. Indeed, it is hard to imagine a more inhospitable pedestrian journey than along an arterial road that crosses Highway 407 and passes through an adjacent major hydro-electric power corridor (see Map 4.1).

Map 4.1   Map of a portion of Toronto's in-between city indicating its complex landscape

The 407/hydro corridor is widely perceived as the physical divide between 'inside' and 'outside' within Toronto's in-between city. The districts just inside this divide are home to substantial and increasing numbers of poor households and stagnant job growth; just outside is the realm of middle-income families and a landscape of post-Fordist industry. Public transit networks in the Toronto region largely operate either inside (the Toronto Transit Commission or TTC) or outside (e.g. York Region Transit) with few north-south links providing connections between, for example, unemployed youth in priority neighbourhoods to the south and potential employment in vast employment districts to the north.[1] Current proposals for improved transit would do little to improve those sorts of connections. For example, the Spadina Subway extension will be routed through York University and on to a future yet-to-be-developed mixed-use office/residential node in the City of Vaughan. While it will somewhat improve the connectedness of the residents of the impoverished Jane-Finch district (which lies to the west of the university) it is noteworthy that the subway is not to be routed through the heart of that district nor to the industrial districts farther north. Instead the 60,000 students and workers at York University and the future thousands of office workers in the Vaughan Corporate Centre are to be connected; the 60,000 residents of Jane-Finch and the thousands of factory workers in Vaughan aren't.

In-between the prime networked spaces in the in-between city low-income single parents will continue to travel with their infants in strollers on overcrowded buses operated by an underfunded public transit system on pot-holed streets. They will do so in sight of huge tractor-trailer trucks fitted with state-of-the-art GPS that are monitored 24/7 from a nationally important logistics complex. Above the slowly moving buses a steady stream of aircraft prepare to land at Toronto Pearson International Airport, recently rebuilt at a cost of $4.4 billion (Keil and Young, 2008).

Transportation

Until approximately 1980 all transportation planning and funding in the Toronto region was premised on the concept of the region having one pre-eminent centre. Downtown Toronto, it was assumed, would continue to play its role as the location of most office employment, as well as of major hospitals, institutions of post-secondary education, major cultural facilities, high end shopping, and major sports venues. A change in planning policy roughly 30 years ago proposed instead the creation of a polycentric urban structure with three suburban downtown nodes outside of downtown Toronto. Additions to the subway system were seen as crucial to implementing this vision of a new urban

---

[1]The City of Toronto has identified 13 neighbourhoods of heightened social deprivation. These so-called priority neighbourhoods are recipients of new neighbourhood-based state interventions and strategic spending initiatives in the realms of education, recreation, social welfare, and policing.

structure; they would link the three suburban downtowns and down-town Toronto as a network of premium spaces.

After several changes of provincial government and funding formulas (in the late 1990s the provincial government reduced its support to capital and operating transit budgets to zero), and the re-ordering of the priority list of proposed suburban subway extensions, one piece of the new network of suburban downtown subway links was completed in 2002. The $1 billion 6 km long Sheppard subway lines runs east from North York Centre in the direction of Scarborough Centre. It was widely considered a 'subway to nowhere' at the time of its completion as it was routed under a suburban arterial road lined with single storey buildings and only reached the half way point to Scarborough Centre. Full-length station platforms were built but knock out walls were installed to shorten the platforms to match the length of shorter than normal trains that are run on this route due to low ridership levels. Substantial redevelopment has occurred in the past few years along the Sheppard line but its perceived waste of precious transit dollars fuels a persistent belief that all suburban subway extensions are 'subways-to-nowhere'.

A regional commuter network of train and bus routes was created by the province in 1967 and called GO (for government of Ontario) Transit. Its hub is Union Station in the City of Toronto's Financial District, the prime space that virtually all routes radiate from. All of the system routes slice through, and some stations are located in, the in-between city, however, the system is geared primarily to connecting distant suburban and exurban residents with jobs in downtown Toronto. Stations are placed several kilometres apart to make the 50 or 80 km journey bearable to the long distance commuter. The in-between city is largely perceived by GO commuters as a grey zone to be passed through as quickly as possible on the way to and from home and work, with iPods helping to further the disconnect between rider and the in-between city's banal visual landscape sliding by outside the train and bus. Funding of GO has been the subject of ever-changing relationships between the province and local municipalities, however, in the Canadian federal government's stimulus spending announced in February, 2009 in response to the economic crisis of 2008–09, GO Transit became the recipient of $175 million earmarked for the creation of parking lot expansion at suburban stations.

The latest attempt at a regional transportation planning authority is an agency established by the province called Metrolinx. In late 2008 it announced an ambitious $50 billion 25 year regional transportation

plan premised on previous commitments from the provincial government of $11.5 billion in transit funding and $6 billion from the
federal government. The balance of $32.5 billion to fund years 8–25 of
the Metrolinx plan have yet to be committed. Debate leading up to the
release of the Metrolinx plan mirrored, in some ways, tensions in the
1950s and 60s regarding TTC service. Should new funds be distributed
on the basis of existing per capita ridership (which would favour the
City of Toronto and its TTC) or should they be distributed on the
basis of per capita population (which would favour the rapidly growing outer suburbs in the Greater Toronto Area and their local transit
authorities)? In the end the Metrolinx plan proposes an amalgam of
the two approaches. Thus the TTC's Transit City project to construct
several new light rail lines through many parts of the in-between city
would be funded, as would enhancement of the VIVA bus transit network, a premium system (buses are equipped with wireless internet)
provided as a subsidiary of York Region Transit in conjunction with
private partners.

It is widely recognized in the Toronto region that public transit has
suffered from many years of underfunding coupled with the lack of
any regional coordination of service. In summary, transportation infrastructure in Toronto's in-between city in the early twenty-first century
can be considered a palimpsest of 60 years of multi-scalar action and
inaction by state agencies in varying relationships with the market and
civil society.

Housing

In 1954, the federal and provincial governments expropriated 655 acres
of farmland in the north west part of Toronto with the intention of
developing 3,000 low cost homes. In 1961 a large portion of the land
assembly was transferred to the recently established York University
for development as a university campus, and a small portion of the
assembly was sold to the Toronto and Region Conservation Authority
on which it developed Black Creek Pioneer Village. The remaining
90 acres were later developed as an experimental modernist housing
project called Edgely Village.

The large-scale roll-out of public housing in Toronto was made possible by changes to the National Housing Act in 1964 which substantially ramped up financial support for public housing. Whereas,
in all of Canada, only 12,000 units of public housing had been
built between 1949 and 1963, almost 200,000 units of government-
owned housing were built between 1964 and 1973 (Hulchanski, 2004,

pp. 180–181). In Ontario, public housing for families was developed, owned and administered by the Ontario Housing Corporation (OHC) which was established in 1964 to coincide with the NHA amendments. OHC built in municipalities that invited them to do so, and many of the growth-supportive suburban municipalities within Toronto did just that. By the early 1970s many parts of suburban Toronto contained relatively substantial amounts of public housing. All of these projects housed only low income households and many were developed according to classic modernist urban design principles: Vehicles and pedestrians were separated and many dwellings were provided in high rise housing in order to free up greenspace and to create a more 'urban' experience of everyday life. One of the iconic modernist developments of the 1960s was Edgely Village. An unusual characteristic of Edgely was its mixing of private and public sector housing in adjacent blocs (Young, 2006).

It is ironic that the socio-spatial landscapes of places like Edgely Village, which were representative of enlightened social policy and leading urban design and architectural thinking in the mid-1960s, would be subject to savage repudiation just a few short years later. The approach to affordable housing – 100 percent Rent-geared-to-income (RGI) housing for all low-income households in large projects initiated by senior government – was rejected. Changes to the NHA made in 1973 introduced funding for a different kind of social housing – small projects of mixed income households initiated from within communities (by municipal housing companies, by ethno-cultural groups, or by non-profit co-operatives). The modernist site planning principles were rejected in favour of revaluing the traditional patterns of cities and high-rise living was demonized. As a consequence of the post-modern turn in planning and urban design, large sections of Toronto's present-day in-between city bear the reputation of being the product of 'bad planning'.

Dramatic changes occurred in the arena of social housing in the mid-1990s. One of the first acts of the neoliberal provincial government elected in June, 1995 was to cancel all social housing programmes. In 1998 the Metro Toronto federation was amalgamated into the single megacity of Toronto and many provincial service responsibilities were downloaded onto municipal governments, including social housing.[2] The new City of Toronto created the Toronto Community Housing Company (TCHC) to act as the local housing authority and landlord to 165,000 tenants in 58,000 dwellings. TCHC acknowledges that

---

[2]Metro Toronto was established as a two tier regional government in 1954.

its current maintenance backlog is several hundred million dollars. The underinvestment in building maintenance of their communities contributes to their stigmatization and marginalization.

The condo frenzy of the late 1990s and early 2000s in Toronto eventually reached several sites in the in-between city, even places that are negatively associated with the planning 'mistakes' of the 1960s. Near York University, for example, two proposals for approximately 1,000 condo units each have been announced. In contrast to those parts of the in-between city that lie within the boundaries of the City of Toronto, the much newer housing developments outside of the city have almost entirely been created by the private sector. Such places present landscapes of tens of thousands of owner-occupied detached single family dwellings. They also present a striking contrast, visually and in terms of housing tenure, to the modernist era neighbourhoods in Toronto (see Figures 4.1 and 4.2). Their explosive growth has been backed up by housing policies of successive federal governments that favour home ownership including capital gains tax exemption on the sale of principal dwellings. Such communities have begun to witness

Figure 4.1   Low density detached ownership housing in the City of Vaughan (photograph, Doug Young)

Figure 4.2   High-rise rental housing in the Jane Finch neighbourhood in the City of Toronto (photograph, Doug Young)

a growing affordability crisis which is partially met by the creation of illegal dwellings in basements of houses. While Canada has largely avoided a subprime mortgage crisis, there are signs of some instability (house values declined in 2008 and 2009 then rose in 2010; volume of sales declined sharply in 2010) and in hot markets (Toronto and Vancouver, for example) fear of an impending burst of the real estate bubble is constant.

Coming back to Wacquant's conceptualizations of French banlieue and American ghetto and the presence/absence of the state in urban social and physical environments, we consider Toronto's in-between city to be a messy mix of public and private. This was true in the initial development of what is now the in-between city and continues to be true today both in an active sense, but also in an embedded sense (urban legacies). Sixty years of varying state and market activity (and we have focused on the realms of transportation and housing infrastructure) have co-generated the connectivities and disconnectivities of the in-between city.

4.4 Governing across the in-between city in Frankfurt

Frankfurt is one of the prime examples of Sieverts' understanding of the in-between city. In fact, a schematic representation of the region is the image used for the front cover of the German original of his *Zwischenstadt* (2003).[3] The polycentric landscape of Frankfurt-Rhine-Main presents a specific mix of challenges in transportation infrastructure and offers a broad palette of housing choices but also of potential ghettos and enclaves. Inside the Frankfurt region, polycentricity is an often acknowledged condition of governance (Hall and Pain, 2006) (see Map 4.2) In the Frankfurt case, polycentricity is the official policy and stated objective of almost every published document. In reality, such public doctrine belies the existing dissimilarity of the city of Frankfurt with all other cities and communities in the region, a dissimilarity which has often plagued political institutionalization of regionalism as discussed above. In practical terms, the region has been built from the inside out through the networking of social service provision and economic development as well as political institutions across the always oscillating territorial image of where Frankfurt Rhine-Main

---

[3]This section is based on a series of expert interviews conducted by Roger Keil in Frankfurt in 2008.

Map 4.2   Map of the Frankfurt region (land use)

Source: Planungsverband Ballungsraum Frankfurt/Rhein-Main 2010:2

begins and ends. The consolidation of the regional regime has taken place around a set of infrastructure and service issues including the provision of hard services such as waste removal but also cultural policy. The subtext is not just governance reform through technical efficiencies but also neoliberal state retrenchment in areas that are costly to government. While these arrangements created the conditions for a certain pacific- ation of the highly politicized regional debate in the Frankfurt region, it did not lay to rest issues of intra-regional coordination of service agen- cies, cost equalization and social redistribution. In some cases, it actually hid or increased tendencies for socio-economic segregation and different- iation among cities and communities in terms of their ability to sustain required service levels for their populations (schools, elder care, etc.).

We propose to characterize Frankfurt Rhine-Main's current philo- sophy and praxis of regionalism as 'internal(ized) globalization'. This means in the first place that globalization as a process has been taken for granted, and has been internalized and largely accepted by actors in the regional political process. This is different from the 'glocalization' (Swyngedouw, 1997) processes of the 1980s and 1990s when the global had to be first established as a discursive and real space in which cities and communities in the region were operating. But the concept also entails that when globalization is accepted as the general condition of existence for jurisdictions today, the work of globalization is done in and by the local and regional regimes. This is different from the frantic attempts of previous years to dress the region up for regional competition (based on the – questionable – assumption that such competition is decided in circuits external to the region. There is now a certain resigned, or relaxed *Gelassenheit* (equanimity) in the discourse of regionalism in Frankfurt. This shift has been supported by institutional, ideological and political moves on the regional stage. Much of this process takes place in the interstices of the spaces that are usually privileged, in the in-between cities that provide the flexibility in land use that the internalization of globalization requires. The shift can be traced through political, economic, social and environmental processes where it has taken hold. 'Internalized globalization' relies on a few preconditions that were created earlier. During the 1980s and 1990s the Frankfurt global city-region experienced a double opening that facilitates the 'internalized globalization' of the region today:

1) the central city economy opened towards the region: the global city went to 'the countryside' as its infrastructural functions (airport, water, transportation) extended beyond the political boundaries of the core municipality. In a strange and somewhat unpredictable recent point to that development, even the Frankfurt Stock Exchange, long almost synonymous with the city's financial prowess, moved its main operations to the edge city of Eschborn; and

2) the global economy: world city formation in Frankfurt was to a large degree a deliberate process set in train by an aggressively internationally-oriented regime which intended and went to work integrating Frankfurt into the extant flows of international investment, capital and service delivery. A recent 'think piece' produced for the Mayor expresses this well:

> The idea of a 'NetworkCity' Frankfurt Rhine-Main is based on the essential core of the small German *Global City*, which draws its significance in the first place from its integration into international, national and regional nets. One peculiarity of Frankfurt is that Frankfurt more than other German cities reflects the idea of networking in its built, functional and ideational constitution. The vision of a

NetworkCity concentrates on the positive opportunities for development of Frankfurt in the context of a polycentrally structured region (AS&P, 2009, p. 15).

Municipal and regional politics have been seen as either supportive of or even generative of developments that would facilitate the integration of Frankfurt as a place into those (not always well defined) networks and in-between spaces where they are found. Some network aspects are taken for granted: the airport, the international fairground, the financial industry, the famous *'Finanzplatz'* Frankfurt, clearly buttressed by the decision to make the Main metropolis the seat of the European Central Bank, which has made the city the core of the Euro financial economy. Others are more hidden and less visible: the amateur sports and multicultural entertainment networks, the bioregional infrastructure of the regional park (Regionalpark), for example.

The multiplicity of Frankfurt Rhine-Main, of its cities and communities, is considered a major strength in the international competition of regions and regional planning which is geared towards supporting the networked division of labour and the 'cooperation (*Zusammenspiel*) of all actors' in the region (Planungsverband, 2005, p. 5). The focus is clearly on segmented integration of land uses and people. The region 'has always been interesting for people of many nations' and has been 'open to the world and liberal'. But it is also 'family friendly' and strives towards presenting a high quality of life: 'culture, urban spaces, recreational areas' (Planungsverband, 2005, p. 5). This and other planning documents play down Frankfurt's centrality. Like the global competition in which the region allegedly finds itself, the core functions of Frankfurt are taken for granted and remain unchallenged. This points to a recalibration of the regime towards an internal process of dialogue and conversation – as well as dispute and conflict – among the 200 cities and communities and countless civic groups and enterprises that make up the region's polity. The appeal for unity among diversity is the predominant programmatic thread that can be seen throughout documents that deal with regional planning and policy. It can also be heard in the statements, public and private, of regional actors.

In social terms, the region has accepted and, at the surface, has embraced its multicultural character. But the planning images for the region and the politics that produce urban and regional space and infrastructure speak a language of segregation and of 'us and them'. Frankfurt continues to emphasize its place in the globalized region as embedded and localized:

> Both the economic orientation and the social reality of the region Frankfurt Rhine-Main are clearly marked as global. At the regional scale, it is even more important what is also true for Frankfurt to a lesser degree: the strength of the internationality must be grounded in place, tied in also into a regionally oriented economic and service structure, into an old cultural landscape. City and region become liveable (*'lebenswert'*) not predominantly through their international networking but through qualities in situ. To find this balance between external orientation and inner strength can only be found in the region in a joint effort and in fair cooperation (AS&P, 2009, p. 14; see also Reiss-Schmidt, 2003, p. 387).

Internalized globalization and the role of the region's in-between city in it can be empirically studied in the fields of transportation and housing which are sketched in the next few paragraphs.

Transportation

The Frankfurt region experiences a host of growth related transportation problems that are to a varying degree governed by regional institutions. There is a strong consensus in the region for an extension of existing infrastructures although there is conflict, for example, over the expansion of the airport which is among the prime issues that have to be administered or governed by regional institutions in coordination with communities at one end and higher orders of government at the other. There are generally two points of view: 'Those who favor the expansion view it as vital of the economic integration of the area into the global economy. Those who oppose it see it as a potential source of health and ecological hazards' (Garcia-Zamor, 2001, p. 417; Geis, 2002). The earlier extension of the western runway, *Startbahn West*, in the 1980s changed the political landscape of the region fundamentally and was a major factor in the structuration of the in-between city south and west of the city. The current extension in the north has been an eight-year megaprocess of public participation, negotiation, mediation and political conflict. The public consultation has seen 127,000 formal objections against the new runway and governmental involvement at all levels. The expansion of the airport is increasingly seen as a questionable enterprise as the economic crisis takes its toll on passenger and freight transportation, and the

Figure 4.3   Frankfurt region southwest view from the city centre (photograph, Roger Keil)

extension is considered a major factor in future socio-spatial discrepancies as communities close to the airport become immigrant enclaves due to falling housing prices (Erlenbach, 2009) (see Figure 4.3).

In contrast to Toronto, public transit has been a regional success story which has integrated the complex labour market of the region. While the peripheral areas of the region are losing employment and population, the regional transportation association RMV has been attempting to create access of remote peripheral regions to the centralized (Frankfurt-oriented) network of public transit in the increasingly decentralizing region.

Housing

The infrastructural and economic development plans in the region have direct impacts on the availability and quality of housing. The expansion of the airport, for example, is predicted to have a direct effect on those residential areas in the flight path, for example in Raunheim, where noise is an issue and ghettoization tendencies are considered a possibility. In this way, the regulation of marginalized housing in the flight path of an expanded airport will be central to the logistical coherence of the Frankfurt region (Erlenbach, 2009; *Darmstädter Echo*, 2009). As the central city continues to experience traditional and new built gentrification, housing for lower income families, and in particular immigrants, has been pushed into less desirable locations in the region such as high rise tower blocks and areas affected by environmental problems such as noise from air traffic. Political actors clearly see this as the central issue of the in-between city's housing landscape. The City of Frankfurt builds new housing in peripheral areas outside of its jurisdiction and in the city but there is no conception or expectation that this housing may be occupied by lower income families or migrants. Frankfurt is the only city in the region that still builds social housing while the peripheral communes have stopped this activity. ABG Frankfurt, the City of Frankfurt's housing and real estate corporation is seen to play a positive role in the region and its activities in building social housing in the region is considered a plus.

4.5 Conclusion: Where is the politics of infrastructure in the in-between city?

Where, then, is politics in the in-between city? In this paper, we have put forward the argument that the conventional city-suburb distinction which has produced understandings of urban regimes and regional and metropolitan structured coherences in which politics were contained, had particular blind spots. Those blind spots, voids of sorts, were where the city nurtured a particular mix of state and market policies and politics. In the in-between city, we see the proximity of single family house privatism and public housing estates, backyards and mega highways, universities and problem schools, woodlots and parking lots, parks and production sites. This endless mix is more or less a reflection of today's post-suburban metropolis but neither political form nor political process of the urban are currently aligned with its socio-spatial and socio-ecological realities. Politics of what, with Sieverts, we have called the *Zwischenstadt*, is produced by myriad rational processes to result in an anaesthetic and seemingly irrational mix of social and spatial realities.

Working empirically, albeit sketchily, through the splintering infrastructures of housing and transportation in the in-between cities of Toronto and Frankfurt, we ultimately arrive at a sense of the place of politics which is very much in line with recognizing the in-between city as the real-political centre, from which the peripheries of downtown and exurb will need to be rethought and re-politicized.

In Toronto, we have seen how the in-between city is just awakening as both a site and a target of policy as well as an arena of contested politics. Both marginalized subsections of the highly mixed in-between landscape of post-suburbia in Toronto, and traditionally suburban areas are experiencing extreme perturbations as two processes collide. On the one hand, there is continued growth, mostly in the form of sprawl, that puts municipalities in post-suburbia on a collision course with larger goals of sustainability and regional planning; on the other hand – and exacerbated in the current crisis – the once powerful job machine of the suburban belt has started to stutter and there are huge issues related to shrinkage, deindustrialization and employment loss that now characterizes the in-between city. The centralization, even the multi-centralization of infrastructures (housing and transportation) has continued to bypass large parts of an increasingly immigrant and often poor crescent of neighbourhoods in the old suburban belt of Toronto. How these can be tied back into the regional political universe will be a central concern of future politics in Toronto's post-suburbia.

In Frankfurt Rhine-Main, the specific set of political actors and institutions has guided the region's insertion into global streams under the guidance of their own ideological, territorial idiosyncrasies. The regionalized growth machine or regional regime includes state, economic and civic actors and its actions are contested by oppositional forces in and outside the ruling elite alliance. Larger processes like globalization and neoliberalization which structure post-suburban development have been shown to be determined by the constraints set for them by collective actors at the urban and regional scale. The post-suburban region is constituted 'politically and reproduced through everyday acts and struggles around consumption and social reproduction' (Jonas and Ward, 2007, p. 170; Roy, 2009). Globalization in the Frankfurt region is not a steady expansion of its aggressive and programmatic deterritorialized insertion into the flows and institutions of global capitalism. Frankfurt's regional political actors seem to want to strive towards re-focusing the region's economic, social and environmental policies around questions of quality of life. It is clear that this new focus has had its own problems as internal differentiation/globalization has ceased to be recognized as a challenge and has become the basis for a classed and racialized segregation of the region in which privileges and disadvantages are distributed at a regional scale.

What we have found in both Toronto and Frankfurt is the need to transcend the illusion of the region as bounded territory (Amin, 2004) with likewise bounded politics which needs to be opened up and reassembled through the metaphorical but also the real sense of in-betweenness that engenders political constitution of social space.

But such a politics also recognizes the constraints of the jumbled, anaesthetic environments of the *Zwischenstadt* as the true playgrounds of a new and potentially productive politics of the urban region.

Acknowledgements

Research has been funded by a grant sponsored under the Peer Reviewed Research Studies (PRRS) program of Infrastructure Canada. Some financial support was also provided by Toronto Community Housing Company, one of the community partners to the project. This chapter also bene-fitted from research sponsored by a standard SSHRC grant on metro-politanization in Toronto, Montreal, Frankfurt and Paris.

Part II
Post-suburbia in the Americas

5
Post-suburban Regionalism: From Local Politics of Exclusion to Regional Politics of Economic Development

Andrew E.G. Jonas

5.1   Introduction

The suburbs seem to occupy a contradictory position in the wider politics of space in the United States (US). One dominant view in the literature is that suburbs are local spaces of exclusion (Danielson, 1976). Suburban voters – often categorized mainly but not exclusively as white and middle or upper income – elect leaders who, in their turn, use local land use authority to keep out locally unwanted land uses and incomers, thereby enhancing the local tax base and protecting local services and property values. This local exclusionary politics produces an intense fragmentation of metropolitan political space which, in turn, contributes to a variety of metropolitan governance challenges. For the most part, solutions to these challenges have involved developing closer inter-jurisdictional relationships between neighbourhoods, suburbs and central cities (Downs, 1981). Nevertheless, despite years of attempts to 'open up the suburbs' to non-whites and lower income households (Downs, 1973), local jurisdictional fragmentation remains a deeply entrenched feature of the metropolitan political landscape in the US (Teaford, 1979).

In recent years, scholars have argued that metropolitan areas across the US have entered a phase of post-suburban development (Kling et al, 1995). New terms and theoretical concepts, such as edge cities, ethnoburbs, technoburbs and post-metropolis, have been put forward to describe the new patterns of growth and economic development occurring at the outer metropolitan fringe (Garreau, 1991; Knox, 1993; Soja, 2000). Yet if such terms and concepts lend some degree of intellectual coherence to what otherwise might seem disorganized and fragmented, none actually challenges the received view of suburban political space as predominantly exclusionary in character. If anything, post-suburban developments are becoming even more detached in a jurisdictional sense from the metropolitan area and its constituent central city and contiguous suburbs.

Emerging alongside the literature on post-suburban development, and yet offering a very different perspective on territorial governance, is the growth of academic scholarship around the New Regionalism (MacLeod, 2001). The New Regionalism refers to recent developments in the ways in which regions are governed from the standpoint of economic development. More specifically, new regionalist scholars believe that the new geography of economic development is based around self-organized and competitive metropolitan regions (Jonas and Ward, 2002). Such metropolitan regions are defined not so much in terms of received concepts of territorial space – e.g. declining central cities, exclusionary suburbs – but instead relationally in respect to processes operating well beyond the boundaries of individual cities and suburbs; processes such as global flows of investment, technological changes, transformations in the labour market, new state spaces, and so forth (Brenner, 2002).

Relational thinking about metropolitan and regional development is often based on the premise that economic globalization represents a serious challenge to extant modes of territorial government based on fixed scalar hierarchies (Brenner, 1998; McCann, 2002). Global economic competition calls for flexible forms of territorial governance, which cut across local jurisdictional boundaries and interests, enhancing the capacity of metropolitan regions to compete and attract investment. One can infer from this that the politics of post-suburban development could be characterized not so much as local exclusion but as regional economic development or what I shall henceforth refer to as *post-suburban regionalism.*

The aim of this chapter is to consider whether these two apparently contrasting concepts of territorial politics operating in the peripheral parts of the American metropolis – the exclusionary local politics of suburbia and post-suburban regionalism – can in any way be reconciled. In the early sections of the chapter, I review those concepts of political space usually associated with suburban development in the US before considering the new regionalist politics of post-suburban development. In subsequent sections, I present two case studies of post-suburban regionalism: one in Greater Los Angeles (the Inland Empire region); and the other Greater Boston (the I-495 region). The time period covered in each case is roughly from the early 1990s to the present day. These examples are discussed and compared in relation to aspects of their constituent politics of space. Evidence of building post-suburban regionalism can be found in both contexts, but this seems to reflect as much an attempt to overcome local exclusionary politics as it is as an attempt to address wider problems of growth and regional development. I shall argue that local political geographies of exclusion and economic development continue to operate in tandem and are assuming new territorial (and scalar) forms in post-suburbia. The chapter concludes with a discussion about how work on post-suburban development could benefit from incorporating a critical perspective on the wider territorial structure of the American state and its associated concepts of territorial politics.

5.2 The politics of space in American suburbia

Since at least World War II, the suburbs have played a crucial socio-regulatory role in the wider US political economy (Beauregard, 2006). Suburban development has provided an outlet for effective demand along with the promise of upward mobility, access to affordable housing, and economic security for many low-to-middle income American households (Bruegmann, 2005). In many discussions about the post-war American metropolis, suburban growth has gone hand-in-hand with central-city decline (Beauregard, 1993). Arguably more pertinent to the present discussion, the burgeoning landscape of suburbia has been constructed in and around hundreds, if not thousands, of local municipalities and special purpose districts, each having independent powers and responsibilities such as land use planning, service delivery, taxation and revenue raising (Burns, 1994; Jonas, 2002; Teaford, 1997).

Local land use planning powers have often been deployed to resist the aggressive annexation policies of central cities, thereby protecting suburban residents and property owners from various 'urban' problems, such as crime, poverty, unemployment and racial tensions (Jackson, 1985). The resulting suburban municipal incorporations and exclusionary zoning practices have contributed to what is known as the phenomenon of metropolitan political fragmentation (Teaford, 1979). This refers to the fact that the governance of the metropolis is devolved to independent local jurisdictions (suburbs), which compete with each other for jobs and tax base and contrive to keep out costly and locally unwanted land uses and incomers. For some scholars of the American metropolis, inter-jurisdictional competition is to be welcomed insofar as it generates economies of public service provision (Tiebout, 1954). However, for others there is the concern that that local exclusionary politics only enhances social and economic inequalities between individuals and groups in different occupational, class and racial categories (Downs, 1973; Danielson, 1976).

In a context of globalization, capital mobility has put increasing pressure on suburbs no less than central cities to compete for jobs and investment (Althubaity and Jonas, 1998). Nevertheless, the persistence of the problem of metropolitan political fragmentation has served only to reinforce the view that suburbs are first and foremost spaces of local political exclusion. That is to say, the main *raison d'être* for local government in suburbia is to keep out locally unwanted land uses and, by implication, incomers having particular racial, social class or income characteristics. There are at least two important sets of interests involved in this process. On the one hand, suburban voters tend to elect local leaders whose views and decisions are broadly consistent with local exclusionary political goals. Suburban political regimes are notoriously conservative on issues like land use and taxation yet at the same time face fiscal pressures to promote development. On the other hand, local economic development interests in suburbia are broadly supportive of local land use outcomes at least insofar as their local economic interests are not threatened. Commercial and residential developers organize around local growth coalitions so as to protect and develop local investments in suburbia (Logan and Molotch, 1987). These coalitions work with municipal and county government to attract necessary revenue to fund infrastructure, investment and jobs and thereby variously promote and shape suburban growth trends. While these growth coalitions frequently encounter local resistance in the form of anti-sprawl and no-growth campaigns or environmental movements, they often find ways of working with – or around – local growth controls subsequently imposed by suburban municipalities (Warner and Molotch, 1995). Consequently, the growth of newer edge cities and suburbs tends to occur in remoter unincorporated areas or where development by-and-large can be encouraged and supported by newly-created local jurisdictional arrangements (e.g. expanded water and sewer service areas, new public school districts, etc.) (Cox and Jonas, 1993; Jonas, 1999).

Juxtaposed to the exclusionary politics of the suburban living place is the concept of an inclusive or integrated metropolitan political space (Danielson, 1976). The emergence of this alternative perspective on political space in the American metropolis can be traced back to struggles in the 1960s and 1970s on the part of civil rights campaigners and housing activists. These groups were interested in opening up the suburbs to racial minorities and those deprived of access to decent and affordable housing in suburbia (Downs, 1973). A key issue here was the harnessing of Federal government to override the constitutional authority of State government and, more importantly, local land use authority. However, issues other than housing affordability, land use and racial integration were also at stake, such as the need to deliver public services and infrastructure more efficiently and cost effectively throughout the entire metropolitan area (Cox and Jonas, 1993). For metropolitan reformers, local government powers of land use control and fiscal autonomy have traditionally been targets of criticism. Such reformers have promoted various strategies of annexation, consolidation, amalgamation, revenue sharing and regional special purpose districts, amongst many other possible approaches to metropolitan reform (Savitch and Vogel, 2004). Regional approaches to economic development might also be included in here.

5.3 Post-suburban regionalism

Interest in the phenomenon of post-suburban development emerges from studies of metropolitan regions where peripheral development seems no longer to be related in any way to traditional patterns of growth based around a core urban centre (Kling et al, 1995; Knox, 1993; Wolch et al, 2004; Scott, 2001). New settlements have spread across municipal and county boundaries, following patterns that do not conform to our received models of the modern metropolis. Importantly, these peripheral spaces appear to have neither formal (jurisdictional) nor functional (economic) connection to the traditional metropolitan core; instead they reflect processes of regional development as driven by global forces of capital accumulation (Soja, 2000). In these so-called post-suburban spaces, taken-for-granted divisions and connections between central cities and surrounding suburbs – e.g. those divisions or connections based on the provision of infrastructure, the consumption of services, jobs, and commuting patterns – no longer appear to hold.

As growth in the form of middle- and upper-income housing developments and jobs has continued to shift to the outer-most parts of US metropolitan areas, the problem of metropolitan political fragmentation has intensified, giving rise to contemporary debates about regional (in)equity and the spatial mismatch of population and jobs across the metropolis (Orfield, 2002; Silverman and Schneider, 1991). At issue here is how globalization challenges the received view of metropolitan politics. For writers like Brenner (1998, 2002), economic globalization has produced a profound 'rescaling' of state territoriality, such that the centralizing functions of the nation state are being replaced by non-hierarchical structures (and discourses) of state space and political authority (see also MacLeod, 2001; Leitner et al, 2002). In a related process, inter-urban competition appears to be fostering the creation of new city-regional institutions of governance (Jonas and Ward, 2007). Perhaps these profound changes in state territorial structure can be associated with the rise of 'metropolitan regions' but in some respects what is in question is the very idea of fixed territorial space (Allen and Cochrane, 2007). Not only has space become stretched out to encapsulate regions and globalization but also the territorial state has fundamentally been reworked by the rules and requirements of global competition and neoliberalism (Brenner and Theodore, 2002; Peck and Tickell, 2002).

It is important to note that there are different strands to scholarship on what is now known as the New Regionalism (MacLeod, 2001). Drawing primarily upon the American experience, some scholars believe that political ties between suburbs – especially those in outer metropolitan areas – are becoming stronger than those between inner suburbs and central cities (Rusk, 1995). Others argue that urban regimes are being replaced by new regional governance arrangements (Hamilton, 2002; Savitch and Vogel, 1996) or perhaps even by putative city-states (Pierce, 1993). It could be the case that regional growth networks are forming around outer-metropolitan areas, which have little or no relationship to the rest of the metropolitan area (Gottdiener and Kephart, 1995). The concept of post-suburban development certainly allows for the possibility that the new geography of economic development is organized around regional governance systems which do not correspond with existing structures of urban or metropolitan government. However, we still know very little about the circumstances under which regional governance takes shape in post-suburbia.

To summarize the discussion thus far, there is some agreement that the balance of academic attention should shift away from the debate about suburban exclusionary politics towards identifying new regionalist processes operating in post-suburbia. However, there is little agreement on what precise form the latter might take other than an acceptance that regional economic development is the driving force. We now turn to our case studies of post-suburban regionalism to flesh out some details relating to the form of, and motives behind, post-suburban regionalism.

The case study of the Inland Empire region of southern California revisits and extends previous work on post-suburban development in this region (Jonas, 1997, 1999). In recent years, there have been various attempts by local economic development interests to construct an economic and political identity for the Inland Empire, which emphasizes its separateness from the rest of metropolitan Los Angeles. Local exclusionary politics is apparent but I shall argue that this is not just about the character of residential development but more to do with building up the economic governance capacity of the region and addressing the fiscal and environmental challenges of suburban growth.

The example of the I-495 region of Greater Boston likewise demonstrates the role of interests in the metropolitan periphery in self-organizing for regional economic development. In this case, we see evidence of how obstacles to housing affordability have become a concern for regional employers and economic development interests. Here suburban political exclusion is seen to be a continuing problem. At the same time, the I-495 region is becoming politically reattached to Greater Boston due to the need to address the problem of funding infrastructure State-wide. Considered together, the case studies reveal that the construction of post-suburban regionalism is an unfolding story; it is not a *fait accompli*.

5.4 Building suburban regionalism in Greater Los Angeles: The Inland Empire

The Inland Empire incorporates a region that corresponds more or less to the Riverside-San Bernardino Metropolitan Area as defined by the US Census Bureau. In 2004, this region had a population of about 1.6 million or 19 percent of the population of Greater Los Angeles (an area covering all or part of the counties of Los Angeles, Orange, Riverside, San Bernardino and Ventura) (US Census, 2006). According to some definitions, the Inland Empire includes cities and unincorporated areas in the desert communities of the Coachella Valley (in central Riverside County) but in this chapter I will refer mainly to developments in the urbanized western parts of the counties of Riverside and San Bernardino (see Map 5.1). In some respects, locating the exact boundaries of this region is less important than showing how the region has been afforded a separate political and economic identity by various local interests.

The Inland Empire region is internally politically fragmented into 48 local municipalities and numerous regional and sub-regional agencies.

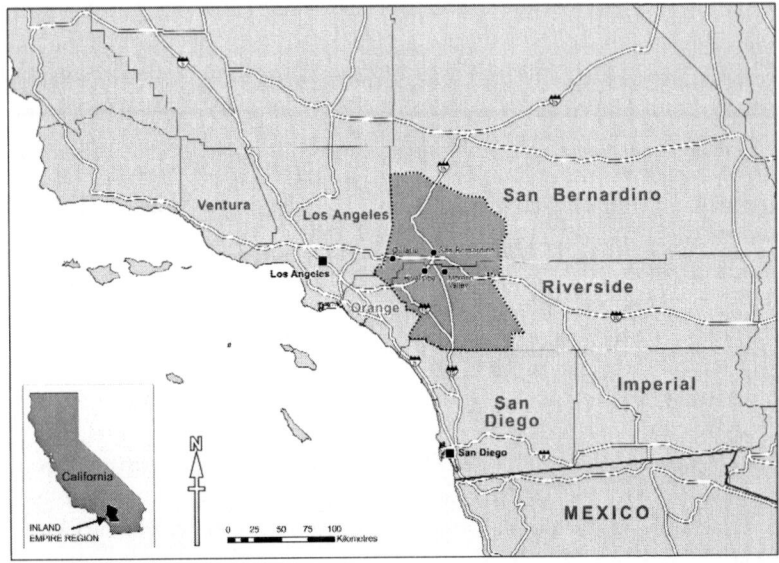

Map 5.1   Greater Los Angeles and the Inland Empire

The latter include special purpose (single-function) service districts, which raise revenue and provide services such as water, sewerage, waste disposal, education (schools and colleges), redevelopment, habitat conservation planning, and so forth. Municipal home rule is a valued principle of local government in the region. However, local autonomy is circumscribed by constitutionally-defined Federal and State authority. The intrusion of direct democracy into State politics in California in the form of voter-led ballot initiatives, such as Proposition 13 (which greatly restricted increases in the local property tax), has provided opportunities for significant cleavages in local voting outcomes, not just along the lines of class and race, but also territory. Previous studies have suggested that voter attitudes to issues like growth control, redevelopment and taxation vary considerably across southern California, and that the Inland Empire is no exception in respect of suburban growth shaping local political outcomes (Neiman and Loveridge, 1981; Warner and Molotch, 1995).

The Inland Empire is sometimes characterized as an amorphous suburban sprawl beset with a variety of problems including lack of coordinated regional planning (Wolch et al, 2004). The region has indeed grown at a remarkable pace and sprawl is a problem that demands governance responses. Some of the region's high growth can be attributed to the lower cost of suburban single-family housing as compared to neigh-bouring counties of Los Angeles and Orange. New housing development across the region increased by 10 percent between 2000 and 2004 and the region's population grew by 20.1 percent between 2000 and 2005 (US Census, 2006), with much of this growth distributed amongst newly incorporated cities and unincorporated areas rather than older free-standing cities (e.g. Ontario, Riverside and San Bernardino). Other reasons for growth include recent immigration trends; but US Census data (op. cit.) shows that the Inland Empire (18 percent foreign born) is not as ethnically diverse as Los Angeles (36 percent foreign born). None-theless, it is perhaps misleading to view this region in racial or class terms as predominantly 'white' or for that matter even as predominantly 'low-to-middle income'. Despite the region's internal social and economic diversity, certain interests both within and outside the Inland Empire want to construct this as a separate region having a unique political identity.

Regionalism and the local politics of economic development

One such identity arises from the region's historic dependence on citrus production, which has formed the basis for the profitable develop-ment of agriculture and resource-based industries over the years. As far back as the 1920s, the Inland Empire was known nationally for its prosperous citrus industry and accessibility to nearby deserts and mountains, factors which encouraged the marketing of the region to visitors and migrants. However, recent attempts to create a coherent economic and political identity for the region reflect contemporary growth trends and economic development problems rather than histor-ical factors. These include attempts to organize and strengthen regional governance (Jonas, 1997).

Since 1992, there has been a regional economic development organ-ization in place known as the Inland Empire Economic Partnership (IEEP). This partnership evolved from two separate county economic development organizations, which were merged into a single partner-ship for the entire inland region. The IEEP represents businesses and communities in the western parts of Riverside and San Bernardino; but it does also include some members from the remoter eastern cities and desert communities. Since the early 1990s, the IEEP has been involved in lobbying for State and Federal assistance to local industry and employers (Jonas, 1997). More recently, the California Center for Regional Leadership has selected the IEEP as one of its model regional collaborative initiatives. It therefore represents a prime example of new regionalist processes at work in this particular region (Jonas and Pincetl, 2006).

Regional economic development practitioners have often referred to a 'population-jobs' imbalance across the Inland Empire. This involves a spatial mismatch between the location of new jobs and new residential growth. Cluster development has been prioritized as a regional economic strategy and local cities have rezoned sites for office and commercial activity. Major employment centres – or edge cities – of regional significance include Pomona, Ontario, Riverside and San Bernardino. However, growth in new sectors is offset by job losses in manufacturing industry, which have tended to concentrate in the older inland cities of San Bernardino, Riverside and Fontana (the site of largest steel mill west of the Rocky Mountains before it closed in the 1980s) (Davis, 1990; Jonas, 1997). Other cities like Palm Springs, Palm Desert and Ontario have attracted new industry and employment, using local powers such as redevelopment and enterprise zones. Likewise, emerging edge cities such as Moreno Valley have experienced rapid growth but have failed to attract corresponding new industrial or service activities (Jonas, 1999).

Perceived (and actual) differences between the Inland Empire and Greater Los Angeles have featured strongly in debates about regional economic development. At 5.7 percent in 2004, the Inland Empire unemployment rate is higher than that for Orange County and Ventura County, respectively, but lower than in Los Angeles (US Census, 2006). Furthermore, a significantly greater proportion of the Inland Empire population is employed in government (21.5 percent) compared to Los Angeles, Ventura and Orange counties (all less than 15 percent). Manufacturing is 10 percent of local employment in the Inland Empire but higher in adjacent counties (ibid.). Mainstream policy discourse represents the Inland Empire as an underprivileged and excluded space relative to an economically dominant and competitive Los Angeles (or LA), as indicated in an interview with a local economic development practitioner:

> ...(T)here has been this very intense frustration with the fact that everything has been LA-centric so there has always been a desire to begin to build the Inland Empire to create its own identity, to create its own image and to build it as a region separate and distinct from LA. And to be able to compete for the appropriate Federal and State funding to grow this region; to compete for businesses to create jobs and to build a strong economic base and an enhanced standard of

living separate from LA... (Economic development official, Inland Empire, May 2003).

Here the economic identity of the Inland Empire is constructed in terms of enhancing regional governance capacities *in situ* and competing for jobs. Indeed, after the Los Angeles riots of 1992 Inland Empire economic development practitioners were quite optimistic about the prospects for attracting industry to the region. In the event, the rate of regional unemployment grew, reaching 11 percent in the mid-1990s. This was due to Federal military base closures and a profound State-wide economic recession (Jonas, 1997).

We can also see ways in which the Inland Empire likes to be excluded from certain dominant representations of Greater Los Angeles. The same practitioner quoted above has simultaneously constructed the Inland Empire as an *inclusionary* political space in respect of affordability and yet also *exclusionary* in respect of not sharing the problems of LA or Orange County that come with over-development:

> If we can balance out the economy by bringing in higher wage paying jobs what I said then we are going to be in a better position moving forward to maintain a certain standard of living and quality of life. What we don't want to do is to tip the scales like they have in LA and Orange County and then start having to deal with those types of issues where you are making a hundred thousand dollars a year and you can't afford to buy the medium price home (Economic development official, Inland Empire, May 2003).

From the standpoint of economic interests in the Inland Empire the governance challenge is not so much co-operation with organizations in Greater Los Angeles since these interests clearly do not want to be a part of a 'global' Los Angeles. Instead, it is a case of drawing in more members from the local cities and businesses into functional regional partnerships, which can address the problems of growth.

Environmental regionalism and exclusionary politics

Alongside economic regionalism, there is another form of post-suburban regionalism operating in the Inland Empire. This has arisen from conflicts in the living place around the competing land use demands of residential and commercial development and protection of biological resources (habitats) for threatened and endangered species, including kangaroo rats, butterflies, lizards, bighorn sheep, etc. These conflicts have been triggered by the listing of species as threatened or endangered under the Federal Endangered Species Act (ESA).

Since the 1980s, the ESA has grown in importance in terms of shaping land use policy and property rights across the region (Feldman and Jonas, 2000). Southern California contains diverse habitats and ecosystems (e.g. sagescrub, desert sand dunes, etc.). These support a variety of endemic species of wildlife and vegetation. New post-suburban developments threaten the region's habitats and ecosystems, and so there have been calls to introduce regional planning as a solution to growing environmental, property rights and land use conflicts. The ESA has encouraged local jurisdictions in the Inland Empire to develop regional and sub-regional habitat conservation plans for private and public land parcels containing habitat under threat of development, thereby providing long-term protection for endangered species.

For Federal and local policy-makers and politicians, it has been important to represent solutions to endangered species conflicts in the Inland Empire in ways that in many respects reflect local concerns. For example, local and national politicians and policy-makers have felt it necessary to differentiate what has happened in the Inland Empire from what has happened in Los Angeles, where conflict and civic unrest have been serious concerns. In signing off on one conflict-ridden regional conservation plan for a single species of kangaroo rat in western Riverside County, Bruce Babbitt, the Interior Secretary under the Clinton administration, spoke to local leaders in the following terms:

> This is a cause to celebrate ... I know it's been a long, tough, arduous process, but this is not just about a rat. It's about multiuses habitat, it's about open space for our kids; it's about a vision which says Riverside County is a lot different from the Los Angeles basin (quoted in *The Orange County Register* (Metro), 9 May 1996, p. 5).

Here regionalism takes on a quite different form and meaning to the previous example. It represents not so much a response to problems of regional economic development but instead a wider struggle over competing visions of life in post-suburban America. It is about being a good steward of the nation's future resources including its land, its native species and its children. For local politicians, in particular, the Inland Empire is *not* Los Angeles; it is not a landscape of uncontained smog and sprawl; it is not a place of crime and unsafe streets. Instead, it is a place or region where kids can play outdoors and have access to open space, and where threatened species can survive. To that end, it becomes necessary to differentiate the Inland Empire from – even to exclude – Los Angeles.

Nevertheless regional economic development interests are still at work here. Notably Federal intervention to get regional conservation plans signed has been prompted by intense lobbying by county-level politicians in Riverside who, working in cross-political party coalitions, have pushed through regional plans that have, in some cases, been bitterly opposed by local property owners, voters and some municipalities. A key incentive for getting local municipalities and developers to support regional conservation planning has been access to revenue for infrastructure. For municipal governments, the provisions of the Federal ESA represent a potential threat to local land use authority; but it also offers an opportunity to access crucial State funds for local infrastructure and transportation. Voters in the Inland Empire have passed bond issues, which tie regional planning for 'smart growth' to conservation planning and infrastructure. Participation in regional habitat conservation plans affords the participating local governments with access to crucial infrastructure funds for freeway interchanges and improved access roads.

For developers, the ESA may be viewed as a threat to their capacity to build houses and sell them at prices that are affordable to the mass consumer due to interim restrictions on land use rezoning. But without investment in infrastructure, housing developments would not happen. Inland Empire developers, too, have come to see economic benefits in regional conservation planning under the ESA because it in fact releases some public and private lands from development controls and restrictions. Likewise, for farmers and private property owners, the provision of the ESA may pose a threat to farming activities and land prices but property owners cannot sell land to developers unless development is an option; and exercising development options across the region can be contingent on participation in regional conservation planning.

In conclusion, it appears that new regional planning and governance arrangements in the Inland Empire have arisen to address a range of economic development problems. Regional infrastructure and environmental planning have also provided ways of dealing with conflicts in the post-suburban living place. They have helped both to overcome local exclusionary politics and to address shortfalls in the funding of regional growth arising from restrictions on the raising of local property taxes and other local revenues.

5.5   Greater Boston: Building regionalism along the I-495 corridor

Greater Boston is often viewed as a successful case of regional economic development. This is due to the presence of strong regional clusters of new economic activities (biotech, ICT, financial services). Clusters include the medical and university complexes in Boston and Cambridge as well as along the Route 128 inner suburban ring of Boston. More importantly, and mainly for our present purposes, new growth has occurred further west of Boston along the I-495 corridor, extending out to the cities of Framingham, Shrewsbury and Worcester and the neighbouring towns and suburbs (Map 5.2). Whilst many of these places are well established local jurisdictions, each with a long history of enforcing local land use planning and control, they also exhibit certain characteristics of post-suburban development: new office space, customized infrastructure, campus-like corporate facilities, covered shopping malls, and the like. Such post-suburban developments have been supported by ongoing efforts to establish a distinct political identity for the I-495 region. Our present focus is on an area

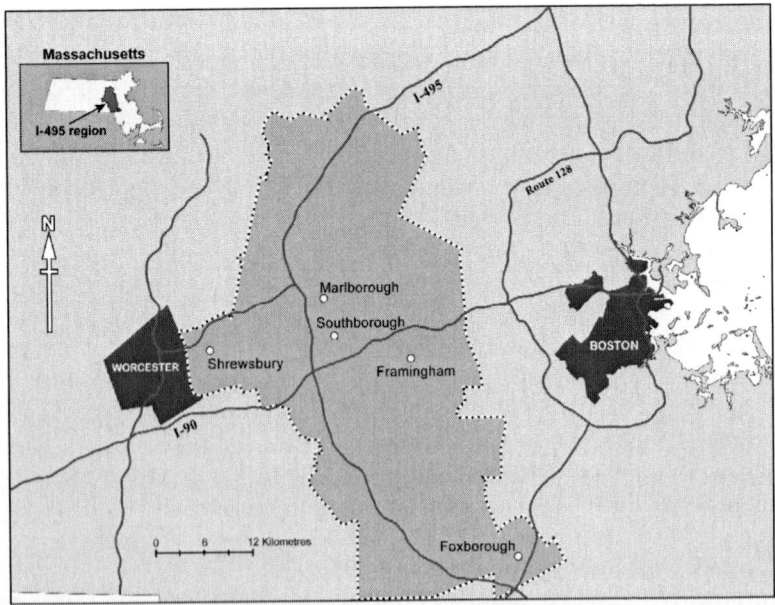

Map 5.2   The I-495 region

comprised of 32 townships (suburbs) known as the I-495/MetroWest corridor region. In 2008, this region employed about 285,000 people, mainly in well-paid high tech and emerging industrial sectors such as renewable energy, but some (c. 44,000 employees) in more traditional manufacturing industries like textiles (Dyer, 2008).

Regionalism for economic development

In providing some context, it is worth highlighting four features of the local politics economic development in this putative post-suburban region. Firstly, there have been significant transformations in the local politics of economic development from corporate welfarism to inter-urban competition. The City of Worcester is illustrative in this regard, with the proactive development of new science and technology parks since the late 1980s (Jonas, 1992). Second, local economies in the region have globalized as a result of local employers coming under external (foreign) ownership. Ensuing local conflicts around economic development have tended to be framed by a discourse of external control, which is seen as a threat to the established political culture of home rule. Third, perceptions of the dominance of Boston's economy and its well-entrenched business organizations are being challenged by the growth of new sectors having different political agendas and spatial interests (Jonas, 1996). As one economic development representative argues:

> If you take a look a decade or so ago, it was pretty much that busi-nesses had to be in Boston…we [didn't] have to do as much because there is so much of a demand coming in here not to need to create incentives and such like that. Well, clearly that's not totally true but that was the attitude. That attitude sort of collapsed, prob-ably around 1990 when we had a recession here… (Greater Boston business representative, September 2007, my inserts).

Fourthly, notwithstanding an entrenched political culture of localism, the I-495 region has developed its own separate regional governance structures in the form of the 495/MetroWest Corridor Partnership. This is a non-profit economic development organization which was estab-lished in 2003 to represent the interests of firms, local chambers of commerce and the local government jurisdictions. It was felt that more of a regional approach was required to address certain growth-induced infrastructural, planning and housing needs (Interview with regional economic development practitioner, September 2007).

In recent years, the I-495 region has been facing some serious economic development issues not the least of which are shortfalls in infrastructure provision (roads, water supplies, commuter rail, etc.) and housing for entry-level workers (Jonas et al, 2010). Given the weak functional linkages with Boston, there are particular concerns about retrofitting aging infrastructure and developing new transport connections to these outer parts of Greater Boston. A Transportation Investment Coalition was recently established to address the infrastructure shortfall in Boston as well as State-wide. It is comprised of Greater Boston business organizations, trades unions and transportation agencies and, as such, is seen by economic development interests in other parts of the State to have a Boston bias. According to the coalition, the State's current 'infrastructure crisis' amounts to $20 billion; this is the estimated deficit in funding for infrastructure renewal. In the I-495 region, talk of the infrastructure deficit has served to highlight local issues, such as improving local connections and reducing travel costs for high tech and service firms and workers within the region. The emerging regional strategy is to improve connections between towns and suburbs along the I-495 and adjoining local routes so that workers can spend less effort, time and money on commuting.

In terms of solutions to the infrastructure deficit, the State of Massachusetts has already been involved in promoting an array of supply-side forms of economic development, many of which have indeed focused on the City of Boston (Horan and Jonas, 1998). For instance, the 'Big Dig' project sought to improve and upgrade existing links between the city's airport, the inner suburbs and downtown Boston, including the city's established biomedical and financial sector firms. From the standpoint of I-495 suburbs and high tech interests, however, the solution to the 'infrastructure crisis' is not a question of making Boston more attractive to business and investment. They want to see money spent on addressing local infrastructural issues, retaining and attracting the workforce to meet a growing demand locally for entry-level high tech and service jobs. In this context, the I-495/MetroWest Corridor Partnership has tried to speak for outer parts of Greater Boston, which have felt inadequately represented by coalitions and debates about infrastructure funding in Massachusetts.

Overcoming local exclusionary politics

Another significant area of concern in the I-495 region is promoting housing affordability for entry-level knowledge and service-sector workers (Jonas et al, 2010). In the case of affordable workforce housing, the problem might be seen as one of a lack of local supply. None-theless, the issue most often highlighted by housing activists and business interests alike is exclusionary local politics. There is a particular concern that addressing demands for workforce housing is not to be confused with the provision of affordable social housing. In reality, levels of 'affordability' are uneven between local political jurisdictions and the problem is especially acute for the outermost suburbs of Boston, where there is a lack of collective memory of how to produce subsidized and low-income housing. Here the problem of metropolitan political fragmentation is seen as part of the context:

> ...[W]e have 351 cities and towns, each of which is a separate political jurisdiction. So that each of those cities and towns sets its own zoning, sets its own design standards. And there is a huge amount of what we call here Not-In-My-Back-Yardism (NIMBYism) going on, so that it is very, very difficult to produce new housing (Massachusetts Housing Activist, September 2007).

In terms of overcoming such local exclusionary politics, one focus of attention is the use of State laws to override local zoning legislation. First enacted in 1969, Chapter 40B is the State of Massachusetts' 'affordable housing' law, which requires suburban municipalities around Boston to relax zoning and enable the development of higher density affordable single-family housing (Jonas et al, 2010). The law in effect allows municipalities to produce more housing on smaller lots than the more typical half-acre and single-acre lots. In the I-495 region, 40B has recently been championed by housing developers as a way of resolving a backlog of housing construction. The housing industry, too, likes to emphasize the obstructive role of exclusionary politics:

> Neighborhoods restrict the growth of new apartments or prevent subdivisions, which causes the demand for housing to disperse over larger areas (sprawl), and drives housing and commuting prices higher...This trend is very evident within the Route 495 area..., where there is virtually no undeveloped multi-family zoned land available outside of cities (Flood and Kablack, 2008, p. 22).

However, there have been some concerns that local voters will override Chapter 40B, not so much on racial and exclusionary grounds, as due to its local fiscal impacts. New family housing units create a demand for services and schools. But there are difficulties of meeting these demands by raising local revenues; difficulties that are compounded by Proposition 2½. This proposition restricts increases in local property taxes to a 2.5 percent annual rate. Suburbs facing such local revenue pressures are generally opposed to the construction of housing at the lower end of the market. But enforced local restrictions on new housing development make it difficult for entry-level workers to afford housing close to work (Dyer, 2008). Developers therefore argue that building more workforce housing to meet employers' demands in post-suburbia helps to redistribute wealth more equitably because workers will not have to devote such a significant proportion of their income to the costs of commuting if homes affordable to workers can be built closer to work.

For I-495 firms and developers, recasting the problem of housing affordability in terms of regional equity offers a powerful weapon in brokering conflict with those public officials and existing home-owners in the I-495 who might, for example, be interested in repealing Chapter 40B (Jonas et al, 2010). There was such an attempt to repeal Chapter 40B in December 2007, but it failed to garner sufficient signatures to appear on a State-wide ballot measure. In this case, regionalism supplanted localism but only because it in effect depended on the leveraging of the higher authority of State government to override political fragmentation and local exclusionary politics.

5.6 Discussion and conclusion

Scholars of post-suburban development have often commented on a *lack* of political identity and representative forms of territorial democracy at the outer metropolitan fringe. Post-suburban spaces and edge cities tend to be run by 'shadow governments' comprised of private-public partnerships and special purpose districts (Garreau, 1991). As a result, it is believed that post-suburban developments have little or no sense of place or political identity. There is certainly evidence of shadow government formation in the two case studies examined in this chapter, respectively, the Inland Empire (Southern California) and I-495 (Greater Boston). Yet at the same time both regions do seem to be developing strong economic and political identities. I have suggested that this is the result of processes operating both within and outwith these two regions. Post-suburban regionalism appears to be a response both to unresolved local political and economic issues resulting from suburban exclusionary processes and to the wider challenges of globalization and regional development.

More importantly, these two examples of post-suburban regionalism have evolved in ways that incorporate, and respond to, the manner in which the American state is organized territorially so as to take into account – or balance – competing local and regional interests. To be sure, the territorial division of powers between Federal, State and local government and the attendant system of checks and balances tends to privilege territorially representative forms of politics (Jonas, 2002). A strengthening of political regionalism is one possibility here; but it is not the only one. In the US, regionalism has involved cross-party coalitions around agendas common to regional political groupings. Examples might include: the States of the North East region organizing against Southern 'right-to-work' states; or the Sage Brush rebellion of western States against Federal management of public lands. As the Inland Empire example shows, regionalism can also involve political coalitions in post-suburbia lobbying against (or, at least, in reaction to) Federal laws, such as the Endangered Species Act. In the case of Greater Boston, regionalism has arisen in response to State-wide debates about infrastructure and workforce housing. Furthermore, one can see how the identity of post-suburban regions is constructed in relation to other concepts of political space: the space of the global city, as in the case of Greater Los Angeles; or the socially integrated metropolitan region, as per Greater Boston.

Instead of it being a case of *either* exclusion *or* economic development, the new regional politics of post-suburban space might be better thought of in terms of struggles *both* of exclusion *and* of economic development. The stories about the Inland Empire and the I-495 region are revealing, not for what they say about the specific geographies of these post-suburban regions, so much as how they exemplify wider struggles around the territorial structure of the American state. Stories from other contexts might be quite different. For example, in Sydney, Australia, the rise of a 'global city' political discourse has served to intensify the autonomous political demands of the outermost (western) suburbs of Sydney in the Australian federal system. If anything, these post-suburban spaces are becoming further detached politically from the otherwise dominant discourse of 'global' Sydney. In other national contexts, the stories might reveal quite different regionalist economic and political processes at work in post-suburbia.

Acknowledgments

The case study of I-495 has benefitted from the financial support of the British Academy and draws in part upon ongoing collaborative research with Aidan While and David Gibbs. The Inland Empire example is based in part on a project, which was originally funded by the National Science Foundation, with research support provided by my former PhD students Tom Feldman and Jim Sullivan. Thanks also to Bob Fagan and the Department of Human Geography at Macquarie University in Sydney, where some of the arguments in this chapter were first presented.

6
Privatization of the Fringes – A Latin American Version of Post-suburbia? The Case of Santiago de Chile

Dirk Heinrichs, Michael Lukas and Henning Nuissl

6.1 Introduction

Latin America is one of the most urbanized regions worldwide (UN, 2008). Urban expansion and suburbanization are well-established and common phenomena, particularly in the larger agglomerations and megacities in the region. However, the profound social, ecological and economic implications of these processes have only recently – with some delay in comparison to the United States (US) or Europe – started to become a major concern of urban analysts and policy-makers across the continent.

The interest in the issue of fringe development has evolved together with urbanization trends that strongly resemble what has been labelled urban sprawl in an attempt to highlight the detrimental effects (Borsdorf et al, 2002; Coy and Pöhler, 2002) of developments such as: large-scale residential complexes that are at best loosely connected to the existing urban fabric, the flourishing of huge retail facilities and exurban office parks on greenfield sites, and the construction of highway systems. These present-day expressions of urban growth profoundly alter the urban physical and socio-spatial landscape: per capita land consumption increases while population densities across urban regions decrease, the demand for transport infrastructure and services rises dramatically, and ecosystem services are reduced considerably.

It seems that these urbanization patterns on the fringes of the largest urban agglomerations in Latin America follow the post-suburban trends in the global 'North', particularly in North America, Western and Central Europe, and Australia. However, one should be cautious with premature conclusions or over-generalization (cf. Hawley, 1971). There has been little discussion so far about whether current edge-urban development in Latin America shares commonalities with or differs from what happens elsewhere. To what extent can we speak of a Latin American version of post-suburbia? What are its shaping factors? These questions are the focus of this contribution. The analysis draws on the discussion of post-suburbia provided by Phelps et al (2010). They depict the characteristic features and attributes of post-suburbia along three dimensions: (i) the general plausibility of a sharp distinction between suburbia and post-suburbia (that allows interpreting the latter as 'a clean break with suburbia'); (ii) the specificity and novelty of particular aspects of post-suburbia, e.g. with respect to urban morphology, land-use mix or location of developments; and (iii) the specificity of patterns of production of post-suburbia, including the constellations of actors that shape these patterns.

Santiago de Chile has been selected as a case to exemplify current development trends on the urban fringes of Latin America's major agglo-merations. The Chilean capital is an excellent case for examining the pressures and consequences of urbanization as well as the political res-ponses. It is typical of Latin American metropolises in terms of spatial structure and growth patterns. At the same time, urban expansion and land use in Santiago show some very recent trends of sprawl (Borsdorf and Hidalgo, 2005; Borsdorf et al, 2007). The advanced stage of urban-ization in Santiago de Chile offers the potential to detect and analyse urban development trends that can be expected to occur later elsewhere. Chile is among the first countries in Latin America that responded to globalization by shifting its macro-economic policy from import substitution to market liberalization and promoting foreign direct investment. Several of its market-oriented urban policy experiments have been exported to other countries of the region (e.g. the housing subsidy system, franchising of highway concessions). Finally, the recent trends of urban development both inside and beyond the limits of the urban area are generally well-documented in the literature, so that the necessary information is available (see contributions to Galetovic, 2006; De Mattos and Hidalgo, 2007; Ducci, 2000; Borsdorf et al, 2002; Green and Soler, 2005; Ducci and Gonzales, 2006; Lopez, 2006; Paz Castro, 2006; Romero and Vásquez, 2006).

This chapter first introduces the case of Santiago with respect to its spatial, demographic and political–administrative features as well as its evolution in terms of urban expansion. This includes the rise of edge-urban megaprojects as perhaps the most visible expression of recent trends. The focus then turns to recent development trends in Santiago looking specifically at their post-suburban quality. While this examination largely follows the lines of analysis introduced by Phelps et al (2010), it also distinguishes between physical features, i.e. morphology and location aspects, and functional issues. With respect to the production of post-suburbia, we pay particular attention to the actors behind the current developments, linking to work which emphasizes the interests that bring about post-suburbia (e.g. Knox, 1992; Teaford, 1997). What then follows is a closer analysis of two illustrative mega-projects – *Piedra Roja* and *Urbanya*. The conclusion reflects on the question of whether and to what extent the case of Santiago de Chile suggests a Latin American version of post-suburbia.

6.2   Santiago de Chile: Recent urbanization trends

Santiago de Chile is one of the most thriving cities in Latin America and occupies a top position in most rankings of the most attractive places for economic activity and investments in the region. Santiago constitutes the centre of one of the most urbanized countries in the world and also one of the most centralized states in Latin America. At the same time, the city illustrates the paradoxical situation in which centralization and decentralization coexist (Siavelis et al, 2002). The 'city' of Santiago does not exist as a political or administrative entity but rather as a conglomeration of local government units *vis-à-vis* the central state. Firstly, the Metropolitan Region (*Region Metropolitana*, RM), is one of the 16 regional entities into which the territory of Chile is divided, with a surface of 15,400 km^2 and a population of around 6.8 million. It consists of 52 municipalities and is governed by a regional government that is neither politically elected nor in possession of many competences or resources. Secondly, and within the RM, Santiago exists as the *Area Metropolitana Santiago de Chile* (AMS). The AMS covers the agglomeration of, depending on the definition chosen, between 34 and 39 urbanized and urbanizing municipalities in the RM. It covers around 2,000 km^2 and has a population of roughly 6.4 million at the time of writing. The AMS is not a political or administrative entity and each municipality has its own local mayor. Thirdly, Santiago exists as a municipality in the heart of the city with a population of some 250,000 at the time of writing. This contribution refers to Santiago as the *Area Metropolitana* (AMS) including 39 urbanized and urbanizing municipalities.

   Santiago has experienced a rapid horizontal expansion in recent decades. The built-up urban area doubled from around 330 km^2 in 1980 to over 600 km^2 in 2004 (Petermann, 2006). Yet urban population growth over the same period slowed down from more than 2 percent per year to less than 1.5 percent per year (Galetovic and Jordan, 2006). In effect, population density of the urbanized area decreased from 93 to 85 people/ha. In this respect Santiago resembles cities such as Buenos Aires, Mexico City or Caracas but differs from the major agglomerations such as Lima or Bogota in the economically less advanced Latin America countries.

The generalized consolidation of population over an expanding physical area masks a highly pronounced intra-urban mobility. Between 1997 and 2002, more than 150,000 persons annually moved within the AMS (Rodriguez, 2007). What adds significance to this number is the trend of relocation towards the peripheral municipalities (Escolano and Ortiz, 2007). On aggregate, almost all central and peri-central municipalities lost population at significant rate. Conversely, peripheral locations realized a dramatic surge in population at rates up to 200 percent.

One of the most peculiar recent urban development trends in Santiago is the frequent appearance of large-scale residential developments on exurban sites that are not contiguous to existing settlements. These so-called megaprojects are known in the Latin American region since the early 1990s. Two types of megaprojects can be distinguished. The first type, 'early megaprojects', are mid-sized developments, planned and constructed on sites of 50 to 250 ha for up to 15,000 residents during a first wave of construction in the 1990s. These projects were designed as exclusively residential gated communities to cater to specific segments of society, from upper to lower socio-economic class. They are located across the entire city, in particular in the traditional upper class districts of Las Condes and Lo Barnechea, in formerly poor municipalities such as Huechuraba and Penalolen, and in the periphery in municipalities such as Puente Alto and Maipú. A second type of development, 'new megaprojects', has emerged more recently. They typically cover plots of 300 hectares or more, and are planned for tens of thousands of residents. Investment volumes sometimes exceed one billion US$ and time horizons for finalization of some megaprojects are beyond 2030. These projects include comprehensive service provision, access infrastructure (motorway connection) and new management structures. Finally, the projects are implemented on the basis of new planning regulations (so-called ZODUC, ADUP and PDUC regulations) which were put in place precisely in order to make these developments possible. Most new megaprojects are designed as gated communities, in some cases for more than 50,000 people, and represent what some authors have called entirely new 'fenced cities' (Hidalgo et al, 2007). They are by no means restricted to high-income groups but address a much wider socio-economic spectrum.

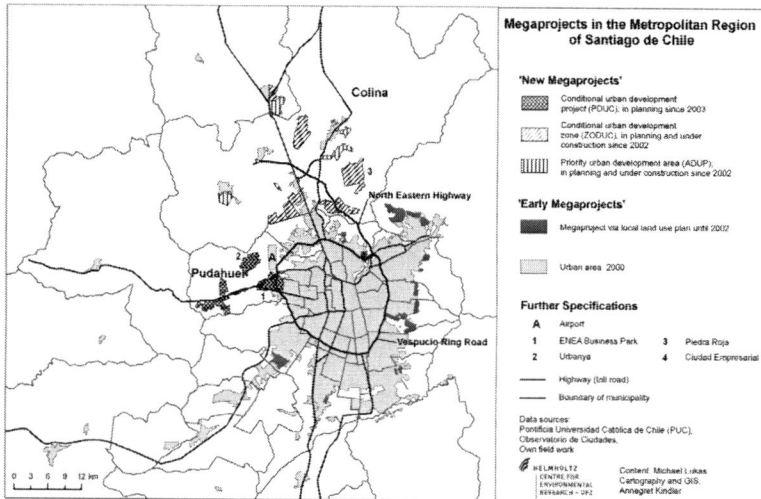

Map 6.1 Megaprojects in the metropolitan region of Santiago de Chile

Map 6.1 illustrates the location of these megaprojects. It shows that the northern periphery and exurban areas are the preferred destination of the most recent and most voluminous real-estate investments. Large-scale developments of the earlier type are physically nearer to the existing urban fabric. Two examples of the most recent form of residential megaprojects, *Piedra Roja* in the municipality of Colina and *Urbanya* in Pudahuel, will serve as exemplary cases in later discussion. In order to allow a broad overview of the physical structure of the Santiago agglomeration, the figure also shows some further features that shape the urban area, such as the airport, the network of urban motorways and the existing municipal boundaries.

6.3 The development of Santiago's urban edges – Leaving traditional suburbia behind?

Over the last 150 years, urban expansion in Santiago has matched that in other Latin American cities. Better-off strata and urban elites who originally lived in the city centre and adjacent areas began to move out to the urban fringes at the beginning of the twentieth century, giving way for Central Business District (CBD) development and less affluent groups that moved in. Around the mid-twentieth century, an industrial belt emerged that encloses the inner city. Within and also beyond this belt, a vast stock of low-standard housing was built, often informally and without official approval, by the immigrant industrial workforce and marginalized groups from rural areas. Although this kind of informal suburban city-building is also known in industrialized countries, its scale was more typical for developing countries.

Generally, the pattern of urban expansion in the twentieth century displayed the features of classical urbanization and suburbanization: the city grew in a concentric and comparatively continuous manner, with little leapfrog development. Adjacent towns and villages were integrated into the growing urban fabric. The boundaries between the urban area and its rural surroundings were clearly visible in most places; the land use pattern of the urban area by and large displayed a zoning of land uses and social strata typical for the big city of modern times.

A characteristic feature of Santiago and other Latin American metropolises was the marked segregation of suburban residential areas: upper- and upper-middle-class suburbanization mainly took place in one segment of the city's fringe – in the case of Santiago in the East facing the Andean mountains – whereas suburbanization of both people with less material resources as well as industry moved into the other directions. This was not least the result of state policy to resolve the problem of illegal settlement by providing social housing on a scale that is perhaps unique in the region. As social housing was mainly provided on low-cost land at the southern, western and northern urban fringes, it contributed to the spatial growth of the city (Tokman, 2006).

With the arrival of the residential megaprojects in the 1990s, the physical-spatial structure of Santiago, and in particular the city's urban edge, again started to undergo a process of transformation which some authors describe as leading towards a fragmented city (Bähr and Mertins, 1995; Borsdorf et al, 2002; De Mattos, 2005). In contrast to the concentric expansion of the urban area, the morphology of recent urban expansion is much more coarse and patchy (see Map 6.1). The new spatial pattern of development reflects the availability of cheap, previously undeveloped land, together with the existing or planned road network (Ducci, 2004). While suburban residential growth has been traditionally treated as the effect of demand patterns, these developments reflect the growing importance of the supply-side in peripheral urban growth, i.e. the mode of planning and realizing new urban areas (Borsdorf and Hidalgo, 2005; Hidalgo et al, 2007).

On aggregate, the traditionally rather compact urban structure is beginning to give rise to a – typically post-suburban – mix of urban and rural land uses in the extending transition zone between the metropolis and its hinterland. Furthermore, whereas new commercial and shopping facilities as well as industrial buildings display the architectural features that are well-known from many parts of the world, most of the more recent mega-developments also involve morphological features previously rather unknown in Santiago, such as artificial lagoons, the post-modern expression of traditional architectural styles, or the huge assembly of detached single-family houses. In places, these new features will soon be complemented by a large-scale pattern of functional mix that strongly resembles some of the prototypical edge cities.

6.4 The functionality and image of new town developments – Delinking post-suburbia from the urban core?

Aside from the physical features and the location of edge-urban developments, the question of whether the urban fringe increasingly acquires specific functions and becomes increasingly independent from the traditional city – and thus constitutes a new form of urbanity in its own right – has been a major concern of recent research. The observation that the rise of edge cities, technoburbs and the like has largely led to a disconnection of fringe developments from their former point of reference in the centre of the old cities is one of the pillars of the concept of post-suburbia. In Latin America, however, it seems that such decoupling has not yet occurred in a pronounced form. In the case of Santiago, the new developments, and in particular those labelled as 'mega', are certainly usually equipped with several facilities and infrastructures. The recently completed motorway ring enables traffic to flow between the various edge-urban zones, bypassing the inner urban areas. There have clearly been incidences of a suburbanization of workplaces due to industrial and commercial developments at the urban edge. Probably the most important examples for the latter are Chile's first green-field office park *Ciudad Empresarial* in Huechuraba and the *ENEA* business park close to the international airport in Pudahuel. However, by and large the centre of economic activity has not yet moved to the urban periphery. Instead, during the last 30 years the CBD of Santiago has largely shifted from the old city centre in the municipality of Santiago to the traditional upper-middle and upper class districts located at a distance of around 5–10 km east of it. These districts used to be sub- or even ex-urban until the first half of the twentieth century, but now form part of the densely built-up inner urban area. This kind of CBD shift towards the socially most favourable direction is a common feature in Latin American cities (Bähr and Mertins, 1995, p. 111ff.). It is in this zone that the current ambition of the Chilean capital to become a 'world class city' becomes tangible with several headquarter buildings and high-rise office complexes.

The expanding CBD in the eastern part of the city is the workplace of many of the residents in the new, gated mega-developments. Therefore the road connection to this zone is one of the most important location factors and a major selling argument for houses in these developments. The *Piedra Roja* megaproject, for instance, is advertised as being located only 'ten minutes from Vitacura' (one of Santiago's most distinguished neighbourhoods), which makes it part of the geographical imagination of the well-off in Santiago. The success of such marketing is crucial for the entire project and in the case of *Piedra Roja* it has already worked. Not only are several celebrities living here or publicly thinking about doing so: from the middle class upwards everybody in Santiago seems to know somebody of the currently (in 2009) 1,000 or so families in *Piedra Roja*. The cultural coding of the new edge-urban settlements that transpires, however, is very close to the traditional suburban dream of white collar workers living in a decent, green neighbourhood remote from their jobs in the city centre and hardly substantiates the post-suburbia hypothesis.

6.5 The production of post-suburbia in Santiago – New constellations of actors?

The producers of edge-urban developments can be assigned to three actor groups, according to the basic distinction of three spheres of society in the literature on governance.

Public sector actors

The actors from the public sector largely aim at facilitating development. In Chile the *national government* generally promotes the growth of the capital city as the country's primary economic powerhouse. Several public institutions are responsible for developing planning instruments and urban development policies, which sometimes are little synchronized. The two national ministries that arguably are most important for urban development in general, and the development of Santiago in particular, are the Ministry for Housing and Urbanism (MINVU) and the Ministry for Public Works (MOP) that are traditionally opposed to each other (cf. Ducci, 2004; Orellana, 2007). While the MINVU has the formal responsibility for most city-building aspects, it is often the MOP that is stronger in practice because of its huge budget to plan and build public works.

Decentralization of the highly centralized state, and transfer of discretionary power and financial resources to the lower tiers of government, is an important element of the state modernization discourse and has been a major goal of Chilean national policy over the last couple of decades. However, in practice there is considerable resistance to decentralization. Although significantly more attention is paid to the sub-national level now, the regional government of the Metropolitan Region (*Gobierno Regional*, GORE) has only limited capacity and authority to coordinate development across the large number of municipalities that together build Santiago. Although GORE is trying hard to increase its influence on the regional development, it is not yet clear if these efforts will succeed.

The *local government* authorities basically form an actor group that usually is not in a position to manage and shape the process of urban development. As with the case of the regional government, this contradicts the goal of decentralization to move decision-making closer to the citizens. However, while potentially increasing the relevance of the municipal level and the importance of local decision-making and services, decentralization also puts substantial demands on local authorities (Ward, 1996). In the light of their weak investment basis (Orellana, 2007), the municipalities' only chance for an improvement of their revenue situation is through investment realized on their territory. Therefore, they enter into partnership arrangements with private (real-estate) actors. While some of the more affluent municipalities (e.g. Las Condes, Lo Barnechea, Vitacura) managed to keep some control over, and even get planning gain out of, the megaprojects (notably in the first wave), in other cases the experience was rather mixed (e.g. Huechuraba, Penalolen). The lack of influence of local authorities on the development in their territory is most pronounced where peripheral communes with a predominantly poor population are affected by the latest wave of megaprojects. These multi-billion dollar projects with their development horizons of 30 years or more, exceed by far the dimensions of spatial developments that could be controlled, let alone planned, by underfunded municipalities.

Private sector actors

Until the liberalization under the Pinochet regime the government housing programmes and individual private actors accounted for the majority of housing construction in the city. Today it is the Chilean real-estate sector that is building the vast majority of new housing stock. Zegras and Gakenheimer (2000) identify around 25 major players in the real-estate business which all arose in the 1980s and 1990s in the wake of liberalization policies and relatively stable economic growth rates in Chile. While some of the firms have their roots in the construction industry, others come from different industrial sectors, such as winemaking or telecommunications; still others are descendants from one of the wealthy families of Chile's traditional plutocracy. In the last few decades, an ever-increasing number of corporate actors and volume of finance capital entered the real-estate market. The result has been the emergence of a new type of real-estate actor, one who is in charge of rent-seeking capital and therefore looking for opportunities to valorize land and to develop attractive products (Stockins, 2004; De Mattos, 2007).

These new actors concentrate a considerable share of their efforts on the development of megaprojects on the urban fringe (Borsdorf and Hidalgo, 2005; Borsdorf et al, 2007). This involves the selection of sites, the development of projects, including master-planning and strategies to commercialize and finance them, and the execution of work. For the real estate sector, thus, the new megaprojects have become a sophisticated tool in a kind of development strategy which Sabatini (2000) has called 'the social modification of place'. It consists of purchasing land in poor peripheral locations for low prices which is then repackaged and promoted as a high-end living environment for the middle and upper classes.

Other actors, in particular specialized consultants, emerged with this new model of urban development. The most prominent examples are two large planning consultancies (URBE and POLIS) with together more than 70 professionals. They offer expertise not only in master-planning and project design but also in the negotiation process with authorities. It is worth noting that both consultancies not only have been important players in pushing many of the megaprojects, but are also working for municipal, regional and national authorities, in particular by elaborating land-use plans. Interestingly, the executives of the consultancies share a special sort of cultural capital with many other high-rank figures in Chilean urbanism in academia, practice and politics: post-graduate degrees in urban design from renowned US-American or British Universities. It is therefore not surprising that land developers in Santiago often claim to have taken US examples of master-planned communities as models for their megaprojects. Furthermore, the involvement of several international architects, landscape designers and consulting firms facilitates the import of global design ideas.

Another sign for the internationalization of the real-estate market is the increasing presence of international capital and joint ventures. A Canadian company, for instance, holds the majority of one of the megaprojects in the commune of Colina, and the *ENEA* business park is entirely in the hands of the Spanish company Enersis. It is no secret that real-estate and building investors in Chile traditionally have strong personal links to the country's political and economic elites. In addition, they have strong organizational and political power. The Chilean chamber of the construction industry (*Cámara Chilena de Construcción*) and the association of real-estate developers (*Asociación de Desarrolladores Inmobiliarios*) are among the most influential economic lobby organizations in the country.

Civil society actors

The sphere of civil society seems to be important for Santiago's urban development mainly in one respect today: it provides the demand for the huge number of new houses being built at and beyond the urban edges. However, it is important to note that this contribution of society to the general dynamics of suburbanization is not necessarily an expression of universal human desires (cf. Bruegmann, 2005). Instead, it is equally plausible to derive it from the inducement of a suburban lifestyle orientation by means of marketing and promotion of suburban houses and resorts by the real-estate sector (cf. Phelps et al, 2010). In other words, the promotion of suburban housing increases the demand of the citizens for sprawl in the same way as, on the other hand, administrative and private actors may feel prompted to meet this demand by residential projects and related infrastructure investments.

On the other hand, there is hardly any opposition to the strong coalition of the public and the private sector for residential sprawl. There is usually no formation of no-growth-coalitions, which are a phenomenon in the US or Europe (cf. Zunino, 2006). Here the simple fact is that with respect to the new megaprojects, new development occurs on former agricultural land and only affects a relatively small existing population. However, the absence of civil society in the dynamics of sprawl also reflects the strong association of the public and the private sector in Chile that frequently leads to non-transparent forms of decision-making and a political framing of projects that discourages participation. Moreover, the planning of private compounds does not require formal citizen participation. Thus, it is often very difficult for the population to get information, let alone information on their democratic rights concerning participation or intervention in the planning process. Nevertheless, in recent years there have also been examples of successful citizen resistance against development and urbanization projects in Santiago (Ducci, 2004; Parraguez Sanchez, 2008). Apparently, such mobilizations require two preconditions: firstly, a sufficient number of people that are directly affected by a project and, secondly, a strong feeling of identity with and belonging to their neighbourhood.

6.6 Privatization of the fringes – The examples of *Piedra Roja* and *Urbanya*

All in all, the spatial and functional features of the current edge-urban developments in Santiago can be read as a marked expression of urban development in times of globalization and hegemony of neoclassical economic thinking (De Mattos, 1999). However, in order to grasp the specificity of the current trends in the transformation of the suburban realm, it also seems necessary to look at the actual processes of planning and decision-making behind these trends. Only then does it become tangible how a liberalization policy together with a legacy of centralism and the absence of civil society bring about a largely privatized form of city building. This final section takes a closer look at two new megaproject cases: *Piedra Roja* and *Urbanya*. It illustrates how the expansion of the urban area has become a largely privatized endeavour, despite the existing planning legislation and the democratic political system in Chile (Zunino, 2006).

Both projects originated in the early 1990s when huge parcels of land in the periphery of Santiago were purchased by individuals and real-estate firms. *Piedra Roja* stands for projects dedicated to the upper class and upper-middle class located in the northern periphery of Santiago. It is one of the biggest and most sophisticated real-estate projects in the history of city-building in Santiago. Located in the municipality of Colina in the north of the Santiago city-region, it consists of around 1,000 ha and six individual residential neighbourhoods or barrios as gated communities that will in the end accommodate more than 60,000 residents. Construction work started in 2002 and the investment will eventually amount to around 1.8 billion US$. The exclusively residential barrios are situated around a commercial centre with supermarkets, shops, restaurants and an artificial lagoon. There is a sailing and horse-riding club. There will be schools, universities, etc. The most exclusive of the neighbourhoods, *Hacienda Chicureo*, is built around an extensive golf course.

Urbanya is a large-scale residential project that is currently in its final planning and approval process located in the municipality of Pudahuel

Figure 6.1 Shopping complex and artificial lagoon in Piedra Roja (photograph, Michael Lukas)

Figure 6.2 Houses in Piedra Roja (photograph, Michael Lukas)

which, until now, has only 5 percent of its territory occupied by urban land uses. *Urbanya* responds to a different market segment than *Piedra Roja* and intends to develop Pudahuel into a new middle-class quarter (*barrio*). The architectural structure and features of *Urbanya* are similarly ambitious to those of *Piedra Roja,* but the amenities and general layout of the project are somewhat less distinguished. *Urbanya* has a prospective investment of 1.3 billion US$ and is planned for up to 70,000 inhabitants.

In order to account for the complexity of private city-building we will use the concept of 'orders of governance' identified by Kooiman (2003) when looking at actors, institutions and their interplay in societal affairs. These orders can be imagined as three nested rings.

> The outer ring deals with day-to-day affairs, and is termed first order governance. The second ring – second order governance – deals with institutions, whereas the third – meta-governance – involves debate on the underlying values and principles. The three orders are closely related and always – even when they are not made explicit – available (Kooiman et al, 2008).

Day-to-day affairs in the production of post-suburban Santiago

The development of *Piedra Roja* began with the real-estate company Inmobiliaria Manquehue acquiring 3,000 ha of agricultural land in Colina and Lo Barnechea in 1993. Some of that land was parcelled into lots of 5,000 m^2 and prepared for extreme-low-density development in accordance with a law from the year 1980 (DL 3.516). The major share of land was reserved for large-scale projects in anticipation that a future change in land-use norms would permit the expansion of urban uses into the rural northern part of the city-region, and especially the municipality of Colina. The case of *Urbanya* in Pudahuel is similar. The municipality is known as one of 'the best corners of Chile' and the real-estate industry has been focusing on it for a while (Zegras and Gakenheimer, 2000) with proposals for three megaprojects (*Urbanya, ENEA,* and a third project, *Praderas*) becoming concrete in the mid-1990s.

From their beginnings, the projects in Colina and Pudahuel have been planned and implemented through collaboration between public and private actors at various levels. In the case of Colina, a coalition of central government authorities and private real-estate investors largely bypassed the local level. In Pudahuel, developers and the local authority created a mixed commission of urbanism in the mid-1990s to elaborate a new local land-use plan that would consider public and private development interests equally. However, this land-use plan was never approved. The incorporation of the location into the PRMS, the metropolitan regulatory plan (*Plan Regulador Metropolitano de Santiago*), under the responsibility of the Ministry of Urbanism and Housing (MINVU) in 2003 removed planning of these projects to higher governmental levels.

In a personal communication with the authors an involved planning official described the relations between public and private actors at the national level, where the two megaprojects of *Piedra Roja* and *Urbanya* were finally negotiated, as close and good. Several of the persons involved changed side – working for the private sector in the beginning and for the public sector or as an academic expert and consultant later, or vice versa. For instance, one of the three owners of ECSA, one of the major real-estate companies in Santiago, was finance minister under Pinochet and one of the leading figures of Chile's neoliberal adjustment in the 1970s. Another example of this 'revolving door' feature of Chilean society is that the crucial modification of the PRMS in 2003, that finally brought the Pudahuel projects on track, was signed by a MINVU official who had worked previously as a private consultant to one of the Pudahuel megaprojects.

In general, the projects have been planned and designed without any meaningful citizen participation. In Colina, where the projects were negotiated and implemented at the highest level, not even the local public authorities had any say and people living in the area were entirely neglected. The *Urbanya* developers in Pudahuel made some voluntary efforts to integrate neighbours and civil society groups, however, participants described the meetings as autocratic and overtly pro-forma in their style, so that social leaders retreated immediately.

Institutions regulating and safeguarding the production of post-suburban Santiago

The recent developments at the periphery of Santiago would not have been possible without the legislative and planning framework. The removal of the *limite urbano*, the urban growth boundary of the metropolitan area, in 1979 can be regarded as a starting point for creating an institutional environment favourable to such developments. At the same time, another law was enacted which prohibits a subdivision of plots in rural areas to a size below 5.000 m^2 with a view to preserving the rural landscape. However, it has had the opposite effect, bringing about a peculiar kind of urban sprawl which is characterized by the acquisition and preparation for development of sites by developers who then sell them to the increasing number of wealthy households who can afford to reside on such large parcels of land (Naranjo, 2006). The abolishment of the *limite urbano* was undone in 1985 and, furthermore, a refined delineation of the urban area was introduced into the new PRMS in 1994. However, this plan only makes prescriptions for the urban area, i.e. zones that are dedicated to urban development; it leaves the rural areas unprotected. Nonetheless, the first version of this plan clearly mirrored what was then the policy of the Ministry of Urbanism and Housing (MINVU): consolidation and densification of the urban area while limiting urban expansion.

In 1993 the 'rival' Ministry for Public Works (MOP) formulated a quite different perspective in its so-called *Macrozona*-Plan, which is driven by a spirit that urban expansion is not only inevitable but highly desirable. Subsequently MINVU modified the PRMS in 1997, thereby widening the scope for peripheral growth especially north of Santiago. The plan achieved this by the introduction of new categories of land-use regulation. It delineated large parts of the municipalities of Colina, Lampa and Til Til as Conditional Urbanization Zones (ZODUC) and Priority Urban Development Areas (ADUP). With this modification the development in these zones was made legally possible, albeit bound by certain exigencies relating to a minimum 300 ha size of developments, the land-use mix (integrating services and social housing) and the financing of infrastructural mitigations (transport infrastructure in and around the development areas). While this solution to some extent permitted MINVU to hold up its claim to provide for a socially inclusive and sustainable form of spatial development, MOP was able to achieve its vision of an expanding polycentric city-region based on transport infrastructure, and the real-estate sector got permission to develop large-scale projects. Although MINVU justified the specific delineation of the Conditional Urbanization Zones on the basis of technicalities (e.g. certain distances of the projects to high-value agricultural land), it is no secret that it closely followed the detailed localized interests of private actors (Poduje, 2006). As one public officer put it in an interview, the pressure to develop projects such as *Piedra Roja* had become so strong that a fast-track mechanism for their implementation was indispensable.

This view is supported by the fact that no clear procedures and responsibilities for the further approval process and the calculation of the mitigation costs for the individual projects had been established. An inter-ministerial Committee of MINVU and MOP was created to define the impact fees that private firms would have to pay for developing projects. MOP took the lead because it had years of technical and negotiation experience with private investors through its system of high-way concessions. Public authorities and nine developers reached an agreement after long negotiation in 2001. For the one-billion-dollar-project *Piedra Roja*, the developers agreed to pay more than 30 million US$ for infrastructure. This included the construction of the Northeast Highway and the *Pie Andino* roads without which the projects would not have been marketable.

In parallel to the negotiations on the new planning instruments regarding conditional urbanization (ZODUC and ADUP), MINVU prepared a further modification of the regional development plan (PRMS) which would enable real-estate development not only in the northern surroundings of Santiago but in almost the entire peri-urban hinterland. This was what the *Urbanya* developers were waiting and working for. Together with the other private actors with vested interests in Pudahuel, they actually sat at the negotiation table with the public authorities elaborating the new regulation mechanism, which was finally approved as Conditional Urbanization Projects (PDUC) in 2003. While following the conceptual idea of the first generation of conditional planning, the ZODUC/ADUP, the PDUC introduced several modifications. These corresponded primarily to public criticisms about the highly non-transparent negotiations and arbitrary procedures that were characteristic of the ZODUC/ADUP processes. The PDUC includes a detailed schedule for, and the involvement of fourteen public authorities in, the project approval process.

Although the increased number of public authorities to be consulted demonstrates that the state has not entirely left the edge-urban realm to the private sector, the leading part of the private sector is a marked feature of projects such as *Piedra Roja* and *Urbanya* and the ZODUC/ADUP and PDUC regulations, which form the legal basis of these projects.

Values and principles underlying the production of post-suburban Santiago

Although the location and design of individual projects at the periphery of Santiago are mainly controlled by real-estate developers, they are embedded in the wider discourse on both the restructuring of the urban region and the streamlining of urban governance promoted by MOP in particular. This discourse, which provides a strong cultural basis for the current transformation of Santiago's fringes, builds on the argument that growth generates jobs and serves societal development (cf. Logan and Molotch, 1987). A central personality in Chilean urbanism, responsible for the macro plan of MOP and for the local land-use plan in Pudahuel in the 1990s, stated publicly that slowing down the expansion of Santiago would put at risk national development (Echenique, 1995).

Another important discursive driver of private towns in Santiago is the naturalization of urban development through the notion that cities just grow. It is accepted as common sense in the urbanism scene in Santiago that the state must not and cannot regulate how people want to live. Discourse in Chile typically does not see the strong orientation of urban policy and spatial planning towards the requirements of the market as selling out development rights and planning competencies to real-estate firms for low prices, but rather as establishing a dialogue with powerful actors in order to achieve planning gains. Conditional planning is understood as part of a public-private-alliance in city-building, as one high-ranking planning official stated in an interview. This can be interpreted as part of a general shift in the conceptualization of the role of the state, which some authors describe as a shift from urban planning to urban governance (De Mattos, 2004). Indeed, public and private actors entered into a wide range of new arrangements since the 1990s such as the introduction of downtown development corporations or the franchising of highway concessions. In this respect, the new planning instruments of ZODUC/ADUP and PDUC are only examples of new policy devices that organize urban governance more along market principles.

However, there are also voices emerging in Santiago and in Chile that oppose the dominating, largely neoliberal urban discourse. As a reaction to the introduction of the ZODUC/ADUP and PDUC instruments, some social organizations are mobilizing against the envisaged reform of the general law of urbanism (LGCU) that would make conditional planning a general means of urban planning. These organizations claim that more participation is needed and that urban sprawl is not inevitable. However, while such critical views are frequently articulated in academic and also public debates, they gain hardly any recognition or support in the political arena. On the contrary, the progenitors of such views are often themselves exposed to harsh criticism. Jaime Ravinet, the former Minister of Housing, labelled the civil society groups that – in part successfully – opposed the approval of the Pudahuel projects as 'slaves of an urban development vision from the 1950s' and as 'bleary-eyed and foreign funded hippies' (La Tercera, 2003). Likewise, the authority responsible for agricultural land, one of the 14 entities that have to approve the PDUC process, is criticized for its occasional disapproval of certain initiatives as not understanding what contemporary urbanism is all about. Politicians, investors and experts have unilaterally declared the discussion about the future of Santiago to be over in favour of a shift in the focus of discussion towards questions of design of infrastructural requirements (e.g. Aravena, 2006). Although these examples may appear anecdotal, they indicate a lasting influence of authoritarianism and technocratic rationality (Zunino, 2006).

6.7 Conclusion: Santiago as a Latin American version of post-suburbia?

This contribution outlines the general patterns of urban expansion and suburbanization in Santiago de Chile. Urban expansion changed in the 1970 due to a mixture of various factors: the liberalization of planning instruments by the Pinochet regime, the government-driven location of social housing on the urban fringes, and, more recently, the modernization and extension of the urban transport infrastructure into the city-region. The return to democracy since 1990 and the corresponding reinforced efforts to achieve a more decentralized political system have brought a significant push for economic and societal development in Chile. However, the framework conditions for urban development that were introduced beforehand, in particular the strong orientation towards market-oriented policies, by and large continued to exist or have even been deepened. New policy and planning instruments have been introduced that facilitated a largely private edge-urban development in the form of new megaprojects.

To what extent can we speak of a Latin American version of post-suburbia and in how far does this suggest a 'clean break' from suburbia? In order to answer these questions, the three dimensions put forward by Phelps et al (2010) and Phelps and Wu in Chapter 1 of this volume are useful.

The first dimension relates to the question whether these settlements mark a clear break form the suburban past. The case of Santiago exhibits edge-urban development that can be assessed as quite similar to elsewhere in the region. The land-use pattern and the (dis-integrated) location of emerging edge development are to some extent driven by new megaprojects, such as *Piedra Roja* and *Urbanya*. They coincide with intensive infrastructure investment, in particular regarding roads for individual transport. However, similarities are much less clear with respect to functional and socio-cultural characteristics. The megaprojects in Santiago are certainly usually equipped with several facilities and infrastructures and, like other notorious examples of edge-urban gated developments in Latin America, such as Alphaville in Sao Paolo or, more recently, Nordelta in Buenos Aires, involve considerable industrial and commercial zones (cf. Coy and Pöhler, 2002). Likewise, the designs of the Chilean examples are geared to globally-spreading standards of this type of post-modern real-estate product (Irazábal, 2006). Furthermore, there have clearly been incidences of a suburbanization of workplaces due to industrial and commercial developments on the urban edge, for example near the international airport in Pudahuel. However, until now the centre of economic activity has largely remained in the inner urban areas and has not yet moved to the urban periphery. In consequence, the residents of the new edge developments continue to maintain strong ties with their traditional locations in functional terms, including not only work but also social networks and education of children. With this observation, that the binary functional relationship between the city and the periphery (as a defining characteristic of the suburb) remains a dominant pattern we can hardly substantiate the post-suburbia hypothesis for the Santiago case. Nevertheless, the edge-urban megaprojects mirror the effort of political and economic elite fractions in Chile to use the entire city-region of Santiago in order to form a 'world-class megacity'.

The second dimension relates to the location and placing of post-suburban development. Clearly, the recent developments of megaprojects such as *Piedra Roja* push the boundary of the city beyond the traditional periphery to new exurban locations. Ironically, *Piedra Roja* in particular seems to follow the old ideal derived from Ebenezer Howard's garden city – of the marriage of town and country – that gave inspiration to suburbia in Europe and North America. The assessment is somewhat different for the case of *Urbanya*, that fits much better to the image of post-suburbia with mixed land uses and an edge-city type of appearance. Despite these differences, a common feature of these two examples and also other developments is that they are placed at major highway intersections and are built for private car use. From this perspective, it seems adequate to state that, while we can identify some post-suburban characteristics, more traditional elements of suburbia also continue to exist.

The third argument relates to the production of post-suburbia and the (new) ideologies and politics of post-suburbia. Partly in a synthesis of the previous dimensions, there is evidence that the dominant image of the new edge communities reflects the traditional suburban dream of life in a decent, green neighbourhood remote from employment in the city centre. That is certainly the case in the *Piedra Roja* type of development that responds to residents' ambitions for upward mobility and economic security, ideals for freedom and quality of life. The actors that shape the production of space in the urban periphery form a coalition of state and private sector interests and instruments. While this is by itself not exceptional, there has been a significant shift in the mode of production of urban space in many parts of Latin America in that private actors have gained paramount importance, and it seems appropriate to label this trend 'post-suburban' (Hidalgo, 2005). The case of Santiago shows that the interplay in which public and private actors produce urban space occurs under distinct and very specific conditions that will be difficult to generalize. On the one hand, national policy-makers are largely supportive of this hegemonic role of investors and real-estate companies. On the other hand, local authorities and civil society are often practically excluded from decision-making processes on the development of edge-urban areas, despite a transfer of power, resources and responsibilities to sub-national units of government in the last two decades. It is in this type of urban governance that we see the clearest signs for a new, post-suburban pattern of urban development.

7
From Country Club to Edge City? Gated Residential Communities and the Transformation of Pilar, Argentina

Sonia Roitman and Nicholas A. Phelps

7.1 Introduction

At first glance the view from the *Panamericana* highway that goes to Pilar is much like that from any highway and could be taken as evidence of 'edge city' (Garreau, 1991) style development and indeed has, together with developments elsewhere in the municipality, been regarded in more general terms as the sort of fragmented urbanism said to characterize post-modern urbanization of the United States (US). However the story of Pilar and the process of suburbanization and any nascent post-suburbanization in Latin American cities is rather different from that occurring in the US. We concentrate on the role of one type of private sector actors and investors – gated communities – and their contribution to processes of post-suburbanization in Pilar – an outer suburb of Buenos Aires metropolitan area (Argentina).

The chapter considers the contribution of gated communities to the urbanization of suburbia, highlighting some of the specificities of the Latin American context. It also examines the case of Pilar – an extensive, third ring, municipality at the edge of the Buenos Aires metropolitan region. The study is based on a synthesis of academic and policy literature on the subject of gated communities as well as interviews with local and national government officials and civic, business and developer groups conducted in Spanish on location in Buenos Aires and Pilar during April 2009. As the site of the very first 'Country Club' in Argentina, Pilar is synonymous with the phenomenon of gated communities. Whilst the growth of Pilar has also been associated with new retail, office and other developments these are, like the gated residential communities, rather separate from the remainder of the municipality and its populations, indicating a powerful dual development trajectory as part of post-suburbia in the Latin American setting.

7.2   Gated community development and suburban growth

The analytical distinction between private and public space becomes more complex when those sites credited with the emergence of public space were originally private and where the benefits of public space may be overdrawn and those of private space overlooked (Kirby, 2008). This question is particularly poignant in the Latin American setting where gated communities are part of a strong privatization process. Several authors highlight the broader significance of gated communities to societies and local government when insisting that the phenomenon of gated communities is cultural (Webster, 2002). Blakely and Snyder (1997, p. vii), for example, argue that 'Gated communities are not merely another form of residential settlement. They are part of a deeper social transformation'. In this respect it is clear that gated communities signal a particular cultural and social transformation. Gated communities embody a 'culture that links ownership of private property with freedom, individuality, and autonomy rather than with responsibility to the surrounding community' (McKenzie, 1994, p. 25) and as such they could be regarded as further evidence of the mutation or refinement of the suburban ideology (Fishman, 1987; Teaford, 1997).

Gated communities are enclaves that tend to be presented as 'opposed to the city, which is represented as a deteriorated world...' (Caldeira, 2000, p. 264). Nevertheless, the large and growing body of empirical studies of gated communities makes it clear that – for all their attempts at containment – these private spaces do have economic, social and political effects. This raises an important open question of whether and in what way these communities contribute to the rounding-out of settlements regarded as suburban.

First, gated communities have important economic consequences for the municipalities in which they are embedded: 'The segregation that gated communities represent is intentionally economic' (Blakely and Snyder, 1997, p. 153). This should alert us to the probably modest economic spillovers created by the emergence of gated communities in any municipal context. Indeed Blakeley and Snyder (1997) argue that gated communities are not very good at producing public goods, while the underuse of common facilities is suggestive of the value of such residences not as clubs, but purely as signifiers of social status (Caldeira, 2000). There is a case for believing that the impact of gated communities

on the fiscal position of local government is on balance likely to be negative since 'In many cities and towns, the wealthy have in effect withdrawn their dollars from the support for public spaces and institutions'
(Reich quoted in McKenzie, 1994, p. 23). However, if the economic ratio-
nale represented by gated communities is one of the preservation of
property values, this has ambiguous implications since it can be argued
that they therefore make some contributions to the local tax base
(Le Goix, 2005). Here the impacts of gated communities reverberate
differently at different geographical scales, with Le Goix (2005, p. 323)
suggesting that 'local governments usually favour the development of
this form of land use to pay for the cost of urban sprawl, while indeed
producing social diseconomies for the whole metropolitan area'.

Second, gated communities have important implications for the practice of community-building within the existing framework of local
government. They are argued to sharpen the focus on important issues
of 'private versus public rights, and responsibilities and the practice of
community' (Blakely and Snyder, 1997, p. vii). The problem is that the
collective interests, or club good properties of the gated communities,
significantly shift the balance that has traditionally held sway in community-building. In gated communities, 'a residents' responsibilities to
the "community" can be satisfied by meeting one's economic obligations' (McKenzie, 1994, pp. 148–149) and we might add beyond the
territorial boundaries of any particular gated community (Massey, 1994).
Even though formally recognized as private corporate entities they themselves are no respecters of legal boundaries – engaging in political behaviour and wielding increasing political power in the public governmental
sphere they have in many respects seceded from. As Pirez (2002, p. 155)
notes, 'each private development is seen as a "city", which hides the
fact that its existence is only possible within the city that provides it with
the means of existence'.

Third, the impacts of gated communities can be considered in connection with issues of social interaction and segregation. Indeed, most
literature that discusses gated communities and segregation links them
with increased social segregation. However, the impacts of gated communities on social segregation at the intra and inter-municipality scale
seem to be different in different national contexts. On the one hand,
gated communities appear likely not to increase intra-municipality social
disparities but to reinforce the relatively homogenous white middle-class
complexion of many US suburbs and hence levels of social segregation
at the inter-municipality scale. On the other hand, gated communities
have increased social segregation at the intra-municipal scale in Latin

American suburbs, with poor and rich neighbourhoods close to each other, but divided by walls (Roitman, 2008).

7.3 Urban Latin American specificities

Some of the generalities of the nature and wider impacts of gated communities were discussed above. However, it is as well to remember that the growth of gated communities and their generative impacts on patterns of urbanization and suburbanization are context specific. Latin America presents several specificities that differentiate it from other regions. Here the development of Latin America is compared to that of the US. In addition, although there are similarities across the Latin American region, there are also important historical, social and economic differences between countries that should be considered. Borsdorf et al have quoted Vidal Koppmann and Dietrich's description of Buenos Aires in translation suggesting that it could apply to the Latin American city in general:

> urban fragments surrounded by illegal marginal settlements, rubbish dumps to open sky next to small and medium units of the traditional urban plot, parks and industrial areas very close to luxury residential quarters, and freeways having been constructed over local earth roads without any maintenance (Borsdorf et al, 2007, p. 370: their translation).

Such descriptions are reminiscent of depictions of the post-modern urban fabric of Los Angeles (Dear and Flusty, 1998) but it would be wrong to regard these patterns of fragmentation as equivalents.

To begin with, the major general contrast to be drawn between US and Latin America is with regard to the socio-economic complexion of the suburbs. Notwithstanding the historic and contemporary diversity of US suburbs which has been recognized, the general affluence of US suburbs contrasts starkly with those in Latin America which are populated mainly by lower social classes. This pattern in the metropolitan periphery of Latin America has shifted somewhat in the last 20 years as middle- and upper-class populations have moved to the suburbs. This has created a situation in which poor and rich families live in close proximity (Roitman, 2008; Sabatini and Cáceres, 2004).

A recent survey of studies of urban sprawl in Latin America and Europe situated gated communities as part of successive processes of suburbanization, periurbanization and post-suburbanization (Borsdorf and Hidalgo, 2008). However, the connection of gated communities to the urbanization of suburbia in Latin America can usefully be specified further in terms of features that set Latin American municipalities apart from their US counterparts.

First, in a fashion not dissimilar to that in the US, Latin American metropolitan peripheries have been concerned to attract gated communities. In order 'to deal with their lagging economy and bring new investment, suburban municipalities relied on their planning autonomy to foster the development of gated communities' (Libertun de Duren, 2007, p. 607). These developments have superficial generic similarities with those in the US, but are probably best thought of as representing a 'temporal disparity' – a difference in the phasing of similar patterns and processes of urbanization in different countries – which makes direct comparison problematic (Phelps et al, 2006). Instead, following Dick and Rimmer's discussion of East Asian city-regions, it may be best to depict Latin American cities as passing through a number of phases of divergence from and convergence on US patterns of urbanization. Interestingly, one such element of convergence taking place simultaneously against other divergent developments is the emergence of what Pirez (2002, p. 157) terms 'a "one dimensional city": use value becomes subordinated to exchange value' in the development of land which is reminiscent of the growth machine (Molotch, 1976) logic that drove the post-war mass suburbanization in the US.

Second, one specificity of the Latin American, and indeed transition economies in comparison to developed economies comes in the contrast in the resources and technical capacities of municipal governments and the newly created private governments of gated communities. Historically, the public sector was heavily involved in the suburbanization process in Latin America through the construction of social housing developments. In this sense the state was intimately involved in producing the particular socio-economic complexion of these areas, and indeed some of the ongoing burdens of suburban municipalities in trying to rectify poor levels of infrastructure and services. More recently, the suburbanization process has been led by private planning activities associated with gated communities (Pirez, 2002), not least since the human resources devoted to forward planning, development control and enforcement in municipalities remains limited, and certainly behind that in most developed countries. The situation is not improved by the lack of regulatory framework on which municipalities can draw. According to Pirez (2002, p. 155), '...the metropolitan area becomes a space for operations seeking, largely or almost exclusively, private economic gain' because there are no clear or consistent regulations on land use.

Moreover, the superimposition of gated communities upon outer suburban districts appears to have curtailed some of the possibilities for grass-roots political movements to shape a viable politics centred on issues of collective consumption and the 'retrofit' of amenities and infrastructure which has been apparent in some prominent instances (Phelps et al, 2006). Caldeira (2000, p. 235) notes how

> At the same time that the working classes became important political actors, organizing social movements and demanding their rights and better living conditions, and at the same time that the infrastructure of the periphery indeed improved significantly, their incomes dropped, and their capacity to become property owners through autoconstruction was reduced.

Indeed, the privatization embodied in these gated communities has coincided with what Pirez (2002) describes as a triple fragmentation (institutional, technical and territorial) in the management of public services. All of these factors present significant challenges to the task of community-building in the public city.

Third, in relation to Santiago de Chile, Sabatini and Cáceres argue that the pattern of large spatial scale segregation in Latin America is changing towards a process of segregation in a lower but more intense geographical scale: 'The multiplication of gated communities that is taking place in Chilean cities is equivalent to a diminishing of residential segregation in a large spatial scale and, simultaneously, to an intensification of segregation in a reduced spatial scale. This reduction of the segregation scale takes place when gated communities are built in the low-income periphery' (Sabatini and Cáceres, 2004, p. 11, our translation). Indeed it may be true to say that the presence of gated communities in suburban Latin America is both more conspicuous and more profound because of their superimposition upon some of the poorest populations within metropolitan areas. Thuillier (2005, pp. 255–256) identifies:

> upper class enclaves, requiring huge areas of land, spring up at the fringes of the metropolis, which in Buenos Aires do not consist of 'edge cities' but of slums concentrating the poorest and more recent immigrants in town, coming from the most under-developed provinces of the country. Therefore a striking contrast appears at the outskirts of the Metropolitan area.

As such 'the two extremes of the social spectrum in Argentina coexist through the settlement of gated communities amongst this desolate suburban landscape' (Thuillier, 2005, p. 263). However, it is relevant to emphasize that Latin American cities have been characterized by social segregation since their development by the Spanish conquerors, yet what it is new now is the appearance of gated communities as symbols of this process of segregation (Roitman and Giglio, 2010).

In sum, taking these specificities into account, there are, as Webster (2002) notes, different challenges posed by the growth of gated communities in different settings. Issues of secession are perhaps most pressing in the US whereas it is the balancing of municipal revenues with the costs of gated communities that is apparent in Europe. However, 'In Asia, South America, and Africa, the issue is one of how to let the market provide the professional middle classes with the urban services they aspire to without critically fragmenting highly unequal cities' (Webster, 2002, p. 400). Borsdorf et al (2007, p. 377) go further to argue that 'Exclusion itself may be regarded as the central structuring force' emerging in Latin American cities in some contrast to the US and Europe, in addition to status and social distinction (Caldeira, 2000; Roitman, 2003).

7.4   The 'boom' of gated communities in Pilar

Pilar lies 58 kilometres to the north west of the centre of Buenos Aires in the third ring of municipalities within the Metropolitan Region of Buenos Aires (Map 7.1). It is vast by European municipal standards, covering some 383 square kilometres.[1] The predominant activity in the municipality is still agriculture, with 58 percent of its land used for this (Barsky and Vio, 2007). However, it is one of the third ring municipalities with highest population growth rate: 55 percent in the period 1960–70, 77 percent in 1970–80, 54 percent in 1980–91 and 78 percent in 1991–2001 (Pirez, 2002; and INDEC website).[2] According to the last census in 2010, it had a population of 298,191 inhabitants (INDEC website, Census 2010 preliminary results).

---

[1]This is the current area of Pilar. In 1994, the provincial law 11.551 (20/10/94) modified the administrative borders of some municipalities of Buenos Aires Province and created Municipalidad de Malvinas Argentinas. Malvinas Argentinas annexed land that was formerly part of Pilar and the Municipality of General Sarmiento (Vidal-Koppmann, 2007).

[2]INDEC – Instituto Nacional de Estadísticas y Censos-, Argentina, www.indec. gov.ar.

Map 7.1 The metropolitan region of Buenos Aires

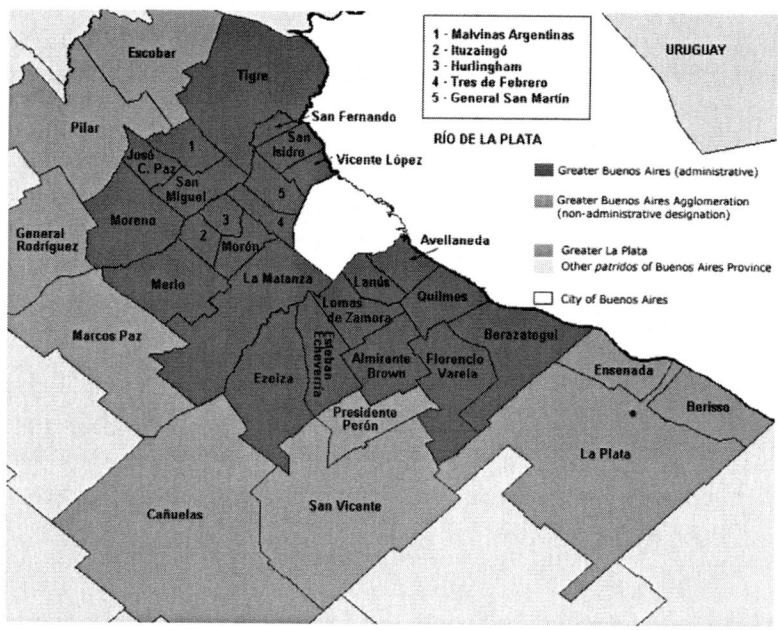

© OpenStreetMap Contributors, cc-by-sa

The city and district of Pilar have existed since the nineteenth century centred historically around the main square – *Plaza 12 de Octubre*. Following the pattern of Latin American cities this historic core has been overlain by self-constructed buildings until recently. Libertun de Duren (2007) reports that in the 1980s a third of houses in the municipality was of substandard condition with two-thirds of houses lacking piped water. By 2006, 25 percent of the population still had unmet basic needs in Pilar but yet coexisted with over one hundred gated communities (Vidal-Koppmann, 2007). As the largest municipal concentration of gated communities in Argentina, now sitting alongside both the existing middle- and lower-class population and the new poor neighbourhoods, it provides an extreme exemplification of the patterns of what has come to be regarded as something of a distinct phase of urbanization of the Latin American city albeit a phase that has its roots in earlier times.

Different definitions of gated communities make it extremely problematic to provide accurate comparable time series figures on the numbers of such developments (Roitman, 2004, 2008). Here we use a variety of sources to provide some very general impression of the growth of gated communities in Pilar, though individual figures cannot be regarded as comparable. The number of gated communities rose from 20 in 1980s, to 30 in 1991, to 115 in 2001 (Libertun de Duren, 2007). The most recent occasional publication '*Guía de Countries, Barrios Privados y Chacras*' put the figure at 98 in 2005 (Publicountry, 2005). While Vidal Koppmann (2007) mentioned there were 117 in 2006, occupying 54 square kilometres (Barsky and Vio, 2007). Such large numbers also translate into a significant part of the land area of the municipality being given over to gated communities with 58 percent of land taken up by agricultural activities, 17 percent by residential development in gated communities, 12 percent by residential development in 'open neighbourhoods', 10 percent by empty land and 3 percent by industrial uses (Barsky and Vio, 2007).

The history of gated communities in Pilar begins with the creation of *Tortugas Country Club* in 1932 as part of *Las Tortugas Polo Club* (Verdecchia, 1995; Svampa, 2001). These 'country clubs' were related to the sports activities of elite groups who lived in Buenos Aires with houses used only during weekends. Later in the 1970s, this type of residential development expanded as people living in the city wanted to have larger weekend houses, with important sport infrastructure and within a green environment. From the late 1990s onwards they became mainly used as permanent residences as families could not longer afford having two houses – one in Pilar and one in Buenos Aires city. Thus the original growth of Pilar as a location for 'country clubs' was limited, exclusive and based on the environmental quality of the area.

The major growth of gated communities in the metropolitan periphery took place from the 1990s onwards. Pilar attracted many of these gated communities and with them a major increase in population. However growth in this phase was based not on the environmental quality that had attracted previous gated community developments, but on a major latent demand for this style of living, coupled with increased accessibility from the periphery to Buenos Aires city centre as a result of the improvement of the *Panamericana* highway.[3]

In general, the recent growth of these gated communities was linked to the search for an explicitly suburban way of life, but also with a

---

[3]*Panamericana*, officially called Northern Access, was formerly a National Route built in the 1970s.

degree of social differentiation. *Barrios Privados* (also called '*barrios cerrados*' – closed neighbourhoods) represented a more affordable version of the '*country clubs*'. This type of gated community was developed since the 1990s. Sport infrastructure is not as significant as in '*country clubs*', but they also usually have tennis courts, a swimming pool, and a football pitch, in addition to a club-house for social events. Security is the most valued service and they are mainly used for permanent settlement.

The newest type of gated communities is called '*condominium*'. It was developed after 2001 as a consequence of the economic and institutional crisis in Argentina to provide a more affordable housing option. They are two or three-storied buildings with security and usually not a significant sport infrastructure for common use. They occupy smaller areas than the other types and are likely to be, along with '*barrios privados*', the most developed type in Pilar over the last eight years.

According to some observers, the now significant congestion on the *Panamericana* highway heralds the end of the 'boom' in gated community development in Pilar. However, the figures for land use reported earlier indicate that the vast majority of land in Pilar is under agricultural use and presumably open to conversion to residential use. As one interviewee described: 'You have the feeling that Pilar exploded and all has been developed but if you see it from the air, you see that in fact 70 percent of the land is agriculture land. There is still a lot, lot, lot to be developed' (Interview: CBRE consultant, 20 April 2009). Moreover, only a modest proportion of many of the largest gated community developments has to date been built-out. The developer of a large gated community indicated that as little as 30 percent of the planned development had to date been completed (Interview: Developer, *Estancias del Pilar*, 15 April 2009).

The economic impacts of gated communities in Pilar

The vast majority of foreign direct investment into Pilar from the 1990s onward has been associated with residential real estate. Yet other activities such as industry, private and public service and commercial activities have grown to a lesser extent (Interview: Director of Planning, Municipality of Pilar). At first glance the growth of gated communities and population in Pilar appear to have been accompanied by other developments that might be considered evidence of the urbanization of the suburb. These include an industrial park, office blocks, hotels, cinemas, shopping centres and university campuses, along the *Panamericana* highway. Doubtless there are some causal connections between the growth of gated communities and these other elements in their spatial arrangement but the fuller sense of how they knit-together the community remains unclear.

Although Pilar has a number of industrial areas, its main industrial park is by far the most important employment and economic activity zone in the municipality. Covering 920 hectares it is home to around 180 companies and 12,000 staff (Interview: Representative, Chamber of Business, Pilar Industrial Park, 7 April 2009). It contributes to 89 percent of the economic structure of Pilar in comparison to 6 percent for commerce and 5 percent for services (Barsky and Vio, 2007). It was located in Pilar as a consequence of a private developer who foresaw the potential of the area, and supported by legislation that encouraged the creation of industrial parks 50 kilometres or more away from Buenos Aires.

The industrial park was actually developed in 1978 prior to the recent growth of gated communities but does provide job opportunities to the same new migrant populations as the existing gated communities. Industries located in this park get tax exemptions if they hire local population. In addition to this, the increasing capital and knowledge intensity of some of the enterprises on the park now also offers important employment opportunities to skilled and professional workers from the gated communities.

The arrival of new populations associated with gated communities in Pilar has created a new demand for bilingual private schools in the area. There are also two private universities and a private university hospital located in Pilar. Pilar has also become home to several office developments and new Sheraton and Howard Johnson Hotels along the *Panamericana* highway. They include the offices of *Grupo Farallón* – one of the major gated community developers active in Pilar and elsewhere in the Buenos Aires Metropolitan Region. However taken in the round, these developments are modest in scale and certainly are not regarded as a separate office submarket within the metropolitan sphere by commercial property brokers because big companies want to stay in Buenos Aires and not in the periphery (Interview: Consultant, CBRE). Pilar also has a major new out-of-town shopping and entertainment centre located at 'Kilómetro 50', which includes two shopping centres, hypermarket, and cinema complex. Another shopping centre is being built at '*Kilómetro 34*'. As such, in formal employment terms it would be very misleading to regard somewhere like Pilar as an edge city in terms of the scale of tertiary activity located there.

However, the physical separation of these various new elements contributes to a sense of fragmentation in the municipal space. This is nowhere more apparent than in the case of the major shopping centre at *Kilómetro 50*. The story of how the location of this major service centre occurred is revealing:

> In 1980 or 1982, I went to a one-day seminar....I listened to all the meetings the whole day. All NyCS – *nacidos y criados*, (meaning born and bred) – were there of course. The discussion was that Jumbo, and Disco – supermarkets – wanted to go to Pilar....The NyCs were saying: '...we won't accept that these people – supermarkets – come here'. So at the end of the meeting the mayor said to the NyCs: 'okay, I accept what you say, but what should I say to the people that want to come here to put a supermarket? Don't you think that this is ridiculous?' So the NyCs said: 'okay, we will make it possible for them to locate in the area between [Route] 234 and the *Panamericana*' [which later became known as '*Kilómetro 50*']. This was a low-lying area that was flooded every time it rained. So all [NyCs] were laughing saying '*mira como los jorobamos*' ['look how we bug them']. So I said to them: '...remember that you have just founded the new commercial centre of Pilar'. All of them laughed and said: 'they will be in canoes' and of course today...they are desperate because '*Kilómetro 50*' was born because of their mistake (Developer, 20 April 2009).

Here, it appears that different municipal stances have resulted in different patterns of incorporating gated communities into their suburban fabrics. Pilar's myriad scattered communities compare less favourably to tightly clustered development in San Isidro and a sector of gated communities that has the potential to be integrated into public infrastructure networks such as the road system in Tigre (Libertun de Duren, 2007).[4]

On the face of it, the scale of development activity – gated residential complexes, offices and hotel developments and shopping centres – ought to confer financial benefits on the municipality and an improvement in its fiscal capacity. Yet studies indicate that the tax position of Pilar has not improved noticeably with the vast growth of gated communities and any associated developments (Goytia,

---

[4]San Isidro is an upper-class residential district in the north of Buenos Aires (first ring) and Tigre is a municipality located also in the north, which is now competing with Pilar in terms of gated community developments.

2005). Some explanation for this comes from the fact that current provincial law allows for between 10 and 15 percent of real estate tax to go to municipalities. As a result local government officials do not see this as a major source of income, and may be little inclined to maximize contributions.

Instead, it is the consumption patterns of new affluent residents and the employment opportunities that gated communities offer that are seen by local government officials as the major economic benefits locally (Libertun de Duren, 2007). One interviewee from the national represent-ative organization of gated communities in Argentina suggested that 'each house provides directly 2.5 new jobs, in addition to all services that could be related to that, like supermarket, newspaper delivery person, cinema, etc' (Manager, Argentinean Association of Gated Communities). Thus, Libertun De Duren (2007, citing Thuiller, 2001) notes how offi-cials in Pilar believed gated communities offered employment for around 30,000 people. These jobs come at a price in that the costs of provid-ing infrastructure and services to these new, often informal, settlements remain the responsibility of the municipality (Interview: Representative, Chamber of Business, Pilar Industrial Park).

Gated communities and community-building in Pilar

The growth in gated communities and associated population changes in Pilar, noted above, have taken place in a context in which there is no national law on gated communities in Argentina. Some projects have been created under the figure of the national law 13.512 of Hori-zontal Property of 1948. This law was originally created to regulate high-rise buildings specifying the difference of individual property from common property. It states that owners of flats are exclusive owners of their flats and co-owners of the land and common spaces within the building. When this law is applied to '*clubes de campo*', the streets and common areas are treated as condominium property. This law also regulates maintenance fees. Due to the growth of gated communities in Buenos Aires, other legal instruments were created later. The pro-vincial decree 8912/77 was written regulating land use in the Province of Buenos Aires in 1977. It was the first legal instrument that consid-ered the legal character of gated communities. It establishes the min-imum plot size, maximum number of houses in each development and gives guidelines for the provision of services and infrastructure. It also states that municipalities are responsible for regulating land use. By the end of the 1990s this province passed more legislation (decrees and resolutions) on gated communities to overcome the legal void at the national level. However, many projects are still considered under the figure established by the national law 13.512. During the 1990s, many municipalities also passed by-laws to legislate on this topic. Pilar was one of the pioneers in a sense with the by-laws 142/94, 148/94, 70/95 and later 2840/05.

Within this legislative context, municipalities are left to create their own regulatory planning and strategic stances toward gated community developments which can vary quite markedly within the Buenos Aires metropolitan region. Pilar is one of the few municipalities with by-laws regulating gated communities although there is some suggestion that it has nevertheless lacked a clear and consistent approach in dealing with, and a strategy to leverage benefit from, gated community developments in comparison with other municipalities (Libertun de Duren, 2007). One of our interviewees described what he saw as 'the absence of the state as planner and regulator because what was not present in Pilar was the making of the city. So anyone came and put up barbed wire and build something' (Interview: Consultant, CBRE).

For some observers, gated communities have brought significant benefits to the local population in Pilar (Interview: Manager, *Fundación por Pilar*).[5] However, this can be contested since improvements in infrastructure have taken place only in the areas where gated communities are located, which are not the poor areas. For instance, Manuel Alberti, one of the poorest localities in Pilar with 40 percent of population under poverty and 20 percent with extreme poverty condition, does not have paved streets, nor water, sewage and sanitation supplies.

The suspicion remains that the 'planning gain' from these large developments has been modest. Developers are obliged to give a proportion of their land back to the municipality as planning gain, but there has been little control over this process with parcels of land being given in return for planning approval which are some distance from the development, in a poor location or areas liable to flooding. Thus improvements that have been made are piecemeal and have yet to knit Pilar together in terms of infrastructure like roads, water supply and service provision, and may ostensibly be to serve the gated

---

[5]*Fundación por Pilar* is an NGO that works mainly on health and education projects carried out in the poorest neighbourhoods of Pilar. It is privately funded by local families and companies and runs annual fundraising events.

communities themselves in the form of access roads and the like. Indeed, only 13 percent of the roads of Pilar are paved (CIPPEC, 2005).

The 'flexibility' of the planning system in Pilar, along with the under-resourced nature of local government, was also an important factor encouraging the growth of gated communities in general and in environmentally unsuitable locations in particular (Interview: Director of Planning, Municipality of Pilar, 7 April 2009). In addition to the burden of remedial work associated with the least suitable sites developed in this way, the growth of gated residential developments also exists alongside a significant and persistent burden of unmet basic needs that falls upon the municipal government (Interview: Councillor, Municipality of Pilar, 17 April 2009). Here it is interesting to note that the relatively modest elements of planning gain 'won' from developers along with any wider sense of social responsibility felt by developers and residents of gated communities have been focused on some of these poorer communities, mainly in the form of charity activities and some tar-mac for the unpaved roads. However, planning gain has not always been won and the process of winning it has not always been transparent (Interview: Director of Planning Municipality of Pilar, 7 April 2009).

The contribution of gated communities in Pilar to resolving these accumulated burdens is mediated through the work of civic bodies and charities. The *Fundación por Pilar* emerged in part as recognition of the apparent socio-economic divides that exist in the municipality. The *Fundación* was created in 2000 and originally had broader aspirations in community-building in conjunction with the municipality. This vision for Pilar promoted through the *Fundación por Pilar* with its strong links to the development community was a very different one to that centred on historic Pilar. As Thuillier (2005, p. 269) describes, 'Insisting on the connection between gated communities and economic dynamism, the foundation does not hesitate to foresee for the area's future "Pilar Valley", a kind of Argentinian edge city, a subtle blend of high-tech corporations, gated housing developments and golf greens'. More recently, the *Fundación* has retreated somewhat from such broader visions for community-building in Pilar in a more pragmatic narrowing of its aims to develop poverty reduction schemes in relation to access to health services and educational development.

Gated communities and social cohesion in Pilar

The phenomenal population growth in Pilar – in which gated communities have been the key dynamic directly and indirectly – has also thrown up some new and significant societal divisions which in turn are suggestive of how the impact of gated communities on society might be judged. As one interviewee summarized:

> The city of Pilar has one of the most polarised social and urban structures. The impact of the development of gated communities and a process of economic growth based on services created a segregated urban fabric and polarised social structure and also the worsening of the historic urban centre (Interview: Secretary of Municipalities, National Government, 8 April 2009).

The society, economy and polity emerging in Pilar as a result of this new round of investment raises important questions regarding the contribution that gated communities make, not least because 'Actually defining *who* the deserving members of the local polity are determines the perceptions of the benefits gated communities provide' (Libertun de Duren, 2007, p. 622 original emphasis).

The job opportunities generated by gated communities meant that people from other areas moved to Pilar and therefore informality and poverty grew alongside the expansion of gated communities even when it was not as visible as the latter: 'Unfortunately Pilar has two Pilars and this is really noticeable. There is a blossoming place where you can live very comfortable and then there is another Pilar which is the 8th poorest localities of the province' (Interview: Manager, *Fundación por Pilar*). In actual fact, the picture is a little more complicated than this suggests. There are some potentially curios divisions and co-existences developing in Pilar. Residents are now informally divided into NyCs (*nacidos y criados – born and bred*) and *Venidos y Quedados* – (meaning came and stayed) – or Non-NyCs. Furthermore, it seems – although it is not recognized – there are two types of Non-NyCs: the visible ones who have moved to Pilar to live in gated communities and the invisible ones, who have moved to Pilar to find job opportunities either in the industrial park or in the gated communities.

This last group consists of many people with unmet basic needs, which has turned Pilar into a poor district with high infant mortality (19%), illiteracy (2%) and school drop-out (93% of children of school age attend primary school and only 50% attend secondary school) and lack of basic services. Twenty-five percent of the population of Pilar has unmet basic needs in 2001 (CIPPEC, 2005). In the same year, 84 percent of total households living in Pilar did not have sewerage, 76 percent did not have water supply, 60 percent did not have gas supply, 7 percent did not have electricity, 24 percent lived in a neighbourhood with no street lighting and no paved streets (45%) or public transport infrastructure (27%) (Vidal-Koppmann, 2007). The relative numbers of households living with unmet basic needs in Pilar decreased from 1991 to 2001, but in absolute numbers this group grew from 7,800 to 12,100 in that period (CIPPEC, 2005). According to census data, between 25 percent and 44 percent (according to the locality) of the population of Pilar were unemployed in 2001 (CIPPEC, 2005).

Moreover, in this picture, the original NyCs population now appear somewhat marginalized. Social divisions now also appear to coalesce around two distinct city visions that orient themselves to two distinct centres within the municipality. There remains the historic centre represented by the public Pilar Square which is used by NyCs and poor Non-NyCs but only very occasionally by affluent Non-NyCs when they need to do legal or bureaucratic activities, or go to the municipality. The second centre is the car-oriented shopping and entertainment complex of *Kilómetro 50*, used by Non-NyCs who live in gated communities. Here then, 'For the newer residents, the traditional centre of Pilar doesn't exist. It is now for other social groups' (Interview: Developer, *Estancias del Pilar*) while some middle-class NyCs also use this second centre. Moreover, the amenity value of an outer suburban area favoured for its environment is largely appropriated within closed communities rather than the open city. Public spaces in Pilar are poorly provided for and are often in poor condition. Although the municipality has plenty of green areas – about 60 percent of the territory – they are mainly privately owned and only less than 10 percent is public (Director of Planning, Municipality of Pilar, 7 April 2009).

7.5   Conclusion

In the course of this chapter we have examined the contribution of one group of private sector interests in the urbanization of suburbia in the Latin American setting, and particularly in the improvement of the urban condition of the 'open city'. For some, the rise of these gated communities in peripheral areas where they were largely absent before is not a break from past patterns of urbanization in the Latin American city (Libertun de Duren, 2007, p. 623). This is a highly schematic view of recent history of the periphery of Latin American cities and our research suggests that important discontinuities may indeed be apparent.

If the case of Pilar can be considered to give an insight into the contribution of gated communities to the urbanization of suburbia then it is a contribution that seems likely to crystallize not soften social inequalities, segregation and spatial fragmentation at the municipal scale. Whilst there is evidence of the contributions that gated communities have made to piecemeal improvements in amenities, services and infrastructure, these do not appear to have contributed to the rounding-out and knitting together of communities at the municipal level. Instead, they appear to be leading to something of a dualistic process of suburbanization. Social polarization has increased because both upper-class and lower-class groups have increased. The municipality has not been able to use planning 'gain' as a tool used for improvement of the municipality outside of the gated communities. Yet again the Pilar case is interesting in highlighting the need to examine carefully the changing dynamics within classes in the metropolitan periphery in light of some unusual cross-class alignments.

Part III

Post-suburbia and Europe's Compact Cities

8
Post-suburbia in Continental Europe

Marco Bontje and Joachim Burdack

8.1   Introduction

In recent decades, the transformation from parts of 'suburbia' into 'post-suburbia' has taken place in several city-regions across continental Europe. Partly the trends here look similar to those that took off in North America and the UK earlier: the rise of new office complexes, 'urban entertainment centres', malls, 'airport cities', and mixed live-work areas at city edges and beyond. Partly also, however, the post-suburban developments in continental Europe are different. Generally post-suburbia in continental Europe is developing closer to and more interrelated with the traditional core cities of city-regions, and most often the developments are also of a more modest scale. That said, also within continental Europe we see striking differences between countries and city-regions. For example, there are significant differences between the 'old' and 'new' EU member states, and also between countries with more and less national and regional planning influence. In our contribution we would like to add a continental European perspective to the theoretical debate on 'post-suburbia'; highlight the main trends across the continent in recent decades and illustrate them with examples across the continent. In our contribution to this volume we focus mostly on post-suburbia as new forms of settlement space and/or the functional transformation of places formerly known as suburbia. We will occasionally also pay attention to other issues related to the post-suburbia debate such as administrative organization, governance and place identity, but refer to other contributions to this volume for more detailed accounts on these issues.

8.2   Recent urban development trends in continental Europe

In a broad perspective two patterns of suburban development can be differentiated in Western Europe (KEG, 1991; Rozenblat and Cicille, 2003). First, urban areas in North West Europe were dominated by tendencies of suburbanization in the 1960s and 1970s and afterwards frequently by de-urbanization, thus a population loss of the whole urban region. The large urban regions in southern Europe experienced high population growth in the central cities until the 1970s due to in-migration from rural areas. Second, since the 1980s, there is a transition to suburbanization tendencies observed, with diminishing population growth rates of the central cities, whereas suburban areas experience further increase. Suburbanization in Central and Eastern European cities effectively started in the 1990s, once socialist planning economies had been replaced by market mechanisms, although first tendencies of de-centralization became already noticeable in cities like Budapest in the 1980s. Meanwhile, in North West Europe since the late 1980s, an 'urban renaissance' has taken place; since then in many city-regions in this part of Europe, both central cities and (post-)suburban zones have been growing in population and economic activities, though the (post-)suburban zones are generally still growing faster than the central cities.

In the late twentieth and early twenty-first century, continental Europe has entered the 'second demographic transition', characterized by low birth rates, a longer life expectation and a greying population (Van de Kaa, 1987). Whether in the short or medium term, all of continental Europe is already or will inevitably be faced with stagnation of population growth or even decline. The differences in timing of this process have resulted in different speeds of diminishing growth throughout Europe. International migration patterns within the continent as well as to and from it have also influenced the effect of demographic transitions on population growth. North West Europe received large groups of immigrants from the 1960s until the late 1990s for various reasons; these migrant groups included 'guest workers' from the Mediterranean, relatives from those guest workers, migrants from former colonies, asylum seekers and refugees. In the aftermath of '9-11', migration regulations have become much more restrictive in North West Europe, which dramatically decreased these migration flows. However, in recent years a new significant migration flow has emerged from Central and East European countries. Most of these successive migration flows have focused strongly on cities, mostly on the largest cities, partly compensating the continuing out-migration of native households from the central cities to the suburbs. In South Europe, the largest cities have become the preferred destination of international migrants much later, in the late 1990s. Before this, they were only receiving migrants from the countryside or smaller cities. Also suburbanization, as mentioned before, started much later in South Europe. Central and East Europe has on the contrary become a mass emigration region since the sudden transformation from socialist to post-socialist regimes in the early 1990s. The exceptions to this are the national capitals and their regions, where the central cities are generally growing fast along with a considerable growth of their suburbs.

Suburbanization of mostly traditional one-earner family households was with some delay followed by suburbanization of employment. Initially this mainly involved personal services (like health care, domestic repair and maintenance, and beauty salons) and small-scale retail on the one hand, and sectors with large space demand and a preference for highway locations like logistics and warehouses on the other. In the 1990s, however, these 'typically suburban' economic functions were increasingly joined by 'big box retail', entertainment centres, and offices. The latter not only included back offices, but increasingly also national or even international headquarters. These changes in the economic geography of city edges and beyond have transformed large parts of continental European suburbia into post-suburbia. Many areas formerly known as suburban have transformed into something in-between urban and suburban. Next to the increasing functional mix, also changes in the population of these places have added to the emergence of post-suburbia: next to the traditional family households (which have meanwhile become rather two-earner than one-earner households), also an increasing share of 'typically urban' household types like singles and single parents lives in post-suburbia. Another remarkable recent trend is that the population of post-suburbia in continental Europe is becoming more ethnically diverse, especially in Northwest and Southwest Europe: ethnic minorities that used to concentrate strongly in the largest cities are starting to disperse across the city-region, similar to the US trend of 'urbanization of the suburbs', already witnessed in US cities in the early 1970s (Masotti and Hadden, 1973; Musterd et al, 2006).

Gottdiener and Kephart describe post-suburban developments as a break with traditional notions of the city: 'For us the traditional concept of the city has become obsolete. Instead, we believe that urban life is now organized in polynucleated and functionally differentiated spaces that are no longer extensions of the traditional city. They are neither suburbs nor satellite cities; rather, they are fully urbanised independent spaces that are not dominated by any central city' (Gottdiener and Kephart, 1995, p. 34). Orange County in California and Suffolk County in New York serve as prime examples. Kling et al (1995, p. 6) emphasize the 'fundamentally de-centered or multicentered nature of these emerging regions'. Based among others on Kling et al (1995), Aring (1999) and Phelps et al (2006), a number of characteristics might be identified to describe the tendencies that differentiate post-suburbia and post-suburban development as from (stereo)-'typical' suburban developments:

- A functional diversification and broadening of the economic base of the urban outskirts: the urban outskirts increasingly become locations for work and spare time activities and experience growth of highly qualified jobs ('technoburbs')
- The emergence of new spatial concentrations of employment in the urban outskirts: these new poles are described for instance as 'edge cities' by Garreau (1991) or 'sub-cities' by Cervero (1989)
- Changing commuting patterns: commuting within the urban fringes gains importance in comparison to commuting between the central city and the urban fringe areas.

So far, post-suburbia in continental Europe is mostly found at the edge of large and medium-sized cities and in formerly suburban or rural communities adjacent to central cities. Next to this, in some countries like France and the Netherlands, also some 'satellite cities' have emerged at a slightly larger distance (usually within 30–40 km) of the largest cities. These 'satellite cities' have most often emerged in the aftermath of the new town policies of the 1960s and 1970s. Starting their new town function with the construction of suburban housing environments for those eager to leave the largest cities, some of the former new towns have grown into medium-sized cities with complementary (rather than competing) economies adding to the city-regional economy. More recently, since the late 1990s, also specialized new centres have emerged in several continental European countries like 'airport cities', 'science cities', and large-scale retail and leisure complexes.

A feature which might (so far) set post-suburbia in continental Europe apart from similar environments across the globe is that city-regions tend to remain rather compact. While increasing distances cannot be denied also in continental Europe, these increases are so far only gradual and in most countries even marginal. Instead of the continuous and often very fast spatial expansion taking place in areas like the South of the US (expressed in terms like 'leapfrogging'), most city-regions in continental Europe rather develop their post-suburbias by intensifying space use within the boundaries of functional urban regions. Mergers of city-regions, despite being pronounced and predicted already for most of the twentieth century, have hardly materialized so far. People, jobs and economic activities have definitely sprawled more since the 1960s, but this happened in a much less extreme fashion than in most North American city-regions. In the case of continental Europe, therefore, internal restructuring of city-regions and redistribution of functions within city-regions are so far much more prominent and influential processes than large-scale expansion or sprawl across large distances. Moreover, since the mid-1980s, as mentioned before, the core cities of large and medium-sized city-regions have spectacularly recovered in most of Northwest and Southwest Europe. The most recent city-regional development trends in these parts of continental Europe are thus a parallel growth of city centres and post-suburbia and a redistribution of people and functions between and across these locations.

8.3 Some perspectives on post-suburban developments

In the last decade the academic and political interest in new post-suburban developments in continental Europe has increased. This was in part due to a reception of North American studies but also due to new developments like large scale business parks, shopping centres, entertainment centres and multiplex cinemas in peripheral locations (for instance the Xanadu project in Madrid).

With reference to the North American debate it seems it seems useful to differentiate between more 'centrist' and more 'de-centrist' perspectives.

- 'centrists' see the emergence of new centralities in peripheral location in the tradition of Garreau's edge city (Garreau, 1991).
- 'de-centrists' see a dominance of decentralized growth the tradition of Robert Lang's 'edgeless city' (Lang, 2003).

The 'De-centrist' perspective

Sieverts (1999) demands that suburban developments should be accepted as a new type of decentralized settlement structure. The concept of the *Zwischenstadt* was developed from its intermediate character, which results from characteristics of the built environment as well as from cultural dispositions. The concept of the *Zwischenstadt* was widely discussed in professional and academic circles in Germany. Thanks to translated editions in several languages, the concept also reached an international audience. At a more analytical level, however, the *Zwischenstadt* left open many questions. It remained unclear what was exactly meant with this term. In fact, the term has different interpretations: it addresses the classical suburban areas at the outskirts of the agglomeration, but also parts of suburbia that lie in between different cities and exhibit rather hybrid settlement characters, and also rural areas with starting densification and urbanization tendencies, which were usually referred to as urban periphery. A similar perspective on peripheral urban growth was adopted in the French research programme on the *ville émergente* (Dubois-Taine and Challas, 1997; Piron and Dubois-Taine, 1998).

The 'Centrist' perspective

In the 1990s and early 2000s, several European authors have undertaken attempts to develop graphic and analytic models of post-suburban developments of European Cities. Most often these authors preferred a 'centrist' perspective instead of a 'de-centrist' perspective, though some of their conceptions of post-suburbia seem to have elements of both perspectives. Perhaps the best known continental European model proposal is Kunzmann's city-regional archipelago model. According to Kunzmann, city-regions across Europe are becoming functional 'archipelagos', composed of 'islands' with distinct functional profiles. The historic inner city is still there, but it is no longer dominant. In fact the central core of a city-region does in his view no longer exist of a narrowly bounded 'city', but consists of several spatial elements spread across the city-region. What is emerging is a 'city-regional core consisting of islands (...) (that is) dealing with the global challenges to meet international ambitions' (Kunzmann, 2001, p. 214; translated by authors). This dispersed 'core' determines the city's global image and functions as 'the city-regional stage'. Concentration areas in the metropolitan periphery add to 'the city-regional functional palette with their distinct profiles, without which the central functions would not be possible' (Kunzmann, 2001, p. 214; translated by authors). Kunzmann describes the functional concentration areas as an unplanned result of a global economy determined by 'economies of scale' and liberalized markets. Spatial clusters are eventually resulting from the demands of specialization and functional differentiation in the global metropolitan competition. Kunzmann's perspective on the twenty-first century city-region is partly in line with Dear and Flusty's model of 'Keno capitalism' (Dear and Flusty, 1998), with one important difference: while Dear and Flusty suggest that the historic city core has disappeared, Kunzmann expects that the city core will remain important next to the specialized centres elsewhere in the city-region.

Burdack et al (2005) compared the spatial-functional structure and dynamics of six European metropolitan regions, dividing these regions in two sub-areas: the inner metropolitan region and the metropolitan periphery. Within the inner metropolitan region, a central core is distinguished, which often in turn can be a composite of several specialized cores in close spatial proximity. This core includes the historic city core, where cultural and tourism functions often dominate, a financial centre which features the main concentration of (multinational) headquarters, and possibly one or some secondary office centres. In the metropolitan periphery, a number of specialized sub-centres can be found. The general pattern emerging from the continental European case study regions (Berlin, Budapest, Madrid, Moscow, Paris and Randstad Holland) is that the domains of knowledge-based industries, high-tech production and logistics each cluster in their own 'growth poles', which may be in close spatial proximity but generally do not develop as an interconnected, integrated whole.

A third example of modelling continental European post-suburbia emerged from the COST-C10 Action 'Insight on outskirts' (Dubois-Taine, 2004). Instead of trying to design a common post-suburbia model, the 11 metropolitan regions studied by this research network were grouped in five models: poly-nuclear urban regions, poly-nuclear agglomerations, patchwork cities, contained towns and a transport corridor model. This typology includes four models connecting to the 'centrist' perspective, but also one which reminds more of the 'decentrist' perspective: the patchwork city. The cases studied by the COST-C10 research network demonstrate the huge variety of possible post-suburbias in Europe. A similar variety, despite the attempt to generalize in one model, is demonstrated between the case studies of Burdack et al (2005). Instead of proposing a new 'model to replace all models', therefore, we will now continue with briefly discussing examples of post-suburban development in various corners of continental Europe illustrating similarities and differences.

8.4   Examples of post-suburban developments across continental Europe

Paris

The Paris Urban region is one of the largest urban agglomerations in continental Europe. The traditional monocentric structure of the agglomeration has been slowly transformed towards a more polycentric structure

Map 8.1   Paris: New economic poles in the metropolitan area

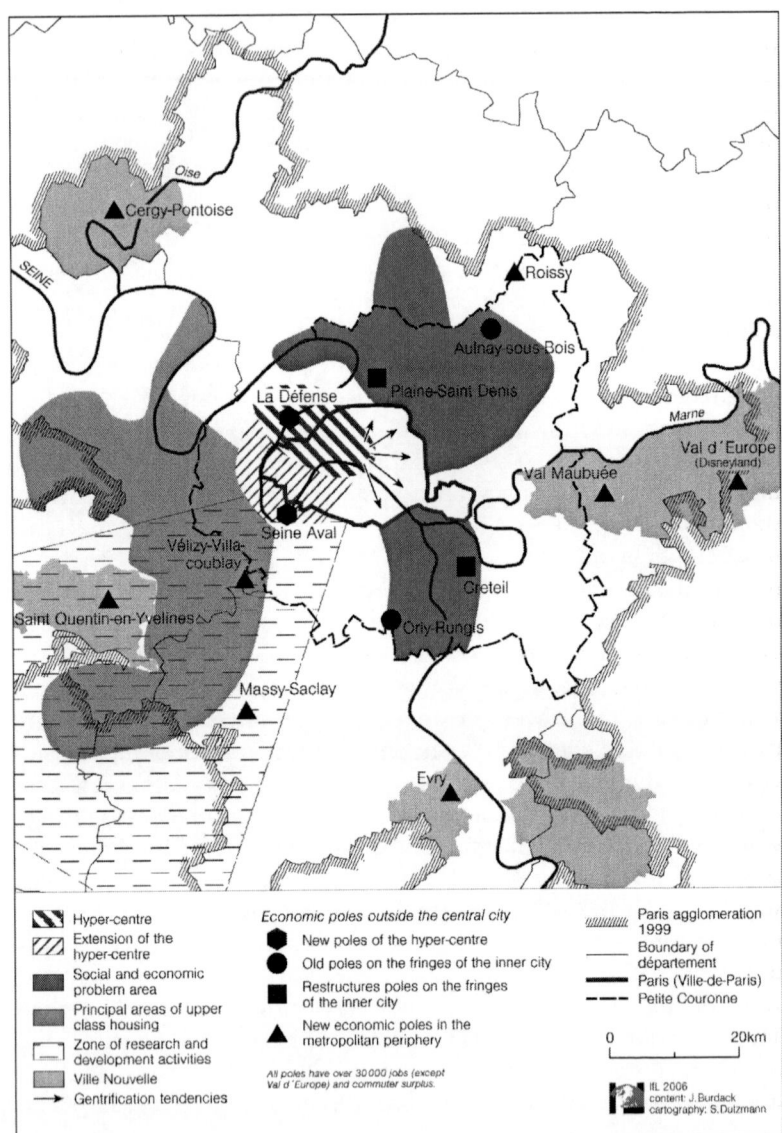

Source: Burdack (2004)

in recent decades. The enlarged 'hypercentre' that now extends from inner Paris to the office centre *La Défense*, however, remains the primate centre (Burdack, 2004). Some of the new poles emerged in the *villes nouvelles* that were built around the capital, while others – like for instance the below outlined Massy-Saclay – result from a more spontaneous market-driven development (Map 8.1).

The new economic pole of Massy-Saclay is located 20 km south west of the centre of Paris. It is one of the most important concentrations of research and development activities in France. Massy-Saclay may be described in settlement terms as a multi-polar settlement structure. Three different parts can be clearly distinguished: the Plateau de Saclay and its fringes, the area around Massy, and the area around Courtaboeuf-les Ulis (Gauvin, 1992). The three parts have complementary structures. Public and private research institutes and institutions of higher education are located in the Plateau de Saclay, research and development and production facilities in the Courtaboeuf area, and Massy is an important transportation node. Integrating factors of the different parts of the economic pole are commuter patterns and synergies of the research and production function and the perception of the area as a unified techno-pole. The Massy-Saclay economic pole has no fixed boundaries: it consists of some 20 communities that total an area of 140 km² and a population of 205,000. There was a total of 107,000 jobs in 1999. It is important to note that Massy-Saclay has a significant commuting surplus of 14,800. This means that it functions as an important employment centre in the Paris region. The number of jobs increased by 65 percent from 1975 to 1999 (from 65,000 to 107,000) (INSEE, 2001).

Val d'Europe is located about 35 km east of the city centre of Paris in a rural setting that was until 20 years ago mostly known for its 'Brie' cheese production. Compared to the other cited examples Val d'Europe stands out as a special case that in many ways bears closer resemblance to the American Edge City model. This is no accident, but stems from the involvement of the Walt Disney Co. as a major actor in the project. The project is in fact the result of the conjunction of two principal actors and their strategic objectives: the French Government that wanted to strengthen the urban and economic development of the eastern part of the Paris Region and the Walt Disney Co., that wanted to export its theme park concept to Europe (Carrel, 1999). The two parties signed an agreement for a joint development of Val d'Europe. Consequently, the European branch of Disney (Euro Disney) received the right to develop 2,000 ha of urban land, which is more than half of the total area of Val d'Europe. In order to accommodate the investors, the French

Government also agreed to finance and build high level transportation links to the area. Therefore Val d'Europe received a high speed train stop (TGV) and two regional commuter train stops (RER-Marne-La-Vallée-Chessy and RER-Val d'Europe) that linked Val d'Europe directly to the centre of Paris.

Amsterdam

In the Amsterdam city-region, a multi-polar settlement structure is emerging as well (Musterd et al, 2006; Martens, 2006), though across much smaller distances than in the Paris metropolitan area. The most dynamic parts of this region are south-west, south-east and east of the core city Amsterdam. Since the 1980s, a kind of corridor development has taken place, expanding between the Haarlemmermeer polder in the south-west and Almere in the east, mostly along highways, with concentrations around multimodal traffic nodes (Bertolini and Le Clerq, 2003). Interestingly, the city of Amsterdam itself is also claiming its fair share of this post-suburban growth on its southern, and to a lesser extent its western, city edges. The prestigious mixed-use development 'South Axis' planned at the southern edge of Amsterdam should in the next decades become the main concentration of national, European and in some cases even global headquarters of multinational companies. This headquarter function should be combined and mixed with luxury apartments and cultural, sports and retail activities. Building activities at the South Axis since the mid-1990s have already been impressive, but to really transform it into Amsterdam's new city centre, much remains to be done, including overarching the infrastructural bundle of highway, rail and subway to link the northern and southern half of the planning area (Salet and Majoor, 2005; Majoor, 2008; Bontje and Burdack, 2005a).

Three other emerging employment concentrations should be mentioned. First, Schiphol Airport, about 20 km south-west of the historic centre of Amsterdam, has not only become one of continental Europe's largest airports and leading transfer hubs, but also attracted and developed several other functions, not all directly related to air traffic. The airport complex also features one of the region's largest shopping centres, several hotels and conference centres, and one of the region's largest office concentrations. The management of Schiphol introduced the term 'airport city' in the mid-1990s to express its airport redevelopment targets, and has exported this concept to other airports across the globe since (Van Wijk, 2007; Bontje and Burdack, 2005a). The airport moreover is surrounded by the Haarlemmermeer, a curious mix of rural, suburban and post-suburban elements. Researchers from the municipality analyse the current development stage of Haarlemmermeer as 'hybrid urbanity': it is impossible to frame this area in traditional concepts like city, suburb, or new town (Suarez et al, 2008). Second, Amsterdam-Southeast, developed as a high-rise suburban satellite of Amsterdam in the 1960s, was expanded with office, leisure and big box retail complexes since the 1990s. The area now features, amongst others, the Ajax football stadium (also one of the country's largest concert stages), a medium-sized concert hall, a multiplex cinema, large-scale furniture, electronics and clothing stores, and the European headquarters of Cisco (Bontje, 2005). Finally, Almere is a good example of the transformation of a former 'new town' into a city in its own right. Almere was founded in 1976 and meanwhile has grown towards the second city of the region with close to 200,000 inhabitants. It is planned to expand further to about 350,000 inhabitants in the next decades. While in its first years, Almere became a typical commuter suburb with huge congestion problems, more recently it is 'emancipating'. The city has managed to attract an increasing number of companies and has invested heavily in upgrading its city centre with retail, cultural, leisure and health care facilities (Bontje, 2004).

After a phase of fast growth in the 1990s, the post-suburban developments around Amsterdam and at Amsterdam's city edges faced a rapid rise of office vacancies since 2000. It soon became clear that estimations of office demand had been way too optimistic. Still, in some parts of Amsterdam's post-suburban surroundings, between 20 and 25 percent of office space is empty, despite the economic recovery of the Amsterdam city-region between 2003 and 2008. A significant part of this problem was caused by a lack of regional co-operation and lack of monitoring of regional demand (Janssen-Jansen, 2006). Both have improved in recent years, but the current crisis only seems to deepen the problems of oversupply.

Frankfurt: Eschborn and the western periphery

The Frankfurt urban region (*Ballungsraum Rhein-Main*) is one of the most important economic centres in Germany and the region has a special significance as international banking centre and airport hub. Post-suburban developments with a mix of office parks, large-scale shopping centres and logistic facilities are of special significance in the western part of the agglomeration, forming a half-circle around the city of Frankfurt from Bad Vilbel in the north to the airport in the south-west and beyond (Bölling, 2004). For instance, large-scale retailing dominates in Liederbach and Sulzbach (*Main-Taunus-Zentrum*), high level producer services in Schwalbach, and airport related activities are concentrated in

Kelsterbach (Bördlein, 2001). The most important office location and new employment centre in the western periphery of Frankfurt is Eschborn (Lange, 2000), which is further outlined below. The developments on the western fringe of Frankfurt follow the motorways (*Autobahn*) around the city almost like pearls on a string. A rapid transit rail system (*Regionaltangente West*) is planned that would connect the different centres and strengthen the development.

Eschborn is located 10 km north west of downtown Frankfurt and shares a common border with Frankfurt. The town enjoys a favourable position in the transport network. It is located close to the A5 and the A66 and linked to Frankfurt by the S-Bahn rapid transport system. The principal business area in Eschborn is the *Gewerbepark-Süd* (Business Park South) which is located with direct access to the Autobahn A66. The business park has an area of 50 ha and contains 20,000 work places, that is about 3/4 of the total employment of the community. There are three more business parks in Eschborn. The Business Park West is oriented towards logistics and the *Gewerbepark-Ost* contains large-scale retail facilities. There are reserve areas for further expansion in the *Phönix-Park*. The suburban town experienced rapid population increase in the 1960s and early 1970s: 4,200 in 1960; 12,000 in 1970; 17,700 in 1974. Today the population remains stable around 20,000. Job growth set in when population growth subsided in the 1970s. In 1997 there were only 7,500 jobs; in 1980 13,000. The job growth peaked in 2001 at 30,600 and then slightly declined to 27,500 (2007). The work force is highly concentrated in finance and business services (47.3%). More than 25,000 workers commute to Eschborn every day (Planungsverband Ballungsraum Rhein-Main/Frankfurt, 2008).

Zurich: Glattalstadt and Limattalstadt

The area between the northern part of the City of Zurich and the Kloten Airport forms an emerging post-suburban landscape that is known as the *Glattalstadt* named after a small river that flows through the territory (Campi et al, 2001). In the 1980s and 1990s the *Glattalstadt* area was one of the most dynamic growth areas in Switzerland. The *Glattalstadt* consists of eight independent (formerly) rural communities (Rümlang, Kloten, Opfikon, Glattbrugg, Wallisellen, Bassersdorf, Wangen, Brüttisellen, Dietlikon, Dübendorf). This rural area experienced rapid growth in the last decades that completely changed its character. The number of jobs increased by 34,000 (55%) between 1985 and 2001 to reach 96,000. The population of the *Glattalstadt* rose from 78,000 to 99,900 between 1980 and 2005. A wider definition of the morphological *Glattalstadt* including the northern districts of Zurich would have a total of 147,000 inhabitants (Statistik Stadt Zürich, 2004).

Morphologically the *Glattalstadt* forms a unit with the northern districts of Zurich (for instance Oerlikon). The area is characterized by very good external transport linkages (airport, train, autobahn). Older housing quarters and manufacturing sites, new office buildings, shopping centres and business parks, university buildings and laboratories and the Zürich Fair grounds and an indoor arena are scattered in the area and connected by roads. Mixed with green spaces (woods and meadows) many headquarters of Swiss companies are located in the *Glattalstadt*, including Swiss television. To strengthen the coherence of the area a tramway ('Glattalbahn') is planned that connects the different centres of the *Glattalstadt* and link up with the Zürich tramway system (Loderer, 2001).

Northwest of Zurich, a similar post-suburban transformation has taken place in the *Limattal*. This is a formerly rural-industrial zone stretching for about 25 km along the traffic gateway to Zurich from Basel. While the transformation from rural to suburban already started with the opening of the first Swiss railway line from Zurich to Baden in 1847, first signs of what we would now call post-suburban developments came in the early 1970s. The first shopping mall in the area opened in 1970, meanwhile followed by many others. Former industrial zones have been changed to leisure complexes and workplaces of artists and creative industries. Schumacher et al (2004, p. 218) describe today's *Limattal* as 'a patchwork of extreme contrasts of scale and characteristics: motorway interchanges next to singly family housing colonies, the shopping mall next to a marshalling yard, historic farmhouses next to functionalistic multi-storey building'. Though the *Limattal* is still very dependent on Zurich for its development, especially on the purchasing power of Zurich's upper class, it is showing signs of 'emancipation', though the development of a stronger independent identity and image so far seems to happen rather at a municipal than at a regional scale, and success differs considerably between the municipalities.

Espoo and Vantaa: Helsinki's edge cities

The Helsinki metropolitan region shows development tendencies that are typical for Northern European capital regions more in general as well. Within Finland, the Helsinki metropolitan region is dominating the scene in terms of population concentration and employment concentration. It is also dominating in a hierarchical sense: the region is clearly the Finnish 'command and control' centre, the country's cultural capital, and the main node of international transport and communication (Vanolo, 2008; Bontje and Musterd, 2009; Vaattovaara and Kortteinen, 2003). However, within the metropolitan region, major shifts have taken place in recent decades. After a phase of 'traditional' suburbanization between the mid-1960s and early 1990s, parts of Helsinki suburban fringe have rapidly developed into important economic hubs. Espoo has emerged as the 'twin city' of Helsinki and Vantaa seems to head in a similar urbanizing direction. Espoo's growing economic importance is strongly connected to Nokia's remarkable rise as the world's leading mobile communication company. Nokia has its headquarters and a part of its laboratories in Espoo. However, Espoo has also become the location of parts of the Helsinki University of Technology, the Finnish technology research centre VTT, and several large finance and insurance companies. Vantaa's growth is rather driven by the international airport and the logistics cluster connected to it. Huhdanmaki and Dubois-Taine (2004) suggest the emergence of an edge-city like cityscape along the E18 highway, existing of Espoo, Vantaa and the northern city edge of Helsinki. The E18 is not only the main highway connection between Scandinavia and Russia, but also functions as a ring road for the Helsinki metropolitan area. Along this highway, a range of specialized clusters (logistics, retail, knowledge production, technology, wholesale) seems to be emerging. While the metropolitan fringes have clearly been the most dynamic parts of the region, the historic metropolitan core has remained vital and dominant though: the inner city of Helsinki is still the main concentration of cultural, political and headquarter functions (Inkinen and Vaattovaara, 2007). Looking at the growth prognoses for Espoo, Vantaa and adjacent (post-)suburban locations, though, it is questionable if Helsinki will be able to retain this regional dominance in the next decades.

Vanolo (2008) analysed the similarities and differences in the promotional images Espoo, Vantaa and Helsinki want to communicate to the outside world. He describes Espoo's strategy as 'aggressive', deliberately aiming for wealthy higher-educated professionals and the high-tech companies they work for. Remarkably, Espoo presents itself mainly as non-urban or suburban, despite its meanwhile more than 200,000 inhabitants. This corresponds with the still recent rural roots of Espoo where urbanization only really took off in the 1950s, and its sprawled and multi-polar structure (Phelps et al, 2006). Vantaa on the other hand seems to present itself almost 'shy' (Vanolo, 2008), taking pride in being well-connected with the globe but not promoting itself as an attractive place to live or visit. The relations with Helsinki are problematic; the three municipalities, but especially Espoo and Helsinki, compete for the better-off inhabitants and the most important headquarters. Espoo is blamed by several academics for not contributing to the regional social housing need, therewith contributing to increasing socio-economic polarization in the Helsinki Metropolitan Area (Vanolo, 2008; Vaattovaara and Kortteinen, 2003). The discussion between Helsinki and Espoo about the extension of the Helsinki subway network across Espoo's border (Helsinki wants this, Espoo prefers road extensions over public transport extensions) illustrates a general lack of city-regional coordination and collaboration. Both Espoo and Vantaa have mostly grown in an unplanned fashion; for Espoo, Phelps et al (2006) even speak of 'dystopian' development and draw parallels with post-suburban developments in California.

Post-suburbia in Eastern Europe? Evidence from Budapest and Prague

As was pointed out above, the transition from socialist planning economies to market economies in the early 1990s marked a distinct break in the spatial patterns of development of Central and Eastern European cities. Budapest and Prague are among the metropolitan areas in Central Eastern Europe that have been most affected by spatial restructuring and peripheral growth. It is debatable to what extent the growth of the outskirts in Budapest and Prague is still suburban or already shows signs of post-suburbia (Map 8.2).

The residential suburbanization of middle-class households has become an important trend in both Budapest and Prague. Both cities now show negative migration balances with their suburban rings, although due to the 'over-bounding' of Eastern European cities, typical suburban developments can already be found inside the administrative limits of the central city (Kok and Kovacs, 1999; Ouředníček, 2005). The new suburban residential settlements do not form complete new rings around the central city, but are concentrated in certain geographic sectors or along the main transport corridors, in Budapest for instance towards the hilly regions to the north and the west. Large parts of the outskirts are still occupied by lower-class populations (Ouředníček, 2005; Burdack et al, 2004; Sykora, 1999).

Large-scale suburban shopping centres have become an important part of the metropolitan retail trade, for instance Cerni Most, Zlicin, Letnany, Sterboholy and Pruhonice-Cestlice in Prague or Budakalász and Fot in Budapest. International retail chains are the principal investors (e.g. Auchan, Metro, Tesco). They were searching for accessible sites along highway interchanges or subway terminal stations. Logistic premises and modern

Map 8.2 Budapest: Suburban and post-suburban developments in the metropolitan periphery

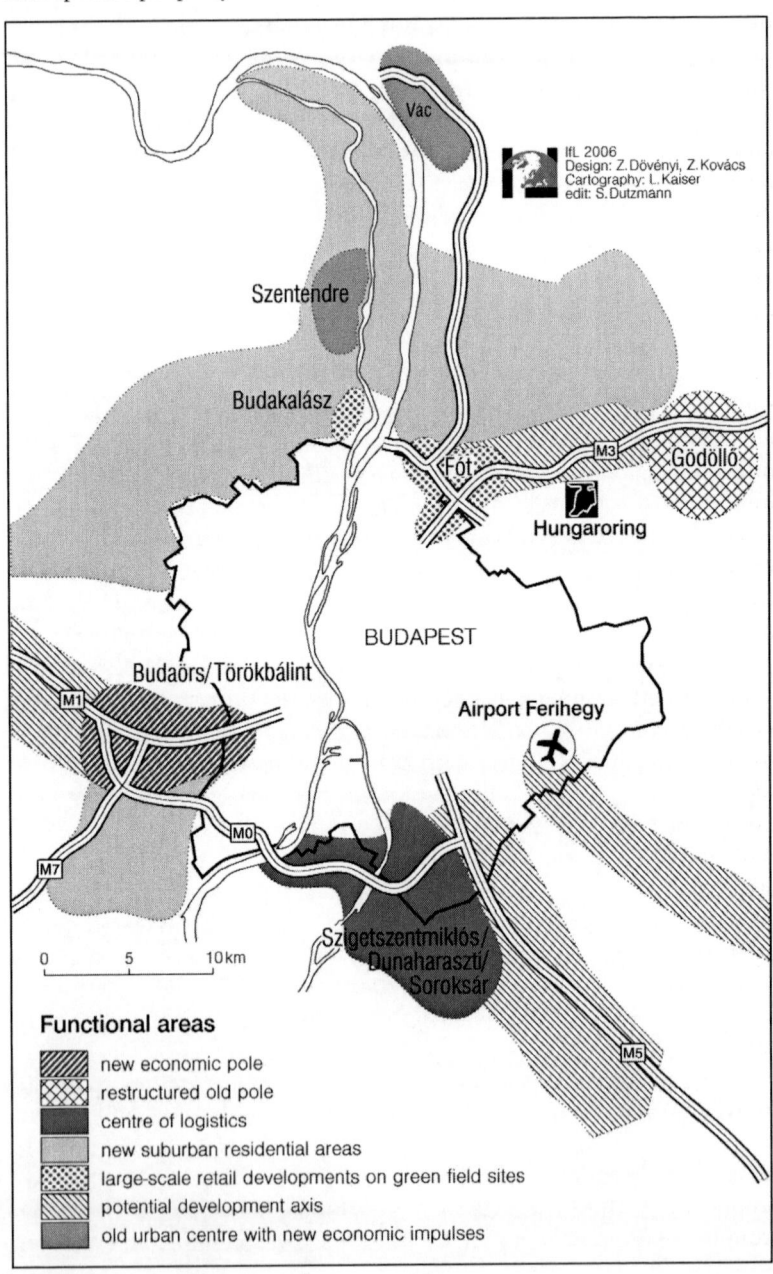

Source: Burdack et al (2004)

manufacturing sites can also be increasingly found in the metropolitan periphery. Warehousing and distribution complexes locate along the major highways and in the vicinity of the airport in the outskirts of Prague (Sykora, 1999). In Budapest a huge logistics centre developed along the M0 motorway in the Szigetzentmiklos-Dunaharaszti-Soroksar area.

Office developments still tend to be strongly attached to the city centre and adjacent inner city locations, although a certain decentralization can be noticed in the last decade. Sykora (2007) even identifies 'a strong trend of office space decentralization to secondary city centres and edge-city-location' in Prague (Sykora, 2007, p. 136). Most of the bigger and more prestigious new projects like Smichov ('Golden Angel'), Pankrác or the BB Center are however still located within the compact inner city only a few kilometres from the historic core of Prague. Only 'The Park', a new office centre with 135,000 sq. in campus style, is situated in a more suburban setting in the Prague district of Chodov (Prague 4) and there are also office projects close to Prague's international airport outside the city limits (Sykora, 2007). A similar pattern of office locations can be observed in Budapest. Office developments outside the city centre concentrate in the former 'rust belt' of old industrial areas that surrounds the inner city of Pest, and along the major roads leading out of the city. An example is the Graphisoft office park on the site of the former Obuda gas works (Burdack et al, 2004).

The pole of Budaörs-Törökbalint southwest of Budapest is a rare example of a large new economic pole in the periphery of Central and Eastern European cities. No similar, large post-suburban centre can be found in the Prague area, although there are some signs of an emerging 'centrist' development near Pruhonice-Cestlice (Sykora and Ouředníček, 2007). The pole of Budaörs-Törökbalint developed without a master plan, 'spontaneously' around the old settlements of Budaörs and Törökbalint and consists of an agglomeration of several business and industrial parks (Izsák and Probáld, 2003). The main reasons for the success of Budaörs-Törökbalint are the favourable geographic location at the intersection of three motorways (M0/M1/M2), the ample availability of land and a business-friendly local political climate with a very low local business tax rate (Dövényi and Kovács, 2004; Bontje and Burdack, 2005b). The multi-functional economic pole of Budaörs-Törökbalint consists of extensive shopping centres, office parks ('Terrapark'), manufacturing firms and recreation facilities. The number of jobs reached 20,000 by 2001. This is an increase of 50 percent since 1991. Two-thirds of the employees commute to the area, more than half of the commuters come from Budapest itself (Dövényi and Kovács, 2004, p. 36).

8.5   Conclusions and remaining research challenges

Our concise catalogue of emerging post-suburban spaces in continental Europe has demonstrated two things at least. First, post-suburbia has emerged across the continent. While our examples are located in North-west, Northern, Central and Eastern Europe, we can add here that several good examples can definitely also be found in South Europe, like Getafe in the Madrid region and Kifissia in the Athens region (Phelps et al, 2006). Second, as small as the European continent is compared to its North-American and Asian counterparts, it does not feature a 'typical European' form of post-suburbia so far; even within continental Europe, variations of post-suburbia are considerable. Comparative European studies like those of Burdack et al (2005), Dubois-Taine (2004) and Phelps et al (2006) have shown that differences in lay-out, functional special-ization and relative importance within city-regions are related to dif-ferences between national, regional and local governance regimes. Even though serious attempts have been made towards European integration in spatial planning and the planning of post-suburban spaces has defin-itely been influenced by European regulations, national and regional planning systems still leave their mark on post-suburbia. In countries with a prominent role for national and/or regional planning like the Netherlands, Germany and France, post-suburban spaces generally are shaped much more compact than in countries where (during the first phase of post-socialist transformation) post-suburban developments were mainly left to market forces. Still, even in those countries with a strong spatial planning tradition, sprawling tendencies and 'highway locations' are emerging next to planned clustered complexes. Furthermore, the shape and growth potential of post-suburban spaces across Europe also depends strongly on the availability of space to develop and expand. In densely populated countries like the Netherlands, especially in its most heavily urbanized western provinces, post-suburbia is almost naturally forced to remain close to historic city centres and infrastructure corridors. Something similar can be said about Switzerland, though there this limited expansion space is mainly related to natural barriers. On the contrary, large parts of Germany, France and Central and Eastern Europe offer abundant potential expansion space. This is even more true for Northern Europe, but there the persisting tendency of people to prefer living in or close to the country's capital results in a concentration of post-suburban developments around the capital cities.

Despite those differences, our case studies also demonstrate some similar features of post-suburbia in Europe, certainly when we would compare it to North American examples. In continental Europe, post-suburbia is generally located closer to the historic city centre than in most North American city-regions. Remarkably, some parts of continental European post-suburbia are even within the municipal boundaries of the central city, though in Central and Eastern Europe this is partly caused by 'over-bounded' local governments of the capital cities. Notwithstanding the differences in spatial lay-out mentioned before, continental European post-suburbia is generally more compact and less sprawled than in North America. It is also often better connected to public transport. A final important characteristic is that although the city edge and periphery have become the most dynamic parts of continental European city-regions, the central city including its historic city core remains vital and dynamic as well. Rather than competing cores, post-suburbia and historic city centres are becoming complementary parts of city-regions in which functions are redistributed. So far we mainly see examples fitting in the 'centrist' perspective, with edge-city-like developments (though much closer connected to the traditional regional cores than in Garreau's perception) and much less evidence of the 'decentrist' perspective of edgeless cities or *Zwischenstädte*. Our case studies in the city-regions of Budapest and Prague, as typical examples of trends in Central and Eastern Europe, may come closest to a 'decentrist' post-suburban model.

Meanwhile, post-suburbia has become an acknowledged phenomenon in Europe. Across continental Europe, urban and regional researchers increasingly agree that the traditional urban-suburban-rural distinction is no longer adequate and that new types of city-edge and edge-city development have emerged which show both urban and suburban characteristics. Also local and regional policy-makers in such areas increasingly acknowledge that post-suburban environments may require different development strategies than suburban or urban environments.

Now that post-suburbia has claimed a prominent position on the research and policy agendas across continental Europe, more than enough intriguing research questions remain. Most of them are connected to the future of post-suburbia. Will post-suburbia remain the most dynamic part of metropolitan regions? To what extent are post-suburban places capable of dealing with economic crises? How sustainable is post-suburbia, not only economically but also socially and ecologically (Bontje, 2004)? How will the functional links and 'division of labour' between post-suburbia, the traditional central cities and the rest of metropolitan regions develop? Will continental European post-suburbia remain polycentric or will a sprawled, 'centreless' landscape result after all? And finally: will differences in post-suburban development between Western and Central and Eastern Europe remain, or will city-regions in Central and Eastern Europe become more like their Western European counterparts? These are only some of many possible post-suburban research themes that are worth exploring more in-depth in the near future. Combining in-depth case studies with an internationally comparative perspective offers the most promising road ahead towards a better understanding of continental European post-suburbia.

9
Post-suburbia in the Context of Urban Containment: The Case of the South East of England

Allan Cochrane

9.1   Introduction

Traditional models of urban development have tended to view it as a more or less 'organic' (almost biological) process growing out from a central core, around which various rings of settlement and economic activity are organized. These approaches seem stubbornly to retain their power in the language of inner cities, outer estates, suburbs and city-regions, but they have been under severe challenge over the last few decades. In recent years a wide range of spatial imaginaries has been called on as attempts have been made (by academics) to understand and (by policy-makers) to manage contemporary geographies of settlement and urban living.

One well-known expression of this shift has been associated with the self-proclaimed 'Los Angeles school' (in contrast to the more famous 'Chicago school') which suggests that it is possible to identify a different set of relationships as underpinning the development of the contemporary – or post-modern – city. From this perspective, it is suggested, in a neat inversion of traditional models, that today it may be the urban periphery that shapes and comes to define the centre. Drawing on the experience of Los Angeles and Southern California, Michael Dear (2000, 2002) puts this position particularly strongly, suggesting that a post-modern urbanism has effectively replaced the old modernist urbanism. In this context, Dear argues that 'the imperative towards decentral-ization...has become the principle dynamic in contemporary cities' (Dear, 2002, p. 3).

This post-suburban imagery is not the only one in contention, however. So, for example, Peter Hall and others (see e.g. Hall and Pain, 2006) have tried to capture the emergent arrangements through the identification of what they call polycentric mega regions (they identify eight in Europe, including the South East of England, the Rhine Ruhr, the Randstadt, Northern Switzerland and Paris). Meanwhile, Thomas Sieverts (2003) has drawn attention to what he calls the *Zwischenstadt* (or 'in-between city'), which he suggests is where the majority of people now live – not entirely convincingly linking the informal settlements of the global South with the low density sprawl surrounding (most of) Germany's major cities. Others have suggested that the focus needs to be on what have been identified as city-regions (see e.g. Hull and Neuman, 2010; Marvin et al, 2006).

For our purposes in this chapter, what matters is that the language and imagery being used is one that goes beyond the identification of megacities (which might simply be seen as bigger versions of the traditional model) to suggest that it may be necessary to begin to think differently, to refocus away from the core city, indeed away from the 'city' towards a more nuanced version of urbanism, in which not only can the periphery no longer be seen as the periphery, but has to be re-imagined as the driver of urbanization, the definer of urbanism as it is actually lived, rather than as Louis Wirth imagined it (Wirth, 1964) – the suburbs as urbs, maybe even the good city (Schoon, 2001; Barker, 2009), in contrast to Jane Jacobs' rather more negative interpretation (Jacobs, 1961, pp. 458–461).

This chapter sets out to explore these issues with the help of some reflections on the experience of the South East of England (here understood to stretch beyond the narrow definitions of government offices and regional development agencies to incorporate a wider space defined by economic and social relations connecting through and across London) (see Allen et al, 1998). While recognizing that other ways of thinking about the South East may also be in contention, the chapter critically considers in turn three distinctive ways in which the South East may be (and has been) understood as an urban region – first as administratively identified 'growth region', then as city-region and, finally, as expanding suburbia, a region of suburbs. All three approaches have something to contribute. All three highlight particular features of the South East as emergent (polycentric) urban space. Each certainly has its own weaknesses, but using a range of spatial imaginaries is helpful in developing an understanding of and in exploring the governance and politics of that space. As well as offering alternative ways of thinking about it, in other words, the chapter concludes by suggesting that the three approaches may be seen to complement each other in providing ways of exploring the complexities and uncertainties of the South East as a lived space.

9.2 Making up the South East

Trying to define, understand and interpret the South East is not a straight-forward task. The changing ways in which it has been imagined and re-imagined in recent years (see e.g. Allen et al, 1998; Cochrane, 2006; Gordon, 2004; John et al, 2002) mirror the extent to which its position in the national spatial hierarchy has shifted or been challenged. In one sense, the very notion that there might be a 'South East', with its own distinct identity, is a relatively recent phenomenon reflecting the extent to which its role as condensation of national (British or English) identity and centre of political power has been called into question (see Amin et al, 2003).

The experience of the new Labour decade encouraged a process in which the South East was increasingly defined in regional terms, in the context of a wider regionalization within England, based around the creation of regionally based Government Offices and a network of Regional Development Agencies. It was (albeit in severely truncated form) given some sort of organizational/administrative structure – even if the government office and the headquarters of the regional development agency were located in resolutely suburban Guildford. Of course, this is a region defined narrowly through the administrative structures of government and quasi-government – and the regional institutions to which reference has already been made. It neither includes London, nor the counties that stretch out to the North East of London, administratively defined as the East of England.

At the same time, the region was given a central role in a form of nationally sponsored regional policy. In the context of this policy, it was understood that the South East needed to experience strong economic growth if growth nationally was to be achieved – in England and possibly even the UK (see e.g. H.M. Treasury et al, 2007; Allen and Cochrane, 2007). Without a successful, competitive, prosperous South East, it was suggested, the UK as a whole would not be successful, competitive or prosperous.

This was reflected in the language of the new regional institutions set up in the early days of new Labour in power. The strap-line of the South East of England Development Agency (SEEDA) promised that it was 'Working for England's World Class Region', and its early reports emphasized that the South East was the 'driving force of the UK's economy' or the 'powerhouse of the UK economy' (SEEDA, 1999, 2002a, b). The aim of the South East's Regional Economic Strategy for 2002–12 was to ensure that the region was acknowledged to be one of the 15 'top performing regional economies' in the world (SEEDA, 2002b, p. 8). The confidence of the early statements was eroded over the years. This may reflect the emergence of a more complex (national) regional politics in which regional triumphalism sat uneasily with stated ambitions (expressed in Treasury led Public Service Agreements) for regional equalization, and also the recognition that it was necessary to identify weaknesses in order to mobilize support from government.

But it also reflected increased realism, even among the regional boosterists. Thus, a more recent Regional Economic Strategy identified the South East as one of 'Europe's most successful regions', but went on to identify a series of major challenges (SEEDA, 2006, pp. 3 and 8–21). This time the Strategy incorporated the vision that 'by 2016 the South East will be a world class region achieving sustainable prosperity' (SEEDA, 2006, p. 44). Even in the face of economic crisis, there was a desperate clinging to the mantra that, 'Whilst times may be harder over the coming months, there is no doubt that the many strengths of the South East economy will help it through this difficult period' (H.M. Treasury et al, 2008), and in the dying days of new Labour the promise remained that investment would be undertaken to deliver 'the double dividend of a better environment and quality of life alongside economic competitiveness' (H.M. Treasury et al, 2008, p. 6).

In some respects, of course, this is a powerful representation of the South East. As Allen et al (1998) note, in the 1980s and 1990s it was increasingly defined through growth of a particular sort in the context of neoliberal economic and political restructuring. Yet in this version it somehow manages to exclude London – the space which in many respects defines the region – as well as the other tightly clustered counties that stretch around it (including Essex and Cambridgeshire). In that sense it is curiously disjointed – a quasi region, defined by what is not included as much as what is. And, of course, dealing with this complexity also meant that references to the importance of London increasingly found a place in the documents of the official regionalism and the need to work with other (bordering) regions, particularly the East of England was also increasingly apparent (clearly reflected in the 2006 strategy, SEEDA, 2006). Formally alongside the regional structures, cross-regional bodies were set up in the 'growth areas' identified in the sustainable communities plan (ODPM, 2003) that stretched out from London to the North and to the East (Milton Keynes and the South Midlands; the London-Stansted-Peterborough Corridor; and the Thames Gateway).

9.3   London's city-region

It may, therefore, be worth revisiting the South East from rather a different perspective, namely one that starts from the notion that it is, in some sense, a city-region – that is, London *and* the South East, or even the Greater South East. In some respects, of course, at least in English policy discussion, London is more or less explicitly excluded from any discussion that focuses on city-regions, because it is by defining other cities (sometimes described as the 'core cities') as city-regions that a case is made for them to be taken seriously as economic players. So, for example, Simon Marvin and others (Marvin et al, 2006) have suggested that that there is an 'implicit' (and active) regional strategy which tends to benefit what they call the 'London super-region' – a 'super-region' somehow, by implication, not being a 'proper' city-region.

In many respects, however, London has the strongest case of all the UK's cities to be understood as the centre of a (global) city-region, precisely because of the way in which sets of spatially concentrated economic activities and social networks are connected through it. In their commentary on the results of the 2001 Census, for example, Danny Dorling and Bethan Thomas (2004) highlight the extent to which this area can be seen as the making of a new metropolis, 'with a dense urban core, suburbs, parks and a rural fringe' (Dorling and Thomas, 2004, p. 183).

In this context, there is a clear understanding that it is necessary to think beyond Greater London's administrative boundaries. Ian Gordon (2003, 2004) argues explicitly that the political focus should be on the 'greater' South East, incorporating the East of England as well as the government regions of London and the South East. His starting point is an understanding of this super region as a city-region, one whose central focus is London. For him, it is the spread of activities building on the strengths of the London economy, coupled with a transport network that focuses on London, that help to define the region. However, Gordon emphasizes that developments since the 1970s have begun to redefine the region, as the spread of business services functions and high tech industry has helped to build a wider range of centres with their own linkages into national and international networks. As he puts it: 'In this regionalized version of London, outer areas now substantially contribute to its agglomeration economies, as well as continuing to benefit from those rooted in central London' (Gordon, 2004, p. 41). Gordon et al suggest that 'the effective London economy extends well beyond the borders of Greater London, encompassing most of South Eastern England and perhaps some areas beyond, in what is for many purposes a single labour market' (Gordon et al, 2004, p. 30) (see also Hall and Pain 2006, which identifies the South East as a 'polycentric metropolis').

Gordon argues that such are the interconnections within this region that it is only through regional success that internal divisions and inequalities can be minimized: 'For spatial equity within the GSE [Greater South East], as well as for its overall employment rate', he says, 'it is the competitive performance of the region as a whole which matters' (Gordon, 2004, p. 42). He maintains that 'it deserves serious attention to its needs and management on a continuing basis and structures which maximize the chance of this occurring' (Gordon, 2004, p. 64). 'The Greater South East,' it is argued by him and others, 'is now effectively one economic and labour market region to which policies need to be developed in an integrated way' (Gordon et al, 2003, Executive Summary).

And, of course, despite the formal administrative boundaries, this is also reflected explicitly in public policy, as a political strategy. London is seen to act 'as an escalator region, attracting capital and people and then dispersing it across the wider South East – meaning that at the regional and local level people are drawn in to the wider South East to live, and increasingly to work' (GOSE, 2008. See also SEEDA, 2006). The sustainable communities plan (ODPM, 2003) explicitly built on these understandings, locating London and the South East within a national politics of growth, with proposals for a housing growth in a series of places on the edge of the city-region. In setting out an agenda for the regeneration of a (mainly inner city) slice of post-industrial Greater London, which has already been the target of many regeneration initiatives, Michael Keith firmly and imaginatively locates it within the wider urban context of the London 'super-region' (Keith, 2009). The whole notion of the Thames Gateway, which has been the focus of major investment and the promise of dramatic housing growth is premised on the need to understand how London stretches out into Essex, Kent and beyond (ODPM, 2003).

Viewing the South East through a lens that locates it as London's city-region is helpful both in highlighting the significance of London – and the local significance of London as 'world city' (Massey, 2007) – as well as in pointing to the possible emergence of a more complex urban system. But there is a danger in the language of city-regions and particularly in the context of the South East of suggesting that a more integrated policy object exists than is actually to be found in practice. This is recognized by Ian Gordon in his acknowledgement that residents may not always accept his view of the need for coherent planning and political leadership for the Greater South East, focused on maintaining its economic strength (Gordon, 2004). There is more tension and uncertainty about the way in which the South East is experienced and lived in practice than the various attempts to imagine it as a region imply. Persuading residents that their own future well-being and prosperity rely on recognizing the linkage between the region's continued economic prosperity and housing and development growth is not quite as straightforward as the regional governance models of the first decade of the twenty-first century might suggest.

9.4   A suburban region – a region of suburbs?

In recent years there has been a marked reluctance to use the notion of suburbanization to capture and explain processes of change and development in the South East. Instead – as we have seen – a range of different spatial metaphors has been mobilized. However, it is possible to identify a longer history in which what has come to be defined as the South East of England, has been popularly understood as a quintessentially suburban space – defined by the Home Counties and the commuter train to the City or Whitehall (there is a strong literary tradition which reflects this, from Wells' *The History of Mr. Polly* – or even the *War of the Worlds* – to Forster's *Howard's End* and *Metroland*, whether explored by Betjeman or Barnes). The relationship between London and its periphery has been understood in terms that celebrate (and sometimes bemoan) suburbia.

So, what if we turn the debate around and begin to approach the question through the prism of suburbia?

It is, first of all, clear that for many of those living in the region, a suburban appellation would fit reasonably well. One survey conducted by MORI for the South East of England Regional Assembly (SEERA, 2004b), confirmed that nearly a quarter of those interviewed identified London as part of their region, despite their placing within a government region which explicitly excluded London (as well as neighbouring suburban counties such as Essex, which was identified as part of the region by an even higher proportion of respondents – 29 percent). From a popular perspective, in other words, the identity of the South East of England continues to be defined in large part by the presence of London as its (formally absent) core. Closeness to London is explicitly identified by residents in the MORI survey as one of the fundamental reasons for their satisfaction with life in the region. And, of course, it remains the place of employment for many of those who live in the South East – over half a million commuters travel in by rail every day. And much of the industry (whether production, financial services, knowledge-based or logistics) in the South East is located there precisely because of its closeness to London. Eleven percent of the residents of the South East who are in employment travel to London to work (Robinson, 2004, p. 14).

The sustainable communities plan (ODPM, 2003) was predicated on an approach which emphasized the need to build new 'communities', as an alternative to the incremental and unplanned spread of private, speculatively built housing estates, supported by little social or economic infrastructure. In doing this, it drew on the US example of the 'new urbanism', with its strong critique of 'urban sprawl' (Duany et al, 2000; Hayden, 2004). Even in this context, however, in practice the vision was one which started from the need to provide 'affordable' housing for the labour force feeding into the South East labour market, which is still dominated by London. For the plan to be successful, the unspoken assumption was, just as in the past with the South East's successful new towns such as Milton Keynes and Crawley, that growth would be underpinned by commuting to London. The fourth 'growth area' identified in the 2003 plan is Ashford, where the building of a fast railway connection into London St Pancras has transformed its potential as a home for commuters.

The example of Milton Keynes, on the edge of the administrative South East, is one that illustrates the ambiguities associated with the attempts to build free-standing communities which nevertheless exist in the shadow of London (see Charlesworth and Cochrane, 1997). It may not be a 'classic suburb' but it can only survive in its current form because of its suburban role – as home to thousands of London-bound commuters. It is this which allows both Barker (2009) and Clapson (1998, 2004) effectively to identify Milton Keynes as a suburb, albeit of a rather peculiar sort, one sufficiently developed to incorporate at least some of the cultural facilities that might be expected of free standing city, yet one which also offers easy access to a surrounding countryside.

There have always been significant tensions between different regional (or local) actors. Historically many of the county and district councils of the South East – the Home Counties – have taken on a very clear anti-growth agenda, seeking to protect the green spaces, and (of course) the amenities and house prices of their residents. This was recognized long ago by Peter Hall and others (Hall et al, 1973) when they highlighted the effects of Green Belt policy on housing markets in London as well as the suburbs. In his discussion of development policy in Croydon Peter Saunders (1979), even if he describes the process as 'urban politics', powerfully explores the way in which the outer suburbs sought to maintain their relative privilege, even as development was encouraged elsewhere. In Buckinghamshire, it was the county council which ensured that new development was concentrated in the North of the county (in Milton Keynes) so that the leafy South (on the edges of one of the fastest growing sub-regions of the UK) could be protected and the dominant politics of South Buckinghamshire throughout the post-1945 period has been (very successfully) to resist development (Charlesworth and Cochrane, 1994). Jonathon Murdoch and Terry Marsden (1994) systematically chart the way in which piecemeal development in the same county was managed to enable a class-based reshaping of village populations, in a process they identify as 'reconstituting rurality', but might equally be described as making up new suburban spaces of privilege.

There may be a broad recognition among those living in them that the relative privilege of the older suburbs, commuter towns and villages, is somehow predicated on successful economic growth, but it is equally clear that this should not interfere with the ways of life of residents. In the high days of regionalism (following Labour's 1997 election victory) it was not acceptable for local politicians simply to stand in the way of new development. They had to participate in one way of another. But this does not mean that the tensions disappeared, rather that more subtle forms of political resistance became the norm. In part, of course, this was reflected in the sustainable communities plan itself – the regional map was used to ensure that the new homes would be to the North far away from suburban heartland. Even here, however, matters were not always so easy – even in Milton Keynes, which had always been defined through growth, opposition emerged from those who saw it as an 'urban Eden' (*Urban Eden*, undated).

Subtle manoeuvring was apparent in the use made of the Regional Assembly, as attempts were made to shift (or modify) the overall agenda. The planning process (the South East of England Regional Assembly had overall responsibility for developing a draft regional plan, at least until its abolition in 2010) allowed for the generation of a whole series of reports which highlighted what were perceived to be problems with the main drive of national policy. In its valedictory annual report, the chair of the assembly quite explicitly and directly challenged the strategy being adopted by central government, questioning not only proposed planning reforms, but also the underlying assumptions around the need for new housing on the scale being proposed (SEERA, 2008). The initial housing targets proposed by the Assembly (almost certainly deliberately set below what was likely to be deemed acceptable by the government) were substantially raised, first following the Examination in Public and then raised further by the Secretary of State (GOSE, 2008), although it was by then clear that the assumptions underlying such projections were highly over optimistic. What matters, here, however, is to recognize the extent to which a process of political challenge was underway. The attempt to construct some sort of regional political space within which conflicts might be resolved (or transcended) through new forms of governance mechanism was ultimately unsuccessful (which, of course, helps to explain the Labour government's decision to abolish the assemblies).

The tensions between the drivers associated with the Regional Development Agency (SEEDA), which was effectively a sponsor of growth, as we have seen defining the region as a 'growth region' and seeking to remove obstacles to growth (in line with national priorities, but with a regional slant), and those associated with SEERA, which came to represent the interests of the suburban residents (represented through – mainly Conservative – elected politicians) eager to preserve their quality of life, were relatively clear cut. The 'Integrated Regional Framework' developed under the aegis of SEERA, but in collaboration with a range of other regional partners, explicitly highlighted the need to find ways of reducing 'the negative effects of economic growth' (SEERA, 2004a), a combination of words which it would have been hard to find in any documents generated through SEEDA.

In the draft South East Plan approved for consultation by SEERA in 2004, the tension was still more explicitly stated: 'On the one hand economic growth and concomitant development has been a necessary condition for prosperity and social and environmental action. On the other, some consider that the price of that growth in terms of resource consumption and other impacts is too high and unsustainable in the long-term' (SEERA, 2004c, p. 4). Despite the care of its authors to present the tension explicitly, when the draft plan was presented to the Assembly itself in November 2004, the range of proposals for housing growth in the region was rejected and a lower range was agreed for wider consultation. In other words, for however brief a moment, the protective instincts of the interests represented in the Assembly overcame the sponsors of growth. Their core concern was to find ways of coping with the 'problems of success' (Foley, 2004).

At the same time, the South East region's county councils also came together to sponsor the Commission on Sustainable Development in the South East (which led to a report being published in 2005 (Commission on Sustainable Development, 2005). The Commission was chaired by one of the Council leaders, and it was prepared by the Institute for Public Policy Research. In other words, the notion of 'sustainability' (supposedly at the centre of the sustainable communities plan) was mobilized to generate rather a different vision and the IPPR (often identified as a 'left-leaning' think tank with links to the Labour government) was drawn in to reinforce the concerns of the County Councils. The conclusions of the report are probably less important than the process (although they suggested that what was needed was 'smarter growth' in contrast to the unproblematically boosterist strategy being adopted by the RDA and government's regional office). More important, however, is the way in which suburban-based authorities were able to come together regionally to present a different agenda, in which 'smarter growth' also implied the need for less housing and more protection for existing residents.[1]

The election of a new UK government in May 2010, which brought a Conservative/Liberal Democrat coalition to power also seems to have brought concessions to the suburban political actors of the South East. The initial proposals included a commitment to abolish all of the Regional Development Agencies in England and replace them with 'local enterprise partnerships'. At the time of writing it is not yet clear how these will be constituted; and it seems likely that regional institutions will survive in some form in a small number of regions. However, it is equally clear that the South East and East of England RDAs will be abolished, while the London Development Agency is likely to survive in some form. The various targets for housing growth that have been determined will no longer be the drivers of policy for local councils in the region, and there will no longer be formal Regional Strategies. In the South East, therefore, this effectively represents a significant concession to the politics of the suburbs.

---

[1] A later piece of work also produced by the IPPR, but with rather a different set of sponsors – the British Property Federation, the Building and Social Housing Foundation, English Partnerships, Land Securities, Multiplex Developments (UK) Ltd, Shelter and Tilfen Land – also drew a rather different set of conclusions, accepting the need for housing growth, but with a stress on the need to ensure that economic development and housing growth in the 'growth areas' moved in parallel (Bennett et al, 2006).

9.5   Conclusion: Beyond the suburb?

But, of course, the notion of 'suburb' remains problematic, and some of the difficulties associated with it are highlighted in the context of the South East. There is a danger of imagining the 'suburb' as a homogenous, undifferentiated space, as if those living in Richmond or Beaconsfield, Reigate or Berkhamsted were the same as, or faced the same challenges, as those living in Milton Keynes or Slough, Stevenage or Gravesend. Issues of class, ethnicity and inequality are expressed quite clearly across the map of London, the South East and its suburbs. It may be possible to look at the South East (including the belt around the London core that is within Greater London) as a patchwork of suburbs, but this is a patchwork which has holes and gaps within it, whose stitching together reflects significant inequalities and internal tensions (see Allen et al, 1998).

Equally important, in much of the literature it is assumed that the suburbs are basically a product of non-plan. For some this is seen to present highly positive possibilities, because of the way in which it is assumed to allow people to make their own decisions about how they want to live (see e.g. Banham et al, 1969; Barker, 2009; Clapson, 1998; Garreau, 1991), while others take a more negative view, highlighting the extent to which suburbs generate conformity and unsustainably swallow up land and resources (Duany et al, 2000; Jacobs, 1961; Pile, 1999). Whatever the arguments about the social possibilities of the suburbs, however, even if it was once possible to view them as products of 'non-plan', it no longer is, at least in the South East. The suburbs of the South East are the product of planning and this helps to explain the sharp differences between them – to the extent that it is apparent that suburbanization cannot be seen as a neutral process, but is rather a contested and deliberate organized one. Some suburbs are carefully protected by planning legislation and its operation – one only has to drive North from Slough to notice the sharp differentiation that occurs once the car moves into South Buckinghamshire. These are protected spaces.

Meanwhile we are also seeing the emergence of what might be described as suburbia beyond the suburbs – the suburbs beyond the greenbelt may be suburbs but they are not simply extensions of the core city, not simply forms of decentralization. Sieverts (2003) tries to capture this in the notion of a city web, linked together in a less linear fashion. But in the English context what is being produced is quite clearly the product of planning, rather than some sort of straightfor-wardly market-based or organic process. This is apparent in two ways.

Reference has already been made to the first of these, namely the mobilization of opposition to development in some places, in some existing suburbs, through the rhetoric of the 'containment of urban England'. In other words, the power of the existing suburbs is transparent in this context, and planning is used to resist the operation of the property market in seeking to extract full value from land. The defence of the Green Belt, however much it has been chipped away, means that the new suburbs have to be built beyond it.

It is in this context that the second aspect of active planning comes into play. The tensions between the anti-development politics of the suburbs and the economic drivers identified by Gordon and others remain, which means that it cannot be assumed that the apparent victory of a suburban politics housing growth is a final one. The development of the 'new' suburbs, the suburbs beyond suburbia, effectively involves the state in the active sponsorship of development. In the last decade this has been particularly apparent in the growth areas identified in the sustainable communities plan and the formation of a range of 'local delivery vehicles' of one sort or another (from partnerships to development companies to development corporations) to enable, encourage and sponsor development and to look for ways guaranteeing the necessary supporting infrastructure (see Raco, 2007 for a longer history).

These particular institutional arrangements are unlikely to survive in quite the same form in the wake of the 2010 election, but we can be sure that some active process of intervention will survive (whether privatized or delegated to the development industry), unless there is a dramatic and highly unlikely shift in the spatial politics of national development that is capable of driving economic growth and investment to the North of England. If current models are retained, then we can expect that the development of the new suburbs will be required both to deliver the housing capable of sustaining labour markets in the South East and also to remove the pressures for housing development in the suburban heartland, that is the protected spaces of suburban privilege within and on the Southern edges of London's Green Belt. In the 1990s some of this was achieved through the extension of existing settlements as housing estates, shopping centres and superstores were tacked on to the edges of villages and small towns, leaving them with the same name but a very different experience, but it is difficult to see how this can be sustained, at least in the longer term, assuming that development demands emerge once more.

This may not quite be the world imagined in the post-suburban visions of the 'Los Angeles School' (not least because there is no straightforward 'imperative to decentralization') but it is one in which the suburbs are active (and differentiated) players. They are not simply the products of, or dependent on, the core city with which they are associated. There is no simple way of characterizing the South East, as 'region', city-region or suburbia. Each of these starting points delivers insights, even if they sometimes point in different directions. The first makes it possible to explore the emergence of forms of regional governance in practice; the second highlights the dynamic emergence of a wider region which remains connected to London, despite the divisions within it; the third points to the practices of urban living and urban politics, beyond the city as traditionally conceived. In their different ways, the first two draw attention to economic drivers – the primacy of economic growth as a focus of public policy that leads inexorably to a politics of housing growth targets; the third, by contrast, draws attention to the possibility that housing development may be a rather more contested phenomenon. In other words, rather than having to choose between particular spatial imaginaries, it is helpful to draw on a range in seeking to understand and explore the emergence of new urban spaces.

10
Khimki in Moscow City-region: From 'Closed City' to 'Edge City'?

Oleg Golubchikov, Nicholas A. Phelps and Alla Makhrova

10.1   Introduction

Many concepts in social sciences sooner or later face 'trial by geography' – a consideration of their applicability beyond specific places and contexts, thus allowing these concepts to be either adjusted or rethought. The interest of this chapter is, then, to bring the analysis of post-suburbia from the Western economies into the former 'Second World' and to consider to what extent the ideas of 'edge city' (Garreau, 1991), 'post-suburbia' (Kling et al, 1995) and associated models of urban growth may apply for the latter. To this end we consider urban development and place-making on the periphery of Moscow. The analysis here is particularly based on the case of Khimki – a former Soviet off-limits 'satellite city' of Moscow and more recently a fast-growing area featuring many new retail, office and housing development projects right at Moscow's edge.

As we will argue, while growth in Khimki features some elements familiar for the transformation towards post-industrial multifunctional 'edge city' and while it may even trigger similar political tensions, the political economy of growth in the post-socialist case is somewhat different from place-centred post-suburban politics characteristic to the West. It is not possible in the case of Khimki to speak of obvious 'coalitions' or 'alliances' of private and public forces that would seek to promote the local city as an individual *place*; these are conceptualized elsewhere as key elements behind both 'growth machine' (Molotch, 1976) and 'urban entrepreneurialism' (Harvey, 1989b) – which commonly configure the post-suburban politics in North America and Western Europe (e.g. Phelps et al, 2006). Rather, growth in Khimki is driven by uncoordinated initiatives of individual developers who are not concerned about clustering their efforts for 'place making' or lobbying government for joint infrastructure, but consider the city as merely a *location* suitable as it is for their business expansion outside Moscow. Meanwhile, local government's planning policy, although pro-growth in general, plays only a limited role in coordinating and balancing growth and making the city a meaningful, consolidated and distinguishable place rather than simply a locus of a number of unrelated projects. We discuss what may be the explanations for these specificities in the context of the relationships between forces and ideologies driving growth on the metropolitan edge in transitional economy.

The paper is a result of our fieldwork in summer/autumn 2008, which involved 50 semi-structured interviews conducted with relevant informants representing local officers in Khimki, planning and development supervision bodies at the Moscow Oblast regional level, federal authorities responsible for urban development, land use and housing, private developers, real estate and other relevant businesses, chambers of commerce, academic experts, as well as local environmental groups.

The chapter is organized as follows. The next section introduces the processes of urbanization and urban change on the periphery of Moscow. We then continue with discussing the case of Khimki. We highlight some similarities between growth in Khimki and the patterns typical to suburban 'growth machine', consider the role of the post-Soviet institution of urban planning in place-making, and discuss the politico-economic dynamics behind growth in Khimki before coming to a final discussion in Conclusions.

10.2   Urban processes on the periphery of Moscow

The introduction of the market economy in the ex-socialist countries in Europe has resulted in a flood of many new urban processes which have been rapidly changing the function and morphology of cities (e.g. Hamilton et al, 2005; Tsenkova and Nedovic-Budic, 2006; Stanilov, 2007). This is no surprise, given that it has long been argued that the logic of socialist urbanization produced a somewhat different type of the city from the Western regimes (French and Hamilton, 1979; Bater, 1980; Andrusz, 1994). Larger cities and inner cities were first and foremost bearing the signs of post-industrial transformation, tertiarization and commercialization (Bater et al, 1998). Moscow, being the largest city in Europe and one of its major economic centres, was particularly well positioned in this respect and especially its central areas were much affected by the rapid deployment of post-industrial economy and the attendant transformation of the built environment (Badyina and Golub-chikov, 2005). However, eventually the processes of change have fallen upon the cities further down the urban hierarchy, as well as the peri-pheries of the larger cities, including areas on the edge of Moscow itself (Rudolf and Brade, 2005).

In the US literature, both inner-city regeneration and 'post-suburban' transformations on metropolitan edges tend to be opposed to the rapid pace of suburbanization of the 1940s to 1960s. Thus, gentrification is often depicted as a 'back-to-the-city movement' by the middle class. In Russia, due to suburbanization the 'built-up' land use had grown twice in the 1990s; and still *in parallel* central urban areas have been renovated and increasingly colonized by the new rich – a recognizable pattern of 'super-gentrification' (Badyina and Golubchikov, 2005). Furthermore, what looks familiar has much local specificity. For example, 'suburb-anization' in Moscow has taken a form of second-home developments rather than permanent residence. People continue to reside in their urban multifamily houses, but have second homes of various standards in less urbanized settings. This is better described as 'seasonal suburbanization', 'quasi-suburbanization' or even 'exurbanization', although more 'per-manent' residential suburbanization is also increasing in the nearest areas surrounding Moscow (Makhrova et al, 2008).

Along with this quasi-suburbanization, the existing built-up fringe of larger metropolitan areas such as Moscow has also been affected by large-scale transformation, although more recently than the inner city. Initially, this was clearly driven by the development of shopping malls along the Moscow Orbital Motorway – MKAD (which for the most part corresponds to the administrative border between the City of Moscow and Moscow Oblast), as well as the development of warehouses along the major motorways running from Moscow. But, increasingly, more complex forms of development, such as major modern office-based employment, including back-offices, emerge in cities closest to Moscow (e.g. Rudolph and Brade, 2005; Makhrova and Molodikova, 2007). These forms of development are also paralleled by intensified residential construction in the same locations, usually in the form of multifamily condominiums.

Khimki was one of the first cities in Moscow Oblast to experience the combination of these processes. Khimki was traditionally considered as one of the 'satellite cities' of Moscow in its 'near belt', while it administratively belongs to Moscow Oblast, a separate 'subject of the Russian Federation' (or Russia's administrative region). In the Soviet period Khimki was host to several R&D centres for aerospace defence technologies, such as surface-to-air missiles, engines for interconti- nental ballistic missiles, satellite launch vehicles and other related types of technology. Most residents were employed by these enterprises and Khimki was off limit for all foreigners. Although the city suffered in the 1990s due to declined state investment, it was one of the first cities in Moscow Oblast to quickly revitalize economically. This is seen to be particularly a result of its favourable location as follows. Firstly, it is well connected with Moscow, being in fact adjacent to the MKAD. Sec- ondly, there are Russia's major transport links crossing Khimki, including the Moscow-St Petersburg motorway (known as Leningrad Motorway) and Moscow-St Petersburg railway. Thirdly, Khimki is located near and on the main route from Moscow to Russia's major international airport Sheremetyevo, which also administratively belongs to the territory of Khimki. Fourthly, the city is located in an environmentally favourable zone to the west of Moscow and near the Moscow Canal.

During the period of economic boom in Russian between 1999 and 2008, Khimki became one of the investment attractions in Moscow Oblast. The projects included not only residential development, but also warehouses, retail and increasingly offices. The city now hosts one of the largest malls in Russia, including by IKEA and Auchan; IKEA has also invested considerable sums of money into the largest office development project in Khimki consisting of six towers (Khimki Business Park), three of which were completed by 2010. While in the 1990s due to the decline of employment in the local industries, Khimki evolved to have mostly a residential suburban character with most people commuting to work in Moscow, more recently Khimki has become a sub-centre for employment itself. This means that the work-home relationships between Khimki and Moscow are now more complex than before.

10.3   Post-socialist growth machine?

No one who travels to and from Moscow to the Sherymetyvo airport through Khimki district can avoid making superficial comparisons with the edge city environment of the US. By now the heavy congestion on the stretch of road allows one ample time to gaze out onto what is a rather chaotic mix of office and apartment blocks and retail outlets that, until the recent financial crisis, were being built at very rapid rates indeed (Map 10.1).

It is tempting to consider this suburban nodal point of car-based accessibility as being subject to the sorts of private sector forces apparent in the United States (US). Growth in the peripheries of major cities in post-socialist countries has prompted Kulcsar and Domokos (2005) to

Map 10.1 The spatial structure and new development projects in Khimki

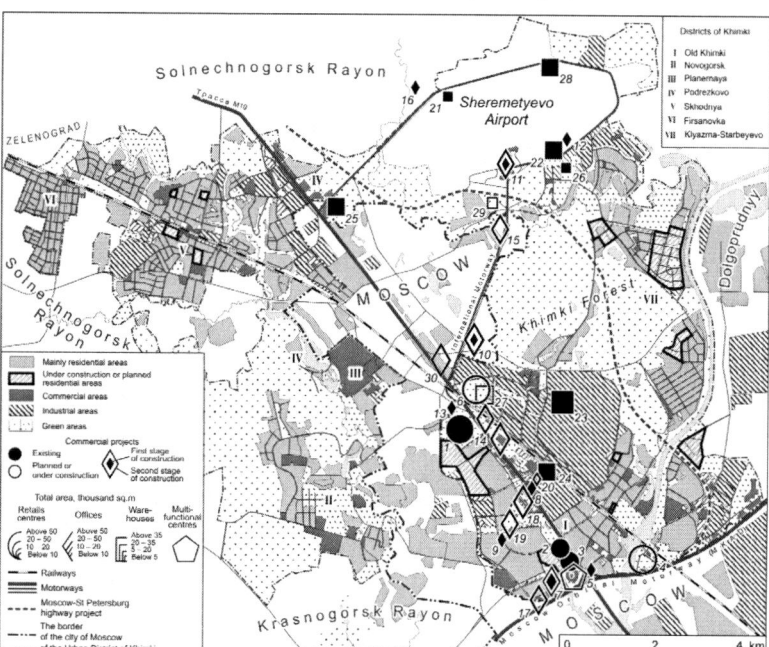

A list of development projects shown on the map

1. Mega-Khimki
2. Liga
3. Ramstor
4. Levoberezhnyy shopping and entertainment centre
5. Khimki City
6. Big Boxes
7. Country Park
8. Office centre, Moskovskaya Ul. 21
9. Office centre, Yubileynyy Prospect, 60a
10. Mercedes Benz Club
11. Sheremetyevskiy Business Centre
12. Sherrizone
13. Business park, Mashkinskoye Shosse, build. 1
14. Khimki Business Park
15. Aeroport Komplex
16. Aeroplaza
17. Khimki Gate
18. Khimki Plaza
19. Business park, Lavochkina Ul. 16
20. Olympus
21. Aeroshare Express
22. Sheremetyevo Cargo
23. National Logistic Company Khimki
24. Khimki Praedium
25. Sheremetyevo Warehouse Complex
26. Sheremetyevo Industrial Park
27. Terminal Europe
28. Vesna-M
29. Vega-Khimki

invoke the term post-socialist growth machine – making use of Molotch's (1976) classic description of the politics of US urban development. The conjoining of the term growth machine is testimony to the concept's ability to travel but it may also conceal more than it reveals. The appearance of rapid land extensive growth has undoubtedly *some* similarities but arguably important dissimilarities with the US pattern. As Kulcsar and Domokos (2005, p. 560) go on to acknowledge 'The nature of the pro growth agenda is primarily political in the post-socialist case. The power core is the local administration and this strongly influences the composition of the growth machine'. Development activity is also almost entirely unimpeded by civil society. Both of which leads Kulcsar and Domokos to suggest that post-socialist constellations of pro-growth interests would exist in the absence of growth, as their motivations centre on the exercise of power and control of the communities.

Some similarities to patterns and processes of urban development in the US do exist, revolving around the speed of development and allied to this the motivation of development in terms of exchange values. Certainly, the initiative, as in the US, does tend to come from the private sector. All interviews with commercial parties indicate that development in recent years was stimulated by developers, who would come to the city with their own projects and realize them as they wished, while the government did not have any thought-out strategy to coordinate these. Many projects were even described to have been in violation with existing planning regimes and approved *ex post*. In some interviews the original strategy of IKEA appeared to conform to such an approach, as some of its building permissions were received already in the process of construction rather than beforehand. This was described in one interview to be a normal practice at least until the early 2000s, although not more recently (DTZ property consultants, Moscow, 20 August 2008, in English).

To be sure, government and its planning and regulatory systems at all levels and especially the municipal level in Russia responds to a newly created market system which was ushered in, albeit in a rather incomplete way, in the early 1990s. Legislation in the early 1990s provided for private property rights, and although incomplete, released a huge suppressed demand for housing from individuals and commercial premises from established and new financial and business services, retail and distribution businesses (including foreign direct investment). This time, until new legislation effectively completing the market system in more recent years, could be considered a period of 'wild capitalism'. In this respect, post-socialist processes of urban development may well be a mutation of the US growth machine. Moreover, this is likely to persist in the Russian case since deficiencies with the new legislation and regulatory systems still promote very rapid urban development and particular types of developer and financing of development in the face of uncertainties over enforceable property rights.

However, in Molotch's original formulation and in subsequent elaborations (Logan and Molotch, 1987), the mutual interests of municipal politicians and officials and private sector, usually land-based business interests, are place-focused due to what Cox and Mair (1988) have further elaborated as local dependency on both parties. The joint actions of the private and public sectors coalesce over the profits and revenues that attend the development patterns centred on uplifts in the exchange value of land and property within a particular jurisdiction. As such municipal economic development strategies and planning policies become a focal point for coalitions of public and private sector interests. In Europe, while the role of the public sector in urban development has traditionally been stronger, the shift towards 'urban entrepreneurialism' similarly articulated the role of public-private partnership concerned with place-making and promotion (Harvey, 1989b) and spatial planning has been used for developing a place-based balance of interests. And here dissimilarities with the Khimki context become pronounced. In the next section, we will start exploring these dissimilarities by firstly discussing why planning policies play a rather limited role for place-making in the context of Russia and Khimki and then in the consequent section we will discuss urban development politics in Khimki in more detail.

10.4 From plan-led development to development-led planning

The Soviet model of urban planning was inscribed into a centralized institutional setting, and land development was part of social and economic regulation. Urban planning was subservient to the complex hierarchy of economic planning. Since the national priority was production, plans largely focused on servicing industrial enterprises. Social infrastructure, including housing and services, was allocated according to some norms based on the needs of production (e.g. Pallot and Shaw, 1981; Andrusz, 1984; French, 1995). One implication of this top-down planning process was that it was largely 'sectoral', while urban plans were to integrate different sectors by the virtue of their location in one place.

With the emergence of market reforms and political and economic liberalization, Russian urban planning fell into a state of crisis, as the new requirements made many inherited principles of Soviet planning for administrative-led development ineffective (Golubchikov, 2004). A series of reforms in relation to the institution of urban planning have, however, not solved this problem but instead considerably emasculated the institution of planning without providing a really workable alternative. Importantly, the 2004 Urban Development Code of Russia stresses the role of legal zoning, thus re-orientating the accent of the Russian town planning from a more comprehensive concept of planning to that of land-use zoning underpinned by narrower development rights interests. The planning instruments, such as General/master city plans still exist, but are assumed to be only 'supplementary' in the new system and in view of Russian planners are largely marginalized by the law. Planning in modern Russia has increasingly taken opportunistic development-led forms. Indeed, in contrast to planning, development control has become a persuasive machine. Today, prior to making an application for a building permit, a developer has to obtain numerous technical approvals with the result that the proposed development is organized in much detail and conforms with infrastructural, environmental and social services norms and policies. Even if a plan exists and developers' proposals are in accordance with it, the developers can be sure about the result only at the end of that administrative process and sectoral negotiations. On the contrary, if authorities are interested in development, plans may be easily violated (Golubchikov, 2004). Apparently, such a system of 'opportunity-led' planning is familiar to many other post-socialist cities in Europe (e.g. Tasan-Kok, 2006).

One result is a lack of a comprehensive and purposeful approach to make coherent places. When asked whether there were any visions at local or regional governments how individual cities in Moscow Oblast should look like in 20–30 years, the head of Moscow Oblast Planning Board replied that such 'visions' are not according to the market regime: 'people who will live in those places in 20 or 30 years time will have their own vision about how they want those places to look like and we don't have the right to impose our views on their wishes' (Head of the Main Department for Architecture and Urban Planning of Moscow Oblast, Moscow, 29 October 2008).

It may be paradoxical to hear such a discourse from a bureaucrat responsible for coordinating all local and regional planning documents, especially given still the extant relevance of city general plans in Russia. However, this reflects the uneasy combination of neoliberal ideology with the tradition of considering urban plans not as the instruments of 'making places', but rather as the tools of providing the basic functionality to the places, mostly in terms of transport infrastructure as in Soviet times. But while the Soviet urban planning was part of the hierarchically-arranged economic and spatial planning for state-led development, which in its totality did provide each place with a sense of its part in the overall system of the national economic production, the loss of the long-term planning perspectives has not been compensated by bottom-up instruments of shaping places.

Thus, the centralized sector-based planning of the Soviet era continues to have an important legacy in that there remains little appreciation of the value of territorial planning at the municipal scale among political leaders and local officials. Furthermore, the capacity for municipalities to integrate aspects of planning for their jurisdictions is also significantly compromised by planning responsibilities and financing that remain fragmented between Federal, regional and municipal levels. The situation contrasts, for example, with China where the State is seen as a coordinator and promoter of development as part of place building at national, provincial and local levels. The Russian local state has rather become an unpredictable holder and releaser of developable land.

10.5   Urban development politics in Khimki

Having considered the institutional limitations of post-socialist planning for purposeful place-making, we also need to discuss the balance of interests in the development processes in Khimki between different parties, including developers, politicians, planners and local citizenry.

For some, at least, aspirations to improve territorial planning at municipal level do exist. One interviewee, a commercial property developer, argued that all local administrations were indeed interested in planning and improving services and infrastructure but that there were different financial possibilities for this. Despite all local administrations having at least some planning, they have limited financial instruments to insure that the actual development is in accordance with it (Marketing Director, REGION Group, Moscow, 21 August 2008).

There is some suggestion that Khimki's mayor has been resistant to powerful real estate company interests with designs on his municipality. Nevertheless it seems that these companies are able to realize development opportunities on the vast land banks they have acquired at the outset of liberalization in Russia by capitalizing on their political connections at the regional or Federal political levels. The clash between local plans and financial interests, with clear dominance of the latter, is exemplified by the development of a previously vacant prime location at the entrance of Khimki from Moscow by the Leningrad Motorway and next to the municipality's first class A office development – Country Park. The site was originally earmarked in the general plan for a new commercial and community centre, and there was a desire by the Khimki chief architect to build a conspicuous office, shopping and entertainment complex, which would also contain new premises for the local administration. However, the plot was suddenly granted planning permission for large residential development by the developer PIK. The interviews with both local administration and neighbouring businesses reveal the discontent about this outcome, which is considered to disrupt what could have been a compatible cluster of office and retail land use. But the pressure for development seems to be linked not only to the lack or availability of money, but also with vested interests involving large development groups with strong backing. As the deputy mayor contended, Khimki administration was often forced to take decisions in contradiction with its policies (Deputy Mayor for Building, Architecture and Land Use, Khimki Administration, 30 October 2008).

One might assume that a municipality like Khimki ought to have a healthy fiscal capacity. In fact, however, due to the tax system in Russia all municipalities are in a relatively weak position relative to the regions in which they sit. As a result, some of the chief possibilities for place-making that are evident at the municipal level have come from the planning gain extracted from developers. For residential developments, the planning gain extracted has been quite significant with 20 percent (and up to 25%) of all units of flats constructed in Khimki being handed over to the municipality in the form of municipal housing. Beyond this, one would have to say that the planning gain extracted so far is modest and far from guaranteed. It has extended so far to the provision or refurbishment of public spaces and parks and the building of kindergartens and schools (Head of the Committee for the Economy, Khimki Administration, 30 October 2008). Even so, the present financial crisis promises to affect the planning gain extracted from even the largest of developers such as PIK who according to one interviewee are now struggling to finance the amenities and services promised for major residential developments in Khimki.

For a number of reinforcing reasons, local officials and politicians operate in a context in which as yet there is little understanding or concern for issues such as rising social inequalities and the costs of rapid urban development. The enormous pent up demand for housing that exists in Moscow coupled with a celebration of unbridled economic growth and the personal wealth that it offers mean that there is little or no popular discourse, and hardly any major grass-roots or civic group action, relating to, for instance, issues of rising social and spatial inequalities, or of the costs of growth. Yet, in some respects this coupled with Khimki's accessibility to Moscow may make politics rather more active in Khimki than many other localities. As one interviewee suggested, Khimki being very near from Moscow was a very politicized city (Chief Architect of the Urban District of Khimki, Khimki Administration, Khimki, 30 October 2008). Described here was less a genuine conflict of developer and preservationist interests than the fabrication of such conflicts by different development interests.

There is some evidence to suggest that the comparatively highly educated population of Khimki has exerted some influence on the municipality. One interviewee commented that the population did have rising expectations of the municipality in terms of improvements to, and refurbishments of, the exiting housing stock (Deputy Mayor for Building, Architecture and Land Use, Khimki Administration, 30 October 2008) and another that the public have been vocal at planning meetings (Chief Architect of the Urban District of Khimki, Khimki Administration, Khimki, 30 October 2008). Yet, this is rather limited evidence that business and civic groups are becoming engaged in any political economy of place with any substantial degree of impact. For example, the very rapidity and haphazard nature of growth in Khimki has created acute transportation problems. Khimki lies at the intersection of major roadways – the north-south Leningrad highway and the MKAD (Moscow Orbital Motorway) but these roads fall under different and multiple jurisdictions and financing arrangements (Federal, Moscow Oblast, and Moscow). The widening of these roads in Khimki is now precluded by the development that has occurred alongside them. As yet there is little sign of business interests having become organized to any significant degree and no real evidence of any such organized business interests lobbying government regarding the need for transport improvements, as would surely be the case in the US and indeed Europe. The only organized action regarding transport issues actually relates to environmental and civic group opposition to a by-pass proposed by the Federal government in order to relieve this bottleneck. A small but tenacious group of people have been trying to raise awareness of the potential destruction of a major forest area and part of Moscow's greenbelt that lies in the eastern part of Khimki which they suspect is driven by the new development opportunities that it would present (Khimki Forest Defence Movement, Moscow, 21 August, 2008).

As Gentile and Sjoberg (2006) describe it, Soviet planning created 'landscapes of priority' across the post-socialist city. In the US, Federal and state government expenditure on roads was pivotal to suburban growth machine politics since it systematically distorted the distribution of locational advantage in favour of suburban locations. Some places like Khimki on the periphery of Moscow have similar advantages conferred by road building programmes but also embody further systematic and potentially negative impacts on the land market and development potential. Khimki was originally built as a closed satellite city along with many other 'company' towns and cities around Moscow as a location for key state enterprises – notably in Khimki's case military production related to missiles and aerospace. Being the key functions in the city, these enterprises had large sites in municipal terms and in many instances were charged with catering for the housing and recreational and service needs of workers and their families, who were the majority of Khimki residents at that time. Especially as many of these enterprises are still controlled by the Ministry of Defence, the insertion of these state enterprises into municipalities represent a freezing in time of industry location, with only some urban adjustment to industrial expansion in the post-Socialist era. Enterprises in accessible suburban settlements now appear as constraints on the alternative use of land but also present significant obstacles to territorial planning. Despite their rationalization over the years there is little prospect of any of the huge site occupied by the three state enterprises – adjacent to the historic centre of Khimki – being released for development. One consequence of this is that the centre of gravity in Khimki is shifting to new Khimki – the essentially previously undeveloped western area of Khimki now subject to massive housing and also new offices developments.

Furthermore, as Khimki has a complicated border and is inter-penetrated by the territory of Moscow. With the collapse of the Soviet system, various administrative borders, which were previously easily changed by central decisions, became important territorial designation of political and economic jurisdictions. Historically, the city of Khimki has been a centre of a larger district with a few other settlements, as well as the countryside. In 1984, the Council of Ministers of Soviet Russia handed over a large part of the territory of the Khimki District to Moscow. This is because Khimki was always an off-limits city; hence Moscow grew around the city rather than incorporating it into its borders. In January 2006, due to the municipal reform in Russia, the Khimki District changed its status; the whole district area which used to consist of several urban and rural parts became amalgamated as the unified 'Urban District of Khimki' (*Gorodskoy Okrug Khimki*), with the total population of about 180,000. The complex and often ambiguous borders of Khimki became the points of tensions between Moscow Oblast and the City of Moscow. Since the borders are uncertain, they remain in flux. A few years ago, for example, the borders for the Sheremetyevo airport were settled in favour of Khimki. It was through the court decisions where the initiator of the case was Moscow Oblast's government, but Khimki administration presented the case in court hearings.

The complicated border also imposes serious obstacles for urban planning and for consolidating it as a single place. There is still a lack of inter-regional planning in Russia, while Moscow in particular is not keen to cooperate with federal government or its neighbour on such issues, as one interviewee indicated (Ministry for Regional Development, Russian Federation, Moscow, 1 September 2008). The new general plan for Khimki, which came into force in 2009, and related land use zoning documentation leave considerable strips of the territory 'in the middle' uncovered. Apart from further erosion of the place as a whole, this negatively affects the infrastructural integrity in Khimki. For example, there is the intent of Inteko, a development company closely affiliated with the Moscow government, to build major residential developments on the Moscow city land which interpenetrates Khimki's territory. The municipality is powerless to prevent this development despite its impact on the planning of the municipal territory and the implications of using and financing utility networks provided from the municipality (Deputy Mayor for Building, Architecture and Land Use, Khimki Administration, 30 October 2008).

Finally what of the political leadership? Again, as yet there is little indication that municipal level politicians are evolving distinctive agendas across the greater Moscow area. The problem is the system and climate of politics that prevails at present is one in which local political leaders are constrained by patronage relationships with the regional governor. This is true of the manner in which political patronage is dispensed within the region in a context of an inverted pyramid of fiscal revenues. Thus 'opportunities' for the building of a sense of place are often allocated by political leadership at a higher tier of government. Whilst Khmki has one of the largest municipal budgets in the Oblast, of more importance in this respect is that Khimki is considered, according to one interviewee, to be the 'locomotive for Moscow Oblast' (Head of the Committee for the Economy, Khimki Administration, 30 October 2008). The close relationship of the Khimki administration and its leadership to the Oblast government and its political leadership has ensured some significant flagship capital investments such as a new basketball and football stadium. However, to one observer from a major com-pany operating in Khimki this relationship between municipal and regional government had provided little in the way of any place-shaping strategy (Vice-President, Director of Operations and Marketing, IKEA Real Estate Russia and Ukraine, Khimki, 6 November 2008 (in English). In sum, Rudolph and Brade's (2005, p. 139) argument that 'the districts of Moscow Oblast have relatively little influence on local economic development, because major economic actors operate at the level of the governor' continues to resonate with the general tenor of observations on the ground in Khimki.

10.6 Conclusions

Rudolph and Brade (2005), while making it clear that contemporary urbanization at the periphery of Moscow can be described as a new phase, suggest that development at the periphery displays hybrid elements, or the co-existence of development of various capital intensity and quality with the emergence of high-quality retail and business centres. As a corollary to this they argue that the economics of transition have perhaps become less powerful as a defining force in peripheral urbanization and that 'Rather, universal economic mechanisms and strategies with global effects are starting to shape the Moscow periphery' (Rudolph and Brade, 2005, p. 148). What we have described above tends to question the diminishing importance of transition and the universality of processes of urban development.

Although the case of Khimki may share some facets and controversies as depicted by the concepts of 'edge city' and '(post-suburban) growth machine', it is still distinctive from these. Particularly, it is 'place-lessness' that must be added to the conceptualization of rapid urban growth in the context of post-Soviet Khimki. The placelessness, or the lack of purposeful place-making strategies and, indeed, visible growth 'coalitions' along, arises from a number of reinforcing reasons, including highly speculative development practices, the minimal interest of local businesses to influence the shape of wider urban development beyond their immediate control, and local government's retreat to standardized planning requirements and to a capricious allocation of developable land as opposed to visionary urban planning and development strategies. Thus, growth in Khimki is fuelled by a spontaneous variety of opportunistic profit-making initiatives that are characterized by short-termism and are essentially disconnected from the 'local' city, at the same time as government maintains a passive pro-growth approach.

This model of growth in fact destroys Khimki's Soviet-era industrial identity as a self-contained city and makes the city into an increasingly fragmented place which may well be hardly distinguished as one city, but rather as several peripheral dormitory districts of the city of Moscow proper. As Khimki is directly adjacent to the territory of the city of Moscow, most of non-government interviewees consider Khimki as *de facto* a district of Moscow. Indeed, Khimki's peculiar borders and location makes it very much interconnected with Moscow and its development is often regarded as part of the continuing expansion of Moscow. In this respect, Khimki ironically follows a reversal trajectory from what is expected in post-suburbia, which would be towards greater self-containment and a greater sense of being an urban place.

However, Khimki does have a separate local government and belongs to a different regional jurisdiction from Moscow, which complicates the political structuration of development interests in relation to Khimki. There is a much stronger and independent role to play by Khimki government than by any local governments within the territory of the City of Moscow proper, because by law the government system in Moscow is much more centralized than in Moscow Oblast – so, while Moscow has the prefects of local districts appointed directly by Moscow Mayor, the Mayor of Khimki is a political popular-elected post. Thus, if by some historical accident Khimki was part of the city of Moscow, then probably the city would have had a very different configuration of political interests and might have followed very different path of development. The separation of Khimki as an individual political unit outside the City of Moscow has indeed created a more distinctive political interest of Khimki government in local development. Rather than being considered a peripheral and (most likely) less well-off district of Moscow, Khimki finds itself in the position of being a 'special' district of Moscow Oblast, effectively one of its wealthiest and investment-attractive (due to the different economic might of the two regions). This also results in a lot of interest in Khimki from the regional government and makes it one of the spatial junctions in the frictions between the regional governments of Moscow and Moscow Oblast. This territorial configuration circumscribes to some degree a place-focused element and creates prerequisites for Khimki remaining a separate place. It remains to be seen, however, whether a growing demand for new urban infrastructure and emerging residents' movements will further re-structure the modes of governing developments in Khimki more in line with what is believed to be proactive place-focused post-suburban politics.

Part IV

Varieties of Post-suburbia in East Asia

11
Post-suburban Elements in an Asian Extended Metropolitan Region: The Case of Jabodetabek (Jakarta Metropolitan Area)

Tommy Firman

11.1 Introduction

Urban development in many Asian countries is characterized by an extensive growth of built-up areas which radiates from city centres in all directions, and extends beyond city and metropolitan boundaries. This process is referred to as the phenomenon of the Extended Metropolitan Region (EMR) (McGee and Robinson, 1995; Leaf, 2002; Firman, 2003; Jones, 2006; Wong, 2006). The development is also characterized by mixing of many different land uses and economic activities, including large-scale housing projects, industrial estates, and agricultural activities. The EMR phenomenon has occurred not only in primate cities and the fringe areas in the Southeast Asian countries, such as Bangkok, Ho-Chi-Min City, Manila, Kuala Lumpur, and Jakarta, but also in their middle cities, including Surabaya, Medan and Bandung in Indonesia, Cebu City in the Philippines, and Chiang Mai in Thailand (see also Rimmer and Dick, 2009). The trend shows that the future of Pacific Asia EMR will see a shift from mono-centric to multicentric EMR with decentred spatial flows (Douglass and Jones, 2008, p. 37).

The phenomenon of EMR in Asian countries is reflected in the development of communication and transportation, increasing flows of direct foreign investments, and the growing diversification and commercialization of agricultural activities (Lin, 1994; Dharmapatni and Firman, 1995; Nas and Houweling, 2000; Firman, 2003, 2009). According to McGee (2005) the globalization of economy has spurred flows of commodities, people, capital and information, resulting in both the detachment of the city core into a wider global market, and integration with its adjacent EMR in terms of using needed resources, such as food and water (pp. 42–43). As Douglass (2000) argues EMR development in Pacific Asia has resulted in urban spatial restructuring, including: (1) the polarization of few urban centres; (2) the formation of large mega-urban around the centres; and (3) the slowing of urbanization rates in inland regions (p. 237) (see also Lo and Yeung, 1996, 1998; Lo and Marcotullio, 2000).

For Dick and Rimmer (1998, 2009) the phenomenon of EMR is not unique to Asia's urbanization, as many big cities in both developed and developing countries world have experienced a similar process, albeit the development of Asian cities has occurred at an unprecedented rate. In fact, the development of Los Angeles in the United States (US) essentially indicates the generality of the process of urbanization in the world (Soja, 2000, p. xvii, see also Webster, 1995).

In contrast to the EMR development in Asia, the recent metropolitan development in Western countries is often associated with the phenomenon of 'post-suburbia' characterized by chaotic polycentric structures, and population decline in former city districts (Soja, 2000; Borsdorf, 2004). In the US context, 'post-suburbia' has also been elaborated in the terms 'edgeless city' (Lang, 2003; Lang and Knox, 2009), and 'technoburb', that is, the favoured location for the technologically-advanced industries which have made the new city possible (Fishman, 2002). As Fishman further argues, the 'technoburb' has lost its dependence on older urban core and now exists in a multi-core region formed by the growth corridors which could extend more than hundred miles, while the suburb became part of a complex 'outer city', and now includes jobs as well as residences (pp. 29 and 30). Nevertheless, studies on transformation of Chinese large cities shows that recent urban development in China displays some of the features of 'post-suburban' growth in Western countries alongside mass suburbanization, albeit the latter is markedly different from that in the West (Wu and Phelps, 2008; and Wu and Lu, 2008).

Against the above background, this chapter is aimed at exploring the extent to which the 'post-suburban' phenomenon characterizes the recent development of Jabodetabek EMR. After the introduction, the chapter is divided into four sections. Section one discusses the phenomenon of post-suburbia to provide a theoretical background to this study. Section two describes the development of Jabodetabek EMR, including in the time of Asian economic crisis and in the era of Indonesia's decentralization reform. Section three will examine the extent to which the elements of the post-suburban phenomenon appear in the recent development of Jabodetabek EMR. Section four will conclude the discussion.

Jakarta Metropolitan Area (JMA) which is also called Jabodetabek, an acronym which stands for Jakarta-Bogor-Depok-Tangerang-Bekasi, is located in the northern area of West Java (see Map 11.1). This region comprises of several administrative units at different levels: First, the Jakarta Special Region (DKI Jakarta) having provincial government status; second, seven municipalities (kota) and districts (Kabupaten), namely the municipalities of Bogor, Depok, Tangerang and Bekasi, and the districts of Bogor, Tangerang, and Bekasi. Although Jabodetabek comprises of only 0.33 percent of the national land area, this region produces about one-fourth of Indonesia's Gross Domestic Products (GDP), and accommodates as much as 12 percent of Indonesia's total population in the mid-2000s (Rustiadi, 2007).

Map 11.1   Jabodetabek region within Indonesia

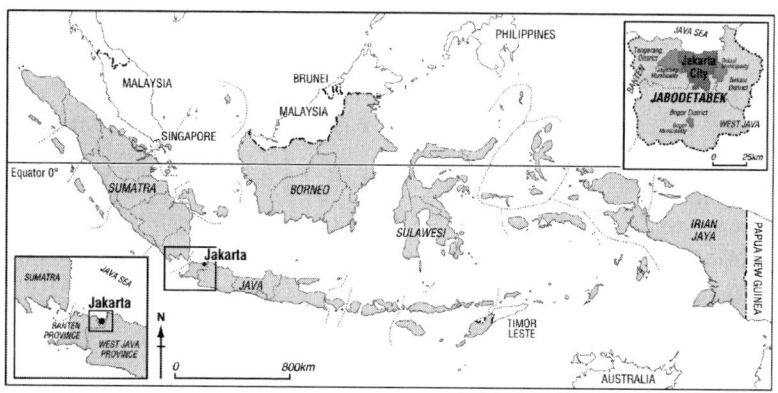

© OpenStreetMap Contributors, cc-by-sa

The GDP (Gross Domestic Product) of the Jakarta City reached Rp. 236,541 billion and Rp. 275,937 billion in 2001 and 2004 respectively, whereas the GRDP of Surabaya City, the second largest city in Indonesia, only reached Rp. 48,947 billion and Rp. 56,020 billion in the same years, which is roughly about two-fifths of Jakarta's GRDP (see Salim and Kombaitan, 2009). This suggests that Indonesia's urban economic activities are greatly concentrated in Jakarta City. As Douglass and Jones (2008) argue, Jabodetabek shows a discernable multi-centre pattern of expansion and daily flows, as a result of urban development around the growth centres in the area, including Tangerang, Bekasi, Bogor, and Depok (p. 37). Urban development in the Jabodetabek region is characterized by several features: First, development of economic activities at a global scale. Second, division of function between the core and the outskirts of the city. Third, change from a single-core to multi-core urban region. Fourth, land use in the city centre and farmland conversion in the fringe. Fifth, large-scale urban infrastructure development. Sixth, a great increase in the production of developed land. Seventh, considerable growth of commuters and an increase in commuting time (Firman, 1998, 2009; see also Firman et al, 2007).

11.2   Post-suburbanization: A general phenomenon of urban development?

Suburbanization in the western countries was characterized by residential development in the outskirts and population redistribution from the urban centre to the peripheral areas. In the 1980s, this process was intensified by decentralization of several economic activities, including commerce, retail especially large shopping centres, manufacturing, and offices, as peripheral locations became attractive, while the central cities increasingly became unattractive for industry (see Champion, 2001). As Feng et al (2008) maintain, the exodus of shopping, offices and manufacturing has resulted in a multi-centred pattern of suburban development, which in turn has made the distinction between urban and suburban areas become blurred. The government has played a very important role in this process, both directly, as in the UK's new town programs since the 1940s, and indirectly, such as the US public sector highway development (p. 85).

As Kraemer (2005, cited in Wu and Phelps, 2008, pp. 465–466) argues, the 'post-suburbia' phenomenon refers to 'a process that deals with a change in the current "suburbanization" phase away from the concentric radial patterns of earlier decades towards new spatial patterns, which are sometimes labelled a "patchwork structure"' (p. 4). Moreover, according to Phelps et al (2010) and Wu and Phelps (2008), post-suburbia might be distinguished from traditional suburban phenomenon in several ways. First, 'post-suburbia' has been used to denote a new era in which inner suburbs have been losing population and have experienced declining resident incomes relative to regional incomes, whereas outer suburbs have benefitted from greater employment-residential balance, and decentralization of service employment from the urban centres. Second, post-suburbia is characterized by mixing of land uses and polycentric development. Third, the development of post-suburbia phenomenon has been induced by government and business interests which play important 'entrepreneurial' role in it (Wu and Phelps, 2008, pp. 465–467).

Post-suburbia in the US, for instance, has been summed up in the phrase 'what was once central is becoming peripheral and what was periphery is becoming central' (Soja, 2000, p. 152; see also Phelps et al, 2006, p. 10). According to Borsdorf (2004), post-suburbia in western countries is clearly reflected in the reality that 'some new areas are much more independent than the former suburbs, but they are not as multifunctional as the traditional center' which has resulted in an emerging fragmented structure of specialized outskirts (p. 13). As Fishman (2002) maintains:

> ...the suburbs now becomes the heartland of the most rapidly expanding elements of the late 20th century economy, [and therefore] the basic concept of the suburb as privileged zone between city and country no longer fits the realities of a post-urban era...Both core and periphery are swallowed up in seemingly endless multi-centered regions... (p. 29).

While the phenomenon of post-suburbia is often associated with metropolitan development in western countries, Wu and Phelps (2008) argue that the term post-suburbia may capture important elements of new trends of suburbanization in Beijing and Shanghai global city-regions (p. 467). The recent urban development in those city-regions are characterized by the following: First, residential suburbanization, as private developers began to promote housing development in the 1990s, especially the construction of affordable subsidized housing in the periphery of city-regions; Second, industrial suburbanization, due to the moving and renovation of polluting industrial enterprises, the establishment of a land leasing system, and the obtaining of more space for industrial enterprises; Third, retail suburbanization, as many big shopping centres have been growing in the suburbs, due to cheaper prices and much more variety of goods offered, cheaper and more sizeable land, and development of residential areas in the suburbs (Feng et al, 2008, pp. 92–94; see also Webster, 2001).

The process of suburbanization in Beijing has resulted in a changing population density and the dispersal of population in the metropolitan area; more commuters in the city, and extended commuting distance, creating more congestion, as enterprises move out from the city centre to the outskirts, but most of the employees remain to live in the city centre. The suburbanization in Beijing and other large cities in China has now become more market-oriented due to the growing role of market forces in the economy (Wu, 2001; Lin, 2002; and Wu and Phelps, 2008).

In general, the Chinese suburban economy and polycentric metropolitan development have been driven by strategic investment and infrastructures in the development zones (Wu and Lu, 2008, p. 390). As Wu and Phelps (2008) note 'very rapid economic growth and urbanization in China has in turn produced the coexistence of different types of suburbs and developments that correspond more closely to post-suburbia closely defined ...' (p. 477). There are some similarities between Beijing's suburbanization and North American suburbanization, but they are not identical processes (Feng et al, 2008). In fact, Beijing's urban development is still at an early stage of urbanization, and the government still plays a dominant role in the process.

In summary, the phenomenon of post-suburbanization has occurred in both Western and developing countries. There are some similarities in the process, but they are not identical processes, as the socioeconomic context is greatly different.

11.3 The development of Jabodetabek extended metropolitan region

Population

The Jabodetabek's share of the national urban population reached 22.5 percent in 1980, 23.6 percent in 1990, 21.2 percent in 2000, and about 20 percent in 2005. The population of Jakarta City, the core of Jabodetabek, was about 8.5 million in 2005, which was two-fifth of the Jabodetabek population. While population plays a very important role in development of Jabodetabek, commuting is also evident. Millions of people commute daily between Jakarta City and the surrounding areas, including the cities and districts of Bekasi, Tangerang and Bogor. The JICA (Japan International Cooperation Agency) estimated that there were more than three million commuters between Jakarta and the adjacent areas by 2002 alone (Hidayat, 2007).

It can be noted that the rate of urban population growth in Jakarta City declined substantially from 3.1 percent over the period of 1980–90 to only 0.16 percent over the period 1990–2000 (see Central Bureau of Statistics, 1991 and 2001). This might reflect the rapid spillover of the Jakarta City to the surrounding areas. A study shows that many former residents in neighborhoods within Jakarta City moved to the peripheral areas of Jabodetabek, which indicates a spatial and functional integration of areas into the metropolitan economy (Browder et al, 1995). The Central Bureau of Statistics (2001) estimates that during the years from 1995 to 2000 about 190,000 to 192,000 Jakarta City residents moved to Bekasi and Tangerang in the peripheral areas of the Jabo-detabek EMR respectively. Meanwhile, another 160,000 of Jakarta residents moved to Bogor and Depok over the same period of time. This situation resulted in the decline of Jakarta City's share of the total Jabodetabek population from about 55 percent in 1971 to nearly 40 percent in 2000, whereas the share of the districts and cities of Tangerang and Bekasi in the fringe of Jabodetabek increased from about 13 percent to nearly 20 percent, and from 10 percent to about 15 percent respectively (Hata, 2003, p. 36).

The cities having the highest population growth rate in the Jabo-detabek over the period 2000–05 were Depok (3.82%); Bekasi (3.72%), and Tangerang (2.03%). This might suggest that while the Jakarta City experienced low population growth, Jabodetabek, as an extended metropolitan region is growing rapidly (Salim and Kombaitan, 2009).

Jabodetabek has been a destination of recent migrants, defined as those who had moved to any cities and districts in this metropolitan region during the last five years (1995–2000) from many provinces elsewhere in Indonesia. In total, there were more than 1.35 million recent migrants in Jabodetabek as recorded by the Population Census of 2000 (Central Bureau of Statistics, 2001), about 30 percent and 33 per-cent of them came from West Java and Central Java respectively. This indicates the attractiveness of this EMR to migrants who search for jobs.

The urban transformation in Jabodetabek is also indicated in the change of number and percentage of urban localities in the region, which increased by more than 28 percent, that is, from 730 to 1,035, over the period of 1999–2005, whereas the proportion of urban local-ities over the total localities increased from about two-fifths to almost three-fifths over the same period of time. The new urban localities are mostly located in the fringes of the Jabodetabek, reflecting a trans-formation of the fringes toward an urban area (Gardiner and Gardiner, 2006).

Land conversion

Over the past 30 years, the development of economic activities in Jabo-detabek has resulted in the extensive conversion of prime farmland into non-agricultural land (Dharmapatni and Firman, 1995; Firman, 2000, 2009), especially by industrial estates, subdivision and 'new town' development in the fringe areas. Meanwhile, in the urban centers many former residential areas have been converted into business spaces, offices, entertainment, and condominium.

Land-use data in the Bogor area of south Jakarta shows that the area of primary and secondary forests, garden, estates and paddy fields have declined substantially over the period of 1994–2001. In contrast, the land area for settlements and agricultural activities increased significantly (see Firman, 2009). Apparently, this conversion has brought significant environmental and socio-economic impacts to the areas. Ironically, the land conversion also takes place in the area of South Bogor (Bogor-Puncak-Cianjur) which has been designated a conservation area because of its function as a water recharge zone, so that land conversion in the area might result in negative environmental impacts in the downstream areas, that is, Jakarta City.

Land conversion in Jabodetabek has also resulted from several violations of land-use plans by the local government and private sectors in the area, motivated by political pressures and interests in placing what are perceived to be profitable economic activities. Many development decisions have been made on the basis of proposals submitted by the developers and other private sector actors who have formal and informal access to authorities, as if the land-use plans are negotiable (Firman, 2009). In fact, the enforcement has been so weak that land-use plans are ineffective in controlling physical development in the Jabodetabek EMR. Another problem is that while pressure from investors is strong, the local government capacity to cope with land conversion is inadequate.

The Asian economic crisis and new decentralization policy

There are several factors that might have affected the recent urban development in Indonesia, including in the Jabodetabek EMR, notably the Asian economic crisis at the end of 1990s (see Chatterjee, 1998), followed by the new policy of regional autonomy and fiscal decentralization in Indonesia which has been started since 2001. The Southeast Asian countries were seriously hit by the Asian economic crises, which started in Thailand in July 1997, and quickly spread to Asian countries, including Indonesia, the Philippines, Malaysia and Korea. In Indonesia, Jabodetabek was the hit hardest and had a significant contraction of its economic growth rate, from 6.0 percent to 8.3 percent during the period 1987–97 to minus 2.74 percent in 1998–99 (see World Bank, 1998 and Firman, 1999).

Before the Asian economic crisis many property companies and developers in Indonesia, most notably in Jakarta City had over-invested using unhedged and prevailing market interest short-term loans, including offshore sources for both acquisition and long-term projects of building construction. The foreign loans for property projects had amounted to US$3.4 billion by 1988, so that when the exchange rate of Indonesian currency against US Dollar dropped significantly, many property firms and developers had a big problem, as they were not able to pay the debts (see Firman, 2000). Due to this problem, a number of large-scale housing developments and new town projects in the Jakarta outskirts were slowed down and many even completely stopped, which resulted in abandoned construction sites in addition to unutilized land that had been acquired by the developers (Dijkgraaf, 2000).

Likewise, a number of office and condominium construction projects had been stopped and delayed, because of the sky-rocketing and unreasonable costs of construction. Meanwhile, the industrial estates in the Jakarta outskirts decreased almost by one-third during the period 1997–98, due to the decline in demand for industrial land, which resulted in nearly 47,000 hectares of idle industrial estate land in 1998.

In summary, the economic crises from the late 1990s to early 2000s saw a decline in economic and physical development in Jabodetabek, which was apparently reflected in a slowing down of the development of large-scale residential areas, new towns and industrial estates, because of significant drop in demand for luxury housing and industrial land.

Under the pressures of democratization and justice, Indonesia's National Parliament passed Laws 22/1999 and 25/1999 regarding the regional autonomy and fiscal decentralization in May 1999. The primary objectives of these two pieces of legislation are to avoid a break up of Indonesia into several small tiny countries and to curb separatist sentiment in the outlying provinces of Indonesia. The other objectives were to improve the quality of public service provisions and to make use of public funds in a more efficient and effective manner according to the local needs; to bring the government closer to the people; and to empower the local governments and the local communities. These laws were then amended in 2004 to become Laws 34/2004 and 35/2004 but did not change the primary objectives. The only matter added in the laws was about the direct election (Pilkada Langsung) for governor, head of districts (Bupati) and mayors (Walikota).

By the late 2000s the progress of decentralization has been uneven and slow, in which some local governments have performed well in fulfilling the management of local and regional development, especially in public service delivery, whereas anecdotal evidence indicates that many others have performed poorly, since the officials are involved in bribery and corruption. In fact, not many local governments, including in the Jabodetabek region, are really prepared to implement decentralized local and regional development, as for the time being most of the local governments do not posses sufficient technical, financial and institutional capacity.

11.4   Post-suburban elements in the recent development of Jabodetabek extended metropolitan region

The recent development of the Jabodetabek EMR clearly shows a transformation from a single-core to multiple-core urban region, and the existence of some post-suburban elements in it. First, while the Jakarta City, as the core of the region, experienced low population growth, the Jabodetabek EMR as a whole is growing rapidly. In fact, many former residents in neighbourhoods within the Jakarta City have moved to the fringes of Jabodetabek. This metropolitan-region also experiences an urban transformation, which is reflected in the great increase of number and percentage of urban localities in the outskirts. The recent development of Jabodetabek EMR has been greatly characterized by an increasingly blurred distinction between urban and suburban areas. In overall, this reflects the attractiveness of the fringe areas for socioeconomic activities, and the rapid spillover of the Jakarta City to the surrounding areas.

Second, Jabodetabek experienced a great land conversion of prime farmland into non-farmland use in the peripheral areas, most notably new towns and large-scale housing projects, industrial estates, golf courses, and recreational areas, while in the urban centers many former residential areas have been converted into condominiums, offices, and business spaces. Some new towns in the peripheral areas grew from being merely traditional dormitory towns, which are largely dependent on Jakarta City as the core of Jabodetabek, to become more independent towns with a strong economic base, such as Lippo City (see Hogan and Houston, 2001) and Jababeka City, which is one of the largest manufacturing concentrations in Indonesia with an area of 5,600 hectares and population of about one million. There are 1,570 companies and 24,300 houses in the city (Kartajaya and Taufik, 2009). Bogor City, an old satellite town with population of about a quarter million in the south of Jakarta City, has now become a centre of agricultural research and higher education. It is home to Bogor Agricultural University, one of the largest state universities in Indonesia, and a national and international convention and congress venue. Likewise, Depok City in the south of Jakarta, the main home of the University of Indonesia, is growing rapidly.

The government and private sectors play a very important role in the development of Jabodetabek EMR. Government-sponsored low-cost housing projects in the peripheral areas have been one of the drivers for development in the region. As a result, many low-income and low-middle income groups in Jakarta City moved to the periphery to live in large-scale low cost housing areas built by private developers. Later, from late 1970s the government with pro-growth economic policy allowed private developers to build 'new towns' with luxury houses in the fringes. During the 1970s until late 1990s, the developers were even largely facilitated by the National Land Agency (BPN) in land acquisition by granting them location permits (ijin lokasi), that is, exclusive right to acquire a sizeable area of land for new town development projects, by which the land owners were only allowed to sell the land to the granted land acquisition developers, not to others. Nevertheless, a number of developers keep the land idle for a long period of time for speculation in order to make high profits from rapidly increasing land prices. In fact, about one-third to one-half of the total area under land development permits in the mid-1990s in Jabodetabek was being held off the market by developers, not actively under development (Leaf, 1994 and 1996). There were too many land development permits granted in the past, while the developers and permit holders were not able to develop fully the sizeable land area that they acquired.

Modern new town development is not a new phenomenon in Jabodetabek. It dates back to the early nineteenth century when the Dutch colonial government built new town in Batavia (now the Jakarta City) which was distinct from the congested setting of the old town, using a new pattern with airy large estates. This was followed a long time after by development of Kebayoran Baru new town, in the south of Jakarta City, planned as a dormitory town, in 1950. Later, in the early 1970s a developer successfully built 'Pondok Indah', a new residential area in southern Jakarta (Firman, 2004). At present, those two new towns have become middle- and upper-income group residential areas in Jakarta City.

The most recent large-scale residential areas and new town development in the outskirts of Jabodetabek are characterized by low density, single-family houses, and exclusive residential for middle- and upper-income groups (Leaf, 1994). They have greatly reinforced spatial segregation and also undermined local government and possibilities for inter-governmental coordination in the area in three respects (Firman, 2004; see also Leisch, 2000); (1) they have polarized upper- and middle-income groups of Jabodetabek inhabitants, resulting in several pockets of exclusive residential areas in which the residents enjoy an exclusive lifestyle, with better infrastructures, security, amenities and facilities; (2) they have embodied elements of social segregation within the new town itself, where the lower-high class and middle class live a part of the area, that is exclusively planned for the highest security possible. They in fact become gated communities (see Leisch, 2000; Hogan and Houston, 2001; Leichenko and Solecki, 2008); (3) the management of city development in several new towns is implemented by the private sector exclusively, instead of by municipal government, excluding residents from outside the new town to use the facilities and amenities. The developers and the companies are greatly concerned with how to maintain the good quality of life in new towns, because this is one of the most attractive factors for the residents.

Industrial estates are also developed in Jabodetabek, including Lippo Cikarang Industrial Estate and City, and Jababeka Town and Industrial Estate. Those locations become centers of urban economic activities in the Jabodetabek. The Industrial estates in the region occupied a total land area of about 11,000 hectares by 2005, approximately 25 percent of it are located in the District of Bekasi, one of the largest concentrations of manufacturing activities in Indonesia (Collier International, 2005). These industrial estates have a strong market demand due to their easy access and proximity to Jakarta City.

The demand for industrial land in Jabodetabek has greatly increased due to development of both domestic and foreign direct investment in the region. The cumulative approved direct foreign investment in Indonesia over the period 2000–04 had reached US$64,803.5 million, nearly three-fifth (US$37,112.8 million) was invested in Jabodetabek (Central Board of Statistics, 2006). Meanwhile, the cumulative approved domestic investment in Indonesia had reached Rp. 265,176.1 million over the same period, about one-third (approximately Rp. 82,342 million) of which was located in the Jabodetabek (Central Board of Statistics, 2006). In addition to industrial estates, large shopping centres are developed not only in Jakarta City, but also in the outskirts of Jabodetabek, like Bekasi Square in Bekasi, and Teraskota in Tangerang. In short, the development of Jabodetabek has been due to market forces, especially large-scale residential areas, new towns, and industrial estates.

Third, commuting is also evident in Jabodetabek. One million people commute between the Jakarta City and the fringe areas daily by trains, buses and personal cars. Likewise, a number of the Jakarta City inhabitants also commute between the city and small and new towns in the outskirts, including Bogor, Tangerang, Bekasi, Depok and Jababeka, as they work there but live in Jakarta.

The development of large-scale residential areas, new towns and industrial estates, and shopping centres in the Jabodetabek has been greatly induced by infrastructure development, especially toll road development, built by private companies and coordinated by Toll-Road State-owned Company (PT Jasamarga), including the toll roads connecting Jakarta City with Tangerang and beyond in the west, Bogor in the south, and Bekasi and beyond in the west (see also Mamas and Komalasari, 2008, p. 123). Moreover, the government has also developed the integrated Transportation Master Plan for Jabodetabek (SITRAMP) which is expected to build a comprehensive rail and road transport system with the substantial assistance of the Japanese government (Hata, 2003). Another toll road connecting Jakarta International Seaport (Tanjung Priok) with Cakarang, one of the largest industrial cities in the east of Jakarta, approximately 34 kilometres long, is now being planned with Rp. 2.4 trillion investment.

In short, the recent Jabodetabek development shows some post-suburban elements in it, although it might be in an early stage of 'post-suburban' growth and one that is partially distinctive from that in Western countries. The Jabodetabek development is characterized by a mixing of traditional 'dormitory towns' in the peripheral areas catering to lower income segments of society in a way that is less familiar in the US (although more familiar in Europe and Latin American), but also the more recent development of some increasingly independent towns and cities with various economic bases, most notably manufacturing (Jababeka City), and education and convention space (Bogor and Depok). The government's pro-growth economic development policy has played significant facilitating role in the expansion of the Jabodetabek region, whereas the private sectors play the most important role in the development process.

11.5 Conclusion

The development of metropolitan areas in Asian countries is characterized by mixing of many different land uses and socioeconomic activities, including new towns, industrial estates and agricultural activities. The physical growth extends beyond the city boundary, radiating from city centres in all direction. This process is referred to as the phenomenon of Extended Metropolitan Region (EMR). In contrast, in Western countries, a similar phenomenon is referred to 'post-suburbia', that is, the process in which there is urban development away from the concentric radial pattern towards polycentric structure. The 'post-suburbia' was marked by residential development in the peripheral areas and population redistribution from the urban centres to the fringes, followed by decentralization of various economic activities, including retail, commerce, manufacturing, and offices. In turn, this has made the distinction between 'urban' and 'suburban' become blurred.

The term 'post-suburbia' may capture important dimensions of new trend urban development in Asia, such as in China's large city-region, although it is not an identical process as in Western countries. The suburbanization in China is physically characterized by a mixed of pattern of both traditional and new suburban residential development, but it unlikely reaches the extent of Western cities (Feng et al, 2008).

The 'suburbanization' of Jabodetabek dates back to the early 1950s, when the early Indonesian government planned and built Kebayoran Baru dormitory town followed by development of Pondok Indah town, a new residential area in the southern Jakarta in the 1970s. These new towns have now become a middle- and upper-income residential areas in the city. The development of new towns in this region slowed during the economic crisis, but it has been growing again since early 2000s. Nevertheless, the recent development of Jabodetabek EMR clearly shows some post-suburban elements in it.

First, while the Jakarta City, the core of the region, has experienced low population growth, the population of the fringes grows rapidly. The region also experiences a rapid urban transformation, which is reflected in the great increase of number and percentage of urban localities in the peripheral areas. It also suggests a rapid spillover of the Jakarta City to the adjacent areas.

Second, the Jabodetabek EMR experienced a great land conversion of prime agricultural land into non-agricultural land use in the peripheral areas, especially new towns and large-scale residential areas, industrial estates, golf courses, recreational areas, and shopping centres, whereas in the urban centres many residential areas have been converted into several kinds of business spaces, condominiums, and offices.

Third, some old and new towns in the peripheral areas have developed from merely dormitory towns to become an independent and strong economic-base towns and small cities, including Jababeka, one of the largest manufacturing concentration in Indonesia, and Bogor City and Depok City, among the largest higher education centres in the country. The new town development in Jabodetabek has reinforced spatial segregation, resulting in several pockets of exclusive residential areas in which residents enjoy an exclusive lifestyle with better infrastructure, amenities, facilities, and security, similar to the 'gated communities' in Western countries.

Fourth, as a result of development of foreign and domestic capital in Indonesia, and proximity and easy access to Jakarta City, industrial estates are growing rapidly in the outskirts of Jabodetabek. Nearly 60 percent of direct foreign investment and 30 percent of domestic investment in Indonesia's manufacturing sectors are located in this region. Because of overcrowding and rising land prices in the core, manufacturing industry and housing development have moved to the cheaper site in the outskirts.

Fifth, one million people commute between the Jakarta City and the peripheral areas, by several means of transportation, such as public buses, trains, and personal cars, while a number of the Jakarta residents also commute between Jakarta and small towns in the outskirts. Meanwhile, the commuting distance is also increasing this region.

Sixth, development of Jabodetabek has been greatly induced by infrastructure, most notably toll-road development. Seventh, the government and private sectors play an important role in development at the fringe of Jabodetabek EMR. Government policies sponsoring low-cost housing development and granting exclusive location permits for private developers have been drivers for development of large-scale residential areas and new towns in the Jabodetabek peripheral areas since the 1980s. Moreover, government pro-growth economic policy has encouraged private sectors to develop industrial estates in the fringes of Jabodetabek. The development is now more market-oriented, because of the growing role of market forces in the economy. The recent Jabodetabek development shows a transformation from a single- to multi-core urban region. There are some similarities between suburbanization in Western countries with that in the Jabodetabek EMR, but the underlying processes are not an identical process.

12
Post-suburban Tokyo? Urbanization, Suburbanization, Reurbanization

André Sorensen

12.1   Introduction

Japanese cities exploded during the rapid growth era of the 1950s and 60s, in a wave of decentralization from their super-high-density central areas into expanding rings of suburban development. In the 1970s and 1980s increasing wealth and rapid growth of car ownership and use fuelled continued suburban sprawl that appeared little influenced by any planning processes, as factories, schools, waste management plants and housing surged outward in search of cheaper peri-urban land. And since the 1990s the deregulation of retail location in response to United States (US) government pressure and with the support of major Japanese retail chains prompted yet another round of unplanned sprawl as new retail forms proliferated on arterial roads and highways in unregulated parts of the urban periphery. Yet in fundamental ways the post-suburbia hypothesis of a qualitatively new metropolitan settlement pattern fits poorly with the experience of Japanese cities. This chapter seeks to understand why this is so, and what lessons may be learned from such differences.

The basic proposition of the post-suburbia concept is the suggestion that in recent decades there have been qualitative changes in patterns of metropolitan development. While different analysts stress varied aspects of these changes, there are also significant areas of agreement. First, whereas the original concept of suburbia was premised on a dominant central city ringed by suburban residential development, for many years that has no longer been the typical pattern of growth, particularly in the US, but also in Europe and elsewhere. Instead, areas on the metropolitan fringe have emerged as the location of most new jobs and retail investment, and in many urban regions the share of jobs in the 'suburbs' has long surpassed those in the old central city, creating the major new employment nodes that Garreau famously labelled 'Edge Cities' (Garreau, 1991). The dynamism and economic importance of such fringe development is accentuated by the collapse of many US central cities, particularly in the industrial heartlands of the Northeast and Midwest. Second, increasing 'automobility' has allowed an ever-farther expansion of scattered urban development, well beyond the edges of the built-up area, creating what Lang has referred to as 'Edgeless Cities' (Lang, 2003), others describe as exurban development (Davis et al, 1994), and Teaford (1997) labelled post-suburbia.

Third, these new, more dispersed patterns of development have transformed the practice of urban governance, creating serious challenges, as urban areas grew rapidly beyond central city planning jurisdictions into areas with limited capacity to manage or regulate growth, or provide necessary infrastructure and services (Daniels, 1999; Calthorpe and Fulton, 2001; Gillham, 2002). They have also generated new political dynamics and challenges as functional urban regions now include dozens or even hundreds of political units that have jealously – though not always successfully – guarded their political independence from the amalgamationist impulses of central cities and counties (Teaford, 1997; Frisken and Norris, 2001). Such regional political fragmentation has been described both as a major generator of sprawl (Calthorpe and Fulton, 2001; Fulton et al, 2001; Gillham, 2002), and as a major obstacle to social cohesion and good governance (Orfield, 2002; Rusk, 1995).

Finally, post-suburban development is also characterized by new patterns of urban form, characterized by large blocks or pods of single-use development – whether residential, commercial or industrial – scattered about the urban periphery leaving extensive intervening areas of undeveloped land, and connected by highways and arterial roads. The prevalence of large pods of development, the use of generous buffers, and road systems that connect development pods only to main roads and not each other, mean that virtually any land uses can be adjacent without serious externality issues except for the reinforcing of automobile dependent travel patterns (Duany et al, 2000; Filion, 2000). Such development patterns are described as displaying a very coarse grain of urban form, in contrast to the relatively fine grain of traditional urbanism (Haughton and Hunter, 1994, p. 103). Residential pods in such developments are routinely designed for a relatively narrow house price band, so that land use is separated out not only by use, but also by class, producing an ongoing and dramatic socio-spatial sorting of population (Benfield et al, 1999; Talen, 2001). As is well known, this sorting process has tended to separate the working class and racialized minorities from the middle class and wealthy, with the former stuck in declining central cities, and the latter escaping to the suburbs and beyond. These processes have had enduring political impacts, the clearest of which is that the suburbs and exurbs tend to be more politically conservative than central cities (Walks, 2004). They also combine to produce a settlement pattern that is quite unlike the familiar city-suburb form.

While Phelps et al (2010) and Phelps and Wu (Chapter 1) are right to be cautious about the extent to which these patterns represent a clean break with earlier patterns of urbanization as many of these tendencies are longstanding, the scale and scope of change appear sufficient to support claims that this represents a qualitatively new form of settlement. The bigger and more difficult question that they pose is whether such trends are also characteristic in countries outside the US. Diverse institutional, historical, and regulatory settings produce different dynamics and outcomes in different places, so if the post-suburban patterns of the US described above are common elsewhere, this would have important implications for our understanding both of contemporary global urbanization, and of the meaning of post-suburban patterns in the US. Some have argued that indeed, the US is merely the furthest advanced along a trajectory of dispersed urban growth permitted by widespread automobile use, which is also increasingly seen in other urban regions around the world (Hack, 2000). There is no doubt that the last few decades have produced profound changes in patterns of urbanization and suburbanization everywhere, and it seems valuable to examine the extent to which such changes conform – or fail to conform – to the concept of post-suburbia.

Japan is an interesting comparator, as it is an advanced post-industrial economy, with similar levels of urbanization as Europe and North America, high levels of automobile ownership, and has seen the proliferation of urban sprawl and new out-of-town retail forms that have generated patterns of suburban sprawl that appear superficially similar to those of the US. In particular, the growth of automobile use over the last few decades has been extraordinary. This, combined with rapid increases in wealth since the 1970s, has had profound impacts on settlement patterns. While the dominant pattern of the 1950s and 60s was a massive outflow of population from the high-density inner cities to suburbs within commuting distance of jobs that remained in the central cities, the 1980s and 90s saw a marked dispersal of jobs and retail to auto and truck accessible areas on the urban periphery. Housing was also increasingly built outside existing built-up areas because of lower land prices, and weak planning regulations (Hebbert, 1994; Mori, 1998; Sorensen, 2000). Metropolitan region development thus displays many of the patterns associated with post-suburbia in the US.

The fundamental proposition of the post-suburban hypothesis is that qualitatively new settlement patterns are emerging, so such patterns in Japan are examined in greater detail in section two. But it is worth noting at the outset that although some elements of the idea of post-suburbia appear to fit the Japanese case well, in other aspects patterns are quite different. Three major issues are worth noting here:

First, it is significant that sprawl in Japan has not led to a collapse of central city areas, although it is certainly the case that central areas, especially in small- and medium-sized towns, have seen a decline of population and market share. The main reason for population decline in central areas, though, appears to be competition from employment uses, not abandonment as in Detroit or Louisville, or so many other rustbelt cities. The long-term and consistent planning and building of radial heavy-rail systems by central and local governments and private-sector transit companies has continued to reinforce the accessibility and economic vitality of central cities, especially in the largest metropolitan areas (Harada, 1993; Ohta, 1994; Cervero, 1998). Of course, continued central city vitality is also the norm in most of Europe and Canada, and is sometimes seen even in the US, for example in Manhattan, Boston, and San Francisco, so perhaps such central city vitality can co-exist with post-suburban patterns of development.

Second, political fragmentation of metropolitan areas has long been a feature of Japanese urban development. Recognizing in the 1920s that political fragmentation and narrow local priorities would compromise attempts to plan at the regional scale, the central government kept local planning powers weak, and established consultative councils managed by central government that brought together representatives of all municipalities in each urban region to manage shared issues. Central government also closely reviewed and retained final approval authority for all local plans (Sorensen, 2002). Political fragmentation therefore did not result in governance fragmentation, as central government retained the decisive role in plan-making, and has continued to actively plan for all urban regions, especially for transport infrastructure.

Also important is that the redistributional advantages of metropolitan region government schemes argued by Orfield (2002) are much less relevant in Japan. Until the Koizumi reforms of 2005 some two-thirds of municipal budgets came in the form of central government grants, that were designed to ensure that all local governments were able to provide a comparable level of services nationwide (Steiner, 1954; Harada, 2002). Even after recent reforms, poorer municipalities still receive larger fiscal transfers per capita than richer ones. Income redistribution thus operates primarily on a national, not a regional or municipal scale.

That said, urban sprawl has been a recurring issue in Japan, with vast areas around metropolitan centers seeing scattered urban land development. It is therefore worth examining Japanese processes of suburban development more closely, to consider whether development fits the post-suburbia model, is different in details, or is different in fundamental ways. The next section reviews suburban development patterns in Japan, and the major institutional structures that shaped them. The third section reviews several major trends of recent decades, and a brief concluding section summarizes the main findings.

12.2   Suburbanization in Japan

In comparing patterns of urbanization, it is important to maintain a distinction between patterns of urban form, and the institutions that structure changes to those patterns. It is quite possible that given different starting positions, a similar change process – for example post-suburbanization – could produce quite different outcomes either if the patterns of urbanization at the beginning of the process are very different from those in another country, or if the institutions governing change respond differently, or both. So it is necessary to understand both the existing patterns, and the structures that shape changes to them to be able to understand the meaning of the changes that are occurring.

In Japan both the fundamental settlement patterns prior to urban growth, and the governance institutions that attempt to regulate it are quite different than those of the US. It is useful to discuss these separately, so the next section looks first at patterns of rural land ownership, land holding and land development that form the context of suburban growth, then looks at structures of governance that shape development patterns.

In Japan as in other Asian rice-growing countries, pre-industrial farming and land ownership patterns are radically different than those of either Europe or North America. The key difference stems from the high rural population densities common in rice-growing regions. The intensive cultivation of rice permitted gross population densities in rural areas that were often higher than those in fully developed

American suburbs. The patterns of urban industrialization in such areas have been described as *Desakota*, a neologism based on the Indonesian words for village *'desa'*, and town *'kota'* created to describe a pattern of urban development that spreads into extended peri-urban areas (Ginsberg, 1991; McGee, 1991). With the growth of the urban economy vast rural areas adjacent to cities are rapidly integrated into urban economic networks and emerge as large mega-urban regions. This integration occurs as formerly rural populations gradually earn an ever-larger share of household income from urban activities, while remaining based in their farm dwelling, and maintaining farm output. *Desakota* thus described a spatial and economic phenomenon whereby urban economic integration and urban land uses spread into high-density rural areas, forming what are now commonly referred to as Extended Metropolitan Regions (EMRs) (McGee and Robinson, 1995).

McGee sees this form of urbanization as a generally positive development. Among the benefits seen to flow from the development of such EMRs are economic vitality and flexibility, and reduced pressure of migration towards existing urban centres, as people can participate in the urban economy while remaining in extended family units on the farm. *Desakota* is seen as a natural and even inevitable form of urbanization of Asia's high-density rural areas, and also as a highly fertile medium for economic growth. McGee and his collaborators have in this work challenged the applicability in Asia of the Western dichotomy between rural and urban, suggesting that Western objections to urban sprawl are primarily a manifestation of a culturally specific preoccupation with a tidy division between rural and urban areas that has no relevance in the Asian context.

The Tokaido Megalopolis of Japan's Pacific coast stretching from Tokyo to Osaka is an excellent example of such a region. In Japan the post-war land reforms transferred ownership of the majority of rice-growing land to peasant smallholders, and created a structure of very small farms averaging about one hectare in size, which has endured to the present day. Small-scale mechanization dramatically reduced the labour required to grow rice, at the same time that rapid economic growth created labour demands which were met to a significant degree by the incorporation of a majority of farmers into the urban/industrial economy even while they continued to farm part-time. By 1985 only 14 percent of Japanese farm households were still farming full-time, 18 percent were farming part-time with the majority of their income from farming, and 68 percent were farming part-time with the majority of their income from off-farm sources in nearby towns and cities (Hayami,

1988). Factories also located in proximity to farmers, in search of both labour and cheaper land than near more built up areas. A result has been that throughout Japan, but particularly in the vast Tokaido Megalopolis, urban industrial, commercial and residential uses tend to be scattered throughout what had been rural areas as recently as the 1950s. This area demonstrates both economic vitality and serious urban problems such as pollution and congestion. Japanese planners have put a positive spin on this form of urban growth, describing these areas as '*Konjuka*' where city and countryside are 'melting' into each other (Hebbert, 1994).

A major difference between land markets on the urban fringe in Japan and in most of the other developed countries is that in Japan farmers have tended to hold on to their land as long as possible, often maintaining it in active agricultural use long after it is ripe for development. So farmers have played a much more important direct role in urbanization in Japan than in other developed countries, where farm land is usually bought by land speculators long before it is actually developed (Johnson, 1974; Bunce, 1985). The reasons for this land holding behaviour include: cultural factors such as the Japanese family system which discourages the sale of family land assets; legal and administrative barriers to the sale of agricultural land; rising land prices which created an incentive to speculate; tax incentives which made farm land assets a highly favourable tax shelter, and weak land development regulations which allowed farmers to subdivide and sell land on a plot by plot basis at fully urban prices with no requirement to provide major services such as sewers. The last two factors are arguably the most important, and are directly related to the almost legendary political power of farmers in Japan.

Farmers' success in preserving tax reductions for farmland in urban areas is both one of the best demonstrations of the influence of the farm lobby over the LDP and national government policy, and one of the clearest cases of the LDP rewarding one of its core client groups at the expense of the public interest (Hanayama, 1986; Mori, 1998; Mulgan, 2000). While since the mid-1960s the central government bureaucracy has repeatedly proposed the elimination of tax exemptions on farmland within urban planning areas, these efforts were largely defeated by farm lobby groups. This contributed to a situation that is unusually favourable for the owners of farmland on the urban fringe. As taxes on farmland have been so low, farmers have been able to maintain their land ownership long after their land was ripe for development. And because land prices rose much faster than other prices until the crash of 1990, landowners had a great incentive to hold on to their land in expectation of future gains. This pushed prospective home buyers ever further from central cities in their attempts to find affordable housing sites, jumping over large amounts of still undeveloped land.

The Japanese 'developmental state' facilitated economic growth by keeping regulatory restrictions on private housing supply to a minimum (Tsuru, 1999; Sorensen, 2002). For example, Japan still has no minimum housing standards – it is legal to rent an apartment without a toilet or windows – and land development controls remain extremely lax in comparative perspective.

The weak development control system allows farmers to exploit broad loopholes in the development control system to convert their land to urban use on a plot-by-plot basis. The current development control system was first introduced in 1968 as part of the New City Planning law of 1968. The new system was designed to prevent urban sprawl by dividing City Planning Areas into two parts: an urban development promotion area and an urban development control area, and a Development Permission System that was to control land development.

Loopholes in the development control system have allowed continued sprawl development. The most important loophole is the exemption of developments of 0.1 hectare or less from the need for development permission, which has encouraged the development of land in small bits. A significant majority of all developments since 1970, including a majority of all land developed, have been small enough that they did not require a development permit. A wide range of other loopholes exists, which have been created primarily to allow small land owners the chance to develop parcels of land with the minimum of restrictions. Examples include exemptions from land development restrictions in control areas for housing built for family members, for buildings built on 'existing housing plots', and for construction of gas stations, churches, schools, and parking lots (Hebbert and Nakai, 1988; Morio et al, 1993).

Perhaps the best description of land development patterns in the Tokyo region is that of Hanayama (1986), who has studied what he calls 'The Ecology of Sprawl' in the Tokyo Metropolitan Area. In his analysis sprawl is a result of the fact that farmers release land slowly, severing small bits of land and selling them as they need capital, for a child's university tuition or wedding, or for building a new residence. Sluggish land supply means that buyers of land for housing are driven further from the metropolitan centre in search of land parcels, thus driving up demand for urban land in ever more distant areas. As the field of residential development spreads however, land values in the inner partly developed sprawl areas rise, because they are relatively more convenient than the areas farther out. This rise of land values has a number of secondary effects:

landowners need sell even less land to meet their financial requirements so they release land even more slowly, and land buyers find it more difficult to buy land in the inner sprawl areas so they either buy smaller plots, or travel farther out in search of cheaper land. Each of these secondary effects compound the central problem of partly developed areas of scattered urban development, which spread ever farther from the metropolitan employment centres.

Scattered plot development and the extended periods for Japanese suburban areas to build up are perhaps the most distinctive features of Japanese urbanization. They have been important contributors to the severe problems of shortages of basic infrastructure in suburban areas, as most suburban development in Japan has up to the present day occurred in haphazard and scattered fashion along rural lanes and has thus avoided obligations to provide contributions to local public goods. Vast areas of Japanese suburbs have substandard local road networks, and lack sewer systems, sidewalks or parks, and a large portion of municipal budgets is spent on expensive remedial measures to correct these problems (Sorensen, 2001, 2002).

One of the most important consequences of the development of EMRs in Japan has been that very early in the process of metropolitan growth huge areas adjacent to the metropolitan cores were already becoming integrated into the urban space economy, seeing scattered urban land development and the spread of urban land values. While Japan certainly has no monopoly on urban sprawl, the particular conditions of fragmented land holdings and a relatively high rural population density before urbanization (both factors central to McGee's EMR theory) have made it extremely difficult to prevent scattered urban development. Indeed, they make it very difficult to plan the urbanization of these urban fringe areas at all, and it is not hard to understand why sprawl has continued. Such patterns of development pose serious long-term challenges for urban policy and planning, and particularly for the provision of transport systems and urban infrastructure.

They also produce very different patterns of suburbanization from either North America or Europe. In contrast to the large pods of development common in the US, or the relatively strict development controls in most of northern Europe that promoted a considerable separation between rural and urban and produced clusters of contiguous development, Japanese suburbs saw a diffuse, overall pattern of residential, industrial, and commercial development throughout extended rural areas surrounding major cities. As-of-right land severance below 0.1 hectares, and as-of-right building on severed plots encouraged huge amounts of single plot development, which has produced a very fine grain of urbanization that appears utterly unplanned and unregulated. Almost all statutory land-use zones accommodate a wide range of uses, so land uses also are very mixed. This regime has produced a suburban landscape with a fine-grain sprinkling of single family homes, small apartment blocks, small- and medium-sized businesses including small factories, shops, service establishments such as hairdressers, the ubiquitous convenience stores, and tiny restaurants. Interspersed with these are some larger public facilities such as schools and old age homes. And everywhere – even in suburbs that first started to build up 80 years ago – are remnant farmers fields, almost always still in production because taxes on farm land are so much lower, and the tax break only applies if the land is productive. Sometimes relatively low maintenance crops such as chestnuts or kiwi fruit are planted, but more common are cabbages and other green vegetables such as onions. In recent years advocates of urban agriculture and local food production have started creative projects to encourage greater productivity of these lands.

This does not, however, mean that patterns of suburban development were entirely unstructured. The main factors shaping large-scale patterns of urbanization have been railways, as particularly in the major metropolitan areas almost all travel-to-work trips have traditionally been by public transit, although that pattern began to change in the 1980s, especially in small- and medium-sized settlements, as discussed below. A second factor has been the gradually strengthening protection of some irrigated farmlands, as while much scattered development still occurs in such protected lands, it is not as easy to get permission as it used to be, and there is an increasingly perceptible difference between areas designated for urban development and those designated for continued agriculture.

12.3 Policy changes since the 1980s

There is no doubt that patterns of metropolitan growth have changed greatly since the mid-1980s. An accelerated construction of expressways and associated uses transformed the urban periphery, as did exponential growth in car ownership. A new extended pattern of metropolitan mobility developed, propelled by the property development boom of the bubble economy years of the 1980s, that produced the new phenomena of large-scale automobile-oriented resort development throughout the Japanese archipelago, emblematically of golf courses, but also of hotels, spas, etc. Although the resort boom went bust in the early 1990s, with the collapse of the bubble economy land boom, in the late 1980s the central government began to revise the formerly strict regulation on the location of large retail outlets such as supermarkets, department stores and shopping malls in response to US pressure for access to Japanese markets. These regulatory changes, and the political battles they initiated, were a major factor in the transformation of Japanese suburban landscapes in the 1990s.

Japanese retail location laws were initiated in the early 1970s, and were designed neither to achieve rational land-use planning, nor to prevent access to Japanese markets by US producers, but were intended to protect the small-scale shop owners and retail districts that were such an important voting block supporting the ruling Liberal Democratic Party. When major Japanese retailers began their first major expansions into large stores in suburban areas in the 1960s, small shopkeepers experienced locally disastrous losses of business to the big outlets that were much cheaper and offered greater variety of goods. In response the small retailers organized politically, and were able to persuade the government to regulate retail location. In 1974 the Ministry of International Trade and Industry (MITI) drafted the Large-scale Retail Stores Law (LRSL) to regulate the location of any retail stores with over 1,500 m² of floorspace. MITI also created a 'consultative council' system in which prospective entrants into a retail market were compelled to negotiate with existing store owners in the area. As a result many new entrants were blocked, and existing merchants were often able to extract a range of concessions on size of store, parking requirements, and even cheap space for local stores in new developments. Retail location was regulated, not to prevent sprawl, but to prevent competition with existing small and medium retailers (Upham, 1993, p. 271).

In 1991, primarily in response to American pressure to relax non-tariff barriers to US exports to Japan – and with strong support from the major Japanese retail chains – the government passed a series of laws effective in 1992 that fundamentally changed the way the retail sector was regulated, abolishing the consultative councils, and bringing the decision-making process into the ministry itself, instead of with the councils. This deregulation prompted a boom of exurban retail development along peripheral arterial highways and arterial roads from the early 1990s. The number of applications for opening large-scale stores jumped from 794 in 1989 to 1,987 in 1990 and peaked at 2,269 in 1996 (Japan Ministry of Foreign Affairs, 2008).

This boom had multiple impacts: it produced strips of big-box stores, gas stations, chain restaurants and auto retailers along exurban arterials in unregulated zones; it prompted major increases in automobile use and traffic congestion in outer urban areas; and it contributed to the sudden decline of traditional retail districts in small- and medium-sized cities throughout Japan. It did not have such a major impact on central city retail in the largest cities, because the urban fringe was too far away for convenient car access. The collapse of downtown shopping areas was a disaster for small- and medium-sized cities, and strongly reinforced the existing trend of depopulation and decline of the walkable, transit-oriented, vibrant centres of Japanese cities. That in turn prompted intense lobbying by local governments for policies to support their commercial centres and regulate fringe development.

Deregulation of retail location was widely considered a disaster during the 1990s. Protest was led by local governments, which saw rapid decline in their established commercial areas, and of course the small- and medium-sized businesses complained. Competition for market share was also intense for the large retailers, who overbuilt as a result of new freedoms, and some hoped for a return to the former days of greater regulation. In response, a policy council was formed by MITI in 1997, and a new LRSL was enacted in 1998, applicable in 2000. The new law passed the responsibility for regulating retail location to municipal governments, and explicitly states that it is not to be used as a way for retail interests to negotiate between each other, as had occurred in the 1980s, and had continued in a transformed way in the 1990s. Instead the goal is to 'foster the sound development of the retail sector as a whole', and protect the living environment in the vicinity of large stores. Explicitly mentioned are traffic problems and parking standards (Japan Ministry of Economy, 2008). The key change is that the permit decision is now by local governments and several are using the system to prevent new large stores from opening in the suburban and peripheral areas where they tended to locate in the 1990s (Takami, 2006, p. 140). Instead an incentive system was introduced in 2002 to induce large retailers to locate in central city locations. The LRSL is now referred to as one of the Three Town Planning laws (*Machizukuri Sanpo*), along with the City Planning Law and Building Standards Law. Many small- and medium-sized governments throughout Japan are now using this law to entirely prohibit large-scale retail location in exurban locations as a way of preventing sprawl.

The last 20 years has therefore seen yet another wave of suburban and exurban sprawl, led first by the resort boom, and subsequently by the out-of-town retail boom. A third significant tranche of new exurban development was of 1000s of new elderly care facilities subsidized by the government's Long-Term Care social insurance scheme from the mid-1990s. These were exempt from most land-use planning restrictions, and located in urban fringe and exurban locations to access cheap land.

12.4   Post-suburban Japan?

A fundamental characteristic of Japanese planning is that it hardly restricted land use at all, with almost all land uses permitted in every land use zone. This, combined with an overwhelming preponderance of tiny developments of a few houses at a time, meant that suburbs continued to be built in what appear to most observers to be an entirely unplanned manner (Hanayama, 1986; Mori, 1998; Sorensen, 2001). These conditions have produced a very different urban form and political economy of suburbanization than in the US. In Japan small-scale farmers have remained in place, remaining the dominant political and development actor in processes of urbanization, and producing extended areas of extremely fine-grained, mixed-use development that include huge areas of remnant farm land.

Detailed tracing of the processes of suburban development in Japan is important because both the motivations of moves to the suburbs, and the land development processes and outcomes were different, as suburban residents were pushed more by land ownership patterns and high land prices than by any notion of a countryside living ideal. In the US the desire for countryside living was widespread, but for many was frustrated by continued suburban development, supplying for some the motivation for a move farther out to exurbia. In Japan the alternative to far-flung suburbs is not a move to rural areas, but a move back to city centers when they became more affordable.

These divergences suggest that while the fundamental drivers of post-suburban development patterns – the increasing mobility offered by growing automobile ownership, improved roads systems, and cheap energy – have produced a transformation of metropolitan-scale urban form in many or perhaps all the developed countries, the specific outputs of processes of dispersal can be quite varied. Japanese suburban development patterns are clearly rather different than those of other developed countries.

There is no doubt that Japanese patterns of metropolitan development changed greatly during the last 20 to 30 years. In particular, there was a vast increase in car ownership and use during the period. Weak planning regulations in rural areas allowed a significant amount of resort development to take place in remote and scenic areas, which also led to increases in car travel. Changing retail patterns saw the rapid growth of urban fringe large-format stores along highways in lightly regulated zones. This again served to multiply car use and congestion. All these processes served to transform the look and feel of suburban areas throughout Japan.

It does not appear, however, that these are qualitatively different patterns than what was taking place during the classic period of suburbanization from 1950 to 1970. Rather, it appears to be more of the same: unregulated development, scattered development in urban fringe areas, shops, gas stations and fast food outlets located along urban fringe highways, and large-scale public institutions such as schools, hospitals, elderly care and waste recycling facilities that take advantage of cheaper land on the urban fringe and the fact that public facilities are exempt from development control requirements.

On the other hand, there are two emerging urban trends that appear to work in the opposite direction to suburbanization or exurbanization. The first, and certainly the most profound change in the context of place-making in Japan is the shift from a context of national population growth to one of population decline. Briefly, Japanese population grew from 44 million in 1900 to 72 million in 1945, and to a peak of about 128 million in 2004, and because of steep declines in fertility during the last 40 years, is projected to decline to 115 million in 2030, to 95 million by 2050, and to 48 million by 2100 in the absence of major changes in birth rates or immigration patterns. A crucial consequence of the end of population growth (amplified by a longer average lifespan), is population ageing. The share of population over 65 has increased from 4.9 percent in 1950 to 19.5 percent in 2004, and is expected to rise to 29.6 percent by 2030 (Japan Ministry of Internal Affairs and Communications, 2005; Ogawa, 2005). The other consequence is a decline in population, and in the number of households, so ever fewer dwellings will be required. From a situation of continual growth, Japan is shifting to population shrinkage.

A second trend that has emerged during the last decade is a significant re-centralization of population, as people move back in to central city areas from the suburbs. In part this is a result of local government efforts to encourage the building of high-rise housing in central city areas. Local governments since the 1970s had identified inner-city population loss as posing serious challenges, including increasing risk of crime, declining neighborhood viability, and loss of vitality (Alden, Hirohara et al, 1994). In response they reduced barriers to high-rise housing, and even provided incentives for buildings that stacked residential uses on top of office functions. These efforts started to bear fruit in the 1990s, and combined with further measures by the central government in the early 2000s initiated a remarkable boom in super-high-rise residential development in inner-city areas during the 2000s in all the larger cities (see Sorensen et al, 2010). These incentives were aided by the continuous decline of land prices in central Tokyo after the crash of the bubble in 1990, so that it has become increasingly viable to build and market residential developments in central areas.

The growth of population in city centers is not a minor shift prompted by gentrification, as seen in the US. On the contrary, the building of large numbers of high-rise condominiums and apartment complexes in central areas is transforming inner city areas that had been declining for decades. Whereas the central downtown area of Tokyo (the three inner wards (Ku) around Tokyo Station, Chuo Ku, Minato Ku, and Chiyoda Ku) lost 220,434 residents between 1960 and 2000 (a 49% decrease), they gained 58,078 (22%) between 2000 and 2005 (Population Census of Japan 2005), and the increase from 2005 to 2010 is expected to be even larger (2010 census results are not yet available at time of writing). And while the central ten Tokyo wards lost over a million residents between 1960 and 2000 (2.8 million to 1.7 million), they increased by 133,698 between 2000 and 2005. The number of households is increasing even faster, because average household size is shrinking, with an increase of 48,150 households in the downtown three wards between 2000 and 2005, representing a 37 percent increase over five years. This represents a huge amount of new housing built in inner city areas. There is no question that a major shift of population towards the inner city is occurring.

As the overall population of the Tokyo region is increasing only slowly, and is expected to soon start shrinking absolutely, the significant growth in the center comes at the expense of the outer suburbs, where many neighborhoods lost population between 2000 and 2005, with some seeing significant losses of up to 25 percent of their population. The building of large numbers of new housing units in city centers, combined with a shrinking population has already produced increasingly large numbers of vacant plots and houses in suburban areas, as people move to central city locations.

The combination of population decline and recentralization of population, if they continue as projected, will clearly have profound impacts on urban patterns. If recentralization of population seen during the last ten years continues, suburbs will see an accelerating loss of population, as total population declines, and people move back to central cities. If so, then the pattern in Japan will be one of Urbanization ⇒ Suburbanization ⇒ Reurbanization, not a shift to a new, yet more dispersed form of post-suburbanization. Accelerating population decline in suburban areas, combined with rapidly increasing numbers of vacant sites where formerly there were houses, and a shift of population back to city center areas suggests that 'post-suburban' may also apply to Japan, but with a distinctively Japanese meaning of the term.

13
New Towns for Suburbs? Developmental State Politics and New Town Development in Seoul Metropolitan Region

Yong-Sook Lee and HaeRan Shin

13.1 Introduction

One prominent feature of the urban landscape in North America and Western Europe is the emergence of what have been variously termed 'technoburbs' (Fishman, 1987), 'edge cities' (Garreau, 1991), 'edgeless cities' (Lang, 2003), 'metroburbia' (Knox, 2008), and 'post-suburbia' (Phelps et al, 2010), arguably embodying new forms of settlement, new urban issues, and a distinctive politics in city-regions. Much has been written on the diverse forms and implications of these elements of contemporary urbanization but there are few studies that address the developmental state setting in East Asia.

This chapter investigates contemporary developments at the edge of the Seoul capital city where there is no direct parallel to the sorts of 'spontaneous' development of settlement space but where instead 15 new towns with huge apartments, new office complexes and gigantic malls have emerged for the last two decades as part of an increasingly polycentric metropolitan area. In this paper, through an analytical angle of local politics, we aim to examine the nature, driving forces, and the outcomes of these new town developments in the South Korean urbanization by illustrating the case of the Pangyo new town development. A closer look at the Pangyo new town development at the edge of Seoul capital city can shed light on how such settlements resemble or differ from the urban patterns and politics of contemporary urbanization in the Anglo-Saxon contexts.

The new town projects in the Seoul capital region have been planned by the state since the late 1980s for the purpose of supplying affordable houses in the Seoul metropolitan region, which has had chronic housing shortages due to massive population inflows since industrialization. In the first five new town projects (1988–1992), the state-invested companies, the Korea Land Corporation (KLC) and the Korea National Housing Corporation (KNHC) – which were merged in 2009 – separately or together have mostly dominated as the main developer. But, after the 1997 crisis, not only did city or province governments and city corporations emerge as new developers, but also multiple actors such as private construction companies, environment groups, citizens, and civil society organizations began to raise their voices in the latter periods of the ten new town projects.

Pangyo new town, which was planned and constructed in the latter periods (2003–2009), exemplifies a new form of governance arrangements, associated with multiple actors' involvement in the development process and fragmentation in consensus-making. The Pangyo new town development process reveals the tension between pro-growth and environmental conservation groups, the friction between the municipal and provincial governments and the central government (including dissenting opinions among ministries), and the conflicting interests among diverse actors in relation to deregulation. Based on the empirical evidence arising from the Pangyo new town development, we argue that a new form of governance arrangements with regard to the city-region formation are gradually emerging while the state still holds the significant institutional power and policy tools in new town development. We also illuminate the peculiar 'publicness' of the South Korean public sector, which embodies a particular kind of compromise with private sectors by building the 'close relationship', which means the coalescence, through formal and informal channels. Our study, draws on fieldwork conducted between December 2008 and January 2009. For general characteristics of Korean new town developments and main issues in the Korean case, we analysed archives including public reports, announcements of the Ministry of Land, Transport, and Maritime, planning reports, consultancy reports, newspaper articles, websites of the participants, and blogs. We also conducted site visits and in-depth interviews with representatives from the public sector, the voluntary sector, and media.

In the next section, we review the debates on city-region developments from a comparative standpoint. In the following section, we provide a historical analysis of the role of the developmental state in the South Korean new town projects. Next, we recount the story of the development of Pangyo New Town and analyse the main issues and politics arising from its development. Last, we conclude with the implications arising from our consideration of the developmental state's new town projects.

13.2   City-region developments and the new urban politics: A comparative sketch

Suburbanization has come to symbolize key aspects of contemporary culture such as 'conspicuous consumption, a reliance upon the private automobile, upward mobility, the separation of the family into nuclear units, the widening division between work and leisure, and a tendency toward racial and economic exclusiveness' (Jackson, 1985, p. 4). It became the American mode of urbanization in the twentieth century, so much so that successive simplifications of the Chicago School models of the modern metropolis have come to be associated with a clear divide between the centrality and spatial fixity of suburbs, that is, the binary of city-suburb, as a form of settlement space. The ideological content of conventional suburbia involves the pursuit of personal and economic freedom and escape from the city. These characteristics of the Chicago School's modern metropolis have been contrasted with those of more recent post-suburbanization by the Los Angeles school (Dear, 2002). The spatial forms of post-suburbia in Los Angeles are far removed from binary divisions between city and suburb and instead posit mixed land uses in extended metropolitan areas with polycentric nodes. Although the Los Angeles case indicates a central role for organized business interests in post-suburban politics, their political coalitions are much more complicated and fragmented as a result of the ideological, cultural and political 'hybridization' (Dear and Dahmann, 2008) apparent in post-suburbia. With a history of local initiative and local private sectors' involvement, the politics of Los Angeles suburbs has evolved from growth machine politics to a more fragmented and contested growth politics. This fragmentation was initiated by the private sector that threatened the public sector's planning and brought the private sector's entrepreneurial norms. Then, the emergence of anti-growth groups in particular made focal issues increasingly ambiguous as various discourses conflict (Fulton, 1997). Social consensus on urban growth became hard to make, and the pro-growth coalition also has increasingly complicated participations.

Extended metropolitan areas have been also developed in Asia, but are quite different morphologically and politically from their Western counterparts in the United States (US) and UK contexts. McGee's use of the term *desakota* indicates that Asia's sprawling urban settlements, which combine the village (*desa*) and town (*kota*), are quite unique. They show the mixed rural/urban character of major urban agglomerations. Hence, inevitable conflicts between urban elites and the rural masses and growing urban-based centralism and authoritarianism are witnessed easily in these settlements (McGee, 1991; McGee and Robinson, 1995). Suburbanization has been also relatively slight, and such suburbanization has been associated with low-income rather than higher-income groups (Laquian, 2005). Another feature of the Asian urban regions is that the core cities remain the primate centres (McGee, 1991; Douglass, 2000). Although Asia's urban regions share these characteristics, they also diverge into several types such as the technologically advanced East Asian cities, the mega cities of China, and the primate cities of Southeast Asia (Laquian, 2005).

The technologically advanced East Asian city-regions such as Tokyo and Seoul have relatively well-defined administrative and political jurisdictions encompassing highly urbanized areas and have experienced substantial economic growth (Laquian, 2005). They are economically, socially, culturally and politically dominant within the national urban system. With this centripetal force, statist systems of land and housing development, stronger national political organizations, and more extensive national land use policies are more distinctive in the development processes of the East Asian city-regions (Bae and Sellers, 2007; Laquian, 2005). Among them, in particular, the Seoul capital city-region has been developed under a centralized governance system, whereby the central government holds the effective power to make policies and local governments merely implement central decisions in urban developments (Kim, 1999). This centralized system was developed under the developmental state. In this system, local units were substantially involved in the implementation of planning, but local governments did not have independent power to make plans in regional development. Moreover, civil society had no place in policy-making.

However, this centralized model of city-region governance has been under challenge in the age of globalization. In particular, after the Asian economic crisis in 1997, both the private sector and local governments began to demand the elimination or significant reduction of regulations governing land use and development in order to enhance the international competitiveness of cities (Lee, 1998; Kim, 1999). Citizens, who have been affected by various government land-related policies, also began to demand that their property rights be restored to them. Among neoliberal reformers, deregulation is believed to be the solution for the ills created by past government intervention (Kim, 1999). In this context of globalization, devolution, and privatization, the new governance arrangements of the capital city-region have evolved in South Korea. The contemporary new town developments at the edge of Seoul capital city were created in this context of changing governance structures.

This comparative analysis offers distinctiveness of the South Korean case, while it reveals some convergence among tendencies in the politics and governance of city-regions in North America, Europe, and Asia, and it also highlights the continuing centrality of the nation state in territorial development processes in city-regions. First, for example, there are political tensions over the pursuit of growth versus conservation apparent in the west. As Teaford (1997) says, it is a tension between suburban ideals and new economic realities in the outer suburbs. Even in South Korea, which has the legacy of the developmental state, this kind of tension has become apparent. Second, tensions over the density and morphology of new towns are quite common in the city-regions across the globe, but they appear very differently in the technologically advanced East Asian city-region. These tensions are mediated primarily by the market in the western context, while they are still mediated via the state in the East Asian developmental state context. As the centripetal force of the capital region is still powerful, and the demand for development is quite strong, pro-growth groups (for high density) and environmental groups (for low density) are sharply divided over this issue. Third, political tensions over the degree of self-containment are intimately associated with planned new towns. New towns are traditionally meant to be self-contained, but in reality, new towns on the edge of metropolitan areas often turn out to be satellite towns. In theory, new towns under the developmental state can be more self-contained and less dysfunctional settlements within a large city-region than those appearing 'spontaneously' in North America for example. However, since the developmental state new town project contains within it the contradictory logic of providing for further growth of the capital city-region then, in the context of the changing governance arrangements, local governments and actors can critically raise this issue of the degree of self-containment.

13.3   New towns in South Korea

South Korean urbanization has been shaped by the state-led land and housing developments. The state determines the characteristics of the Seoul city-region through its new town projects. The Seoul city-region (Seoul, Incheon, and Gyeonggi province) was strictly regulated and managed by the state government based on the Capital Region Management Law, which had been enacted in 1984.

State-led land and housing development under the developmental state

A distinctive characteristic of the South Korean land and housing development is extensive state involvement. Large-scale land and housing development projects are virtually monopolized by the public sector (Grange and Jung, 2004; Kim and Kim, 2002). We do not examine here whether the current South Korean state is a developmental state or not. The state continues to utilize many policy tools to regulate land development/use and housing development. Our aim is thus to investigate which state tools are still effective in new town development. In this respect, the state's involvement in these development projects has been justifiable as the developmental state has considered land and housing as public goods.

The South Korean state was a developmental state with autonomous power during the state-led industrialization periods of the 1960s and 1970s. The power and autonomy of the developmental state was based on the weakness of other classes. The developmental state orchestrated the processes of industrialization and urbanization that accelerated after 1960. To pursue and implement its industrialization and urbanization projects, the state needed a large amount of land and thus enacted the Land Expropriation Act in 1962. Based on this act, the state was able to wield its expropriation power very widely for 'public projects' (Kim and Ahn, 2000)[1] and thus to access land for its industrial and urban development projects. Unlike in most developed market economies that have strict limitations on state expropriation of land, the state was able to expropriate land not only for industrial development but also for commercial residential development in South Korea. To control the allocation of land and housing effectively, the state also rationed through public or quasi-public mechanisms in a way that sustained state-invested companies (Kim and Ahn, 2000).

---

[1]Land can be expropriated for national defence or military purposes, for public infrastructure (transport, environmental controls, water supply facilities, sewage systems, electricity, telecommunications, broadcasting and gas), for public facilities (public offices, factories, research centres, public parks, plazas, playgrounds, markets, cemeteries, crematoria, slaughterhouses, and other public facilities), for social education or arts, for housing construction or housing sites preparation for the purposes of lease or transfer, and for iron manufacturing, fertilizer or other important industries determined by Presidential Degree (this item was excluded when the 2001 law was enacted).

The state set up the Korea Land Development Corporation (KLDC), which can expropriate private lands and develop them into building sites that were sold to the public and private builders. For public housing construction, the state also established the Korea National Housing Corporation (KNHC). Both KLDC and KNHC have monopolized land and housing development projects, while the private sector has been excluded from the land development process and restricted to housing and infrastructure construction. Thus, the purpose of this institutional setting of public agencies was to prevent the private sector and private developers from collecting large windfall gains.

During the state-led industrialization periods of the 1960s–1970s, the state's priority was on industrial development for high growth rates under the slogan of 'growth first and distribution second'. For industrial land development, the state heavily relied on the Land Expropriation Act. However, as the state could not easily pay compensation due to the steeply risen land prices with industrialization, the state enacted the National Land Use and Management Act in 1972. This act introduced the Basic Land Prices System, which aimed to promote efficient land use by maintaining an adequate level of land prices, so called Basic Land Prices, which were much lower than market prices (sometimes only one-tenth of market value) (Kim and Ahn, 2002). Between 1975 and 2001, the land expropriation scheme established a two-tiered system: contract-based land acquisition by agreement and compulsory expropriation procedures. Only land which could not be acquired by mutual agreement was subject to compulsory purchase according to expropriation procedures.[2]

Due to the state's priority on industrial development, the state paid little attention to land development for residential use until housing problems arose. As it was faced with chronic housing shortages and unaffordable rising housing prices, it began to develop land for residential use. For this, the state enacted the Land Readjustment (LR) Act in 1966 and pursued the LR projects (Grange and Jung, 2004). These LR projects were mainly used in urban development during the 1960s and 1970s.

However, the state replaced LR with public management development (PMD) projects as housing speculation was rife in big cities. For this shift, the state enacted the Residential Site Development Promotion Act in

---

[2]In 2001 these processes were combined in the Act on the Acquisition of Land for Public Projects and their Compensation, which integrated the existing Land Expropriation Act and the Act on Special Cases concerning the Acquisition of Land for Public Uses and the Compensation for their Loss (1975).

1980 and prohibited the use of LR within big cities such as Seoul and Pusan from 1984 (Grange and Jung, 2004). The Residential Site Development Promotion Act permitted not only the purchase of land in project areas from landowners at appraised prices (usually less than market prices) for site formation purposes and resale to private developers for the construction of dwellings but also compulsory expropriation procedures. Since the 1980s, PMD based on the Residential Site Development Promotion Act has become the basic tool for creating residential sites for housing and infrastructure. The private sector was not allowed to conduct PMD projects until 2000 (Grange and Jung, 2004).

In housing development processes, the state also directly regulated the housing markets through various tools. The price control on new apartments and the advanced sale system were the key elements of the state's regulation tools (Kim and Kim, 2000). To control prices of new apartments, the state introduced ceiling prices for newly built apartment units in the late 1970s. House buyers benefitted from this apartment price ceiling system as it guaranteed low construction costs and subsidized sales prices. Through this system, they enjoyed the gains from the difference between the controlled price and the market price.[3]

For housing construction, the state did not have to enlarge public funds through the introduction of the advanced sale system (ASS). Instead, home buyers had to pay in advance for their flats in monthly installments over several years before taking occupation of their homes.[4] These utilized civilian savings became the main source of construction finance and enabled the state to make serviced land available at no cost to itself.

Although the state monopolized land development, it sold building sites to public and private construction companies for housing construction. The private sector became involved in housing construction, especially new apartment construction. To maximize its profits in housing

---

[3]The 'new apartment price ceiling system' was introduced in 1982. In 1989, this system was replaced by a new type of price control, called 'construction cost linkage system with new apartment price' whereby sales prices were varied in accordance with land values and standard construction costs adjusted annually with rises in the retail price index (Grange and Jung, 2004).

[4]Based on the ASS, home buyers had to pay 20 percent of the whole purchase price when signing a sale-purchase contract with the construction company and then pay another 60 percent of the purchase price in three installments while the housing unit's construction was in progress. The remaining 20 percent was paid when the apartment was ready to be occupied.

construction, construction companies and private developers continued to lobby for the removal of the price control and regulations on the size distribution of apartments. For effective housing supply on a massive scale, the state has built up close relationships with construction companies, especially the chaebol (Park, 1998; Kim and Ahn, 2000). Although large-scale land and housing development projects have been dominated by the public sector, the private sector also enjoyed windfall gains based on the close relations with the state. Thus, the state's housing policies embody a particular kind of compromise between a market and a non-market approach.

Democratization, financial crisis, and the New Town Development Projects

With democratization since the late 1980s, as the Korean people have raised critical questions of housing shortages and land and housing speculation, the state began to pay attention to issues of housing. The housing system became a political target in the late 1980s. However, the state rarely regarded housing as a component of a social welfare system but attempted to meet Koreans' housing needs in order to appease the dissatisfaction of the urban population. To avoid public dissatisfaction, the state under the Roh Tae Woo government (1988–93) pursued the first New Town Development Project, which constructed two million housing units in five years in the capital metropolitan region.

The main aims of the project were to stabilize housing prices, increase housing supply, and promote the equity between various social classes. The five new towns located within a 25 km radius from the city centre of Seoul were constructed. Bundang, Ilsan, Pyeongchon, Sanbon, and Jungdong were built as the first generation new towns with planned populations ranging from 166,000 to nearly 400,000 in the case of Bundang. 2,000,000 dwelling units were constructed on average during 1988–92. The public sector was to construct 900,000 dwelling units (45%) and private sector was to supply 1,100,000 dwelling units (55%) (Chu, 2000). The two million unit target was achieved one year ahead of the scheduled five-year period.

During the construction of these new towns private sector involvement in housing development increased. Construction companies and private developers lobbied for those developments already under way in the 1990s. In particular, the Asian Financial Crisis accelerated these processes of deregulation and marketization, and land and housing development was thus becoming more market oriented. During the crisis, over-regulation and over-planning were criticized for the negative effects on international competitiveness. In particular, high land prices were attributed to the central government's policy failure, including the tight land supply policy imposed by strict planning schemes such as the greenbelt policy and the decrees regulating the Seoul Capital Region based on the Capital Region Management Law. Private sectors and local governments strongly demanded deregulation of land use and planning to enhance the more international functions of the Capital Region (Kim, 1999). During the crisis, many financially weak construction companies were bankrupt, many apartment blocks under construction went unfinished, and many newly built apartment units went unsold. To rescue these construction companies and support the housing industry, the state abolished eligibility conditions for people applying for newly built apartment units and

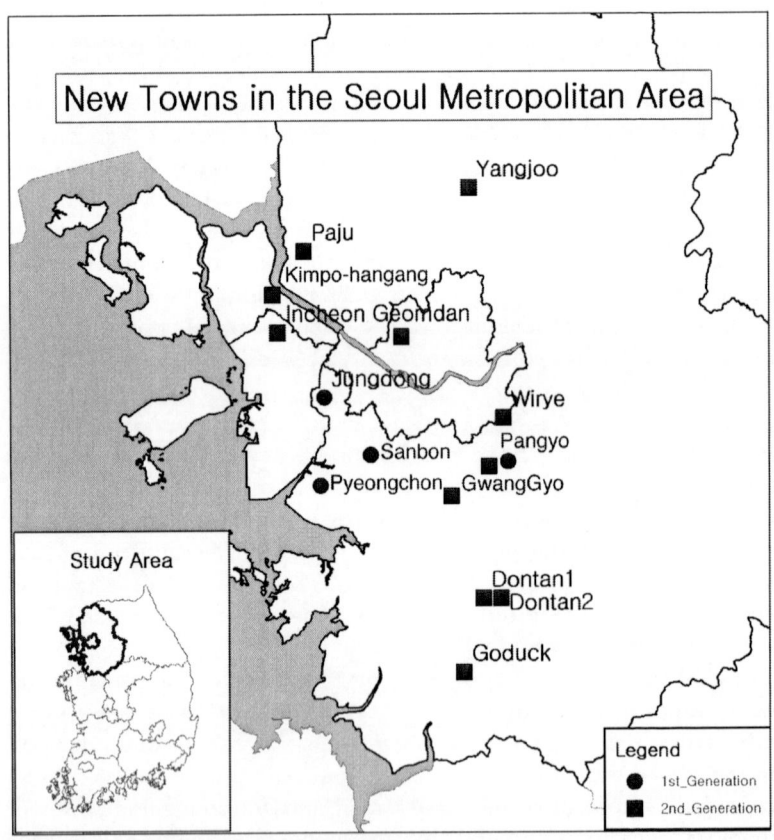

Map 13.1 New towns in the Seoul metropolitan area

ceiling prices on newly built apartment units. Furthermore, the state removed the ban on resale within a specified time period for recently purchased apartment units. The state also deregulated the greenbelts where previously construction activities had been prohibited for the construction of the second generation of ten new town projects which contribute, along with the five earlier new towns, in a distinctive way to the polycentricity of the Seoul metropolitan region (Map 13.1).

Overall, the state stimulated speculation on land and apartments through the new town construction as one method of boosting the economy as a whole. The general tendency in policy after the 1997 crisis was deregulation and marketization. As a result, a few years after the financial crisis, floating capital was concentrated in the stock and real estate market, and the price of stock and real estate began to jump. Such a rising tide of housing speculation, the skyrocketing price of land and housing units, and unearned land-based incomes of large companies and the wealthy threatened the legitimization of the state under the Roh government (2003–08). In the process, the Roh government seriously reconsidered the publicness of the Panyo new town development.

13.4   The case of Pangyo new town

New town development has been at the centre of growth politics in South Korea due to its enormous impact on the housing market, transportation, and the environment. The Pangyo case particularly involved all of the issues that have appeared in the 30-year history of new town policies in South Korea.

(Re)articulating Pangyo new town development

The very location of Pangyo was one of the reasons that made this new town development a hot issue. It is located between Seoul and Bundang, which is an existing new town, and its locational benefit was considered significant as it is closer to Seoul than Bundang is. Therefore, it has been an attractive candidate for real estate development for a long time. But, any development within 66.8 km^2 of Pangyo area was restricted until 2001 since it had been designated as Nam Dan Green Area by the central government in 1976. Although the legal base was weak as it was not a greenbelt, it was possible because the military president, Park Jung Hee's power was enormous at that time. The planned end of the restriction was 2001 which provided a time horizon for the various state and developer interests. The City of Sung Nam, where Pangyo geographically belongs, initiated a development plan for the area in 1999. The Ministry of

Construction and Transportation (MCT) and the majority political party (Minjoo Political Party) under the Roh Moo Hyun Administration, which had cooperative relations with NGOs, took a year to approve the development.

Four participants were officially involved in the development while MCT led the whole process. They include Gyeonggi province, the City of Sung Nam, Korea Land Cooperation, and Korea Housing Cooperation. The process in which four participants were involved in the development by dividing land into four pieces was not easy. As a former director in the MCT recalled 'Everyone wanted to have a good portion and pay little' (MCT, Former Director, 5 January 2009). The same interviewee noted how different options were explored and how compromises were made so that each key stakeholder has its own boundary to develop. This negotiating process alone was intense prompting raised voices in meeting rooms (National Assembly, Assemblyman, 31 December 2008). The role of the Korea Land Cooperation was to prepare land for the development by buying from previous owners. The Korea Housing cooperation was involved in actual construction as a developer along with private developers. As each of the four participants had a different approach on the future of Pangyo, an agreement was made that the land was divided among the four so that each of them could develop the designated land in its own way. The Korea Land Corporation established the basic plan and developed 50 percent, the Korea Housing Corporation 30 percent, and the City of Sung Nam 20 percent. In terms of the number housing units, the Korea Housing Corporation provides about 18,000 households, while the Korea Land Corporation does the rest. The division among the four participants was a result of a complicated set of conflicting interests which resulted in 11 revisions of the development plan.

The politics of the Pangyo new town development

As the planning and development of Pangyo new town proceeded a number of key controversies became apparent. Transportation was a big issue in the Pangyo case, with Bundang residents and the Seoul Metropolitan government being against the Pangyo development because of the increased traffic jams. However, the tensions over transportation were solved easily once the Korea Land Corporation proposed to construct high-level roads and extra roads so that there would be no impact on traffic conditions of Seoul and Bundang. Here instead we concentrate on less tractable debates regarding growth and conservation, density, and self-sustainability.

Growth versus conservation

The Pangyo case shows how the struggle between the pressure for and reluctance over further development resulted in increasingly fragmented interest groups. The main contest here was between big pro-growth construction groups and anti-growth groups who preferred conservation and public housing. However, the divided interests were much more complicated than those between public and private sector in the Korean context. Some public sectors such as MCT and local governments have advocated growth alongside the private sector. In addition, MCT, ME, the Blue House, and the assembly approached Pangyo differently based on their different interests, and even within MCT, different divisions (departments) have been in conflict with one another on some issues.

Private developers are clearly supportive of a new town development. Although their participation and influence do not appear explicitly, some interviewees pointed out that they shared an ideological goal towards land and development with MCT. The impression that there is intensive lobbying of governmental staff and politicians by private developers is supported by the fact that, between 1993–2005, 320 out of 584 bribery cases were related with construction, and 64.2 percent of the total arrests pertained to construction (Citizens' Coalition for Economic Justice, 2006, pp. 620–621). Private developer associations (Land Association and Housing Association) have had regular meetings with MCT staff members, so official channels to MCT remain open to private developer associations. Informal, but crucial collaborations also exist. It is quite popular for the private sector associations to recruit those who used to work in the ministry. Thus, the central government officials regard the private association as a place for themselves after retirement (Daily Newspaper, reporter, 26 February 2009).

Within the public sector, MCT was the leading growth participant in collaboration with the private developers. In addition, semi-governmental agencies such as Korea Land Corporation and Korea Housing Corporation as well as local governments were on the side of pro-growth. They argued that new town development is necessary in order to resolve housing problems by providing more housing. MCT in the central government was commonly said by interviewees to have significant influence. As one interviewee explained,

> We [MCT] lead the whole process. The Ministry of Environment is passive, The Ministry of National Defense and the Ministry Agriculture also only respond rather than lead... We fight with every

one and persuade media, the National Assembly, and the Ministry of Culture, Sports and Tourism. The city of Sungnam and the Gyeonggi province are all passively playing their roles. ... The Blue House looks at the whole and helps (MCT, former director, 5 January 2009).

Although MCT has been a strong advocator in pro growth agendas, their voice was not quite united in the case of Pangyo, according to another interviewee (Government project organization, commissioner, 7 January 2009). Within MCT, the Land department that develops land and the Housing Department that is concerned with house prices supported the Pangyo development. In contrast, the National Planning Department and the City Department of MCT argued that the Pangyo location should be sustained and protected for the next generation. The conflict between the two made the decision-making process complicated.

Furthermore, there was strong criticism arising from civil society, which was supported by the majority party, Minjoo political party. In this conflicting context, the Planning and Management Office of MCT was asked to mediate the conflict in the rhetoric of environmentally-friendly development being able to satisfy both needs. Nevertheless, MCT as a whole was motivated by economic growth and housing supply for the future, so ultimately they sided with the pro-growth agenda. This shows the peculiar publicness of MCT, which is a public organization, but represents its own organizational interest rather than public interests. The media's role in the growth politics deserves an attention as it plays a role as a bridge between the MCT and private developers. Another former staff in the central government also confirmed that 80 percent of his weekend schedule was arranged for meetings with media people because it was very important to be supported by them (MCT, former director, 5 January 2009). Some reporters regularly visit the Ministry of Land, Transport and Maritime Affairs and private developers and so end up playing a role of messengers (Daily Newspaper, reporter, 26 February 2009). He said '...we pass messages of the market to the Ministry of Construction and Transportation. In fact, they know what the market wants better than anyone else...The private developers' needs are regularly passed through the associations.' One of the reasons why the media is considered to have a friendly relationship with private real estate developers is that apartment advertisement contributes the bulk of revenues from total advertising (Daein Sun, 2005, http://blog.daum.net/cityhiro/1775517; accessed May 2009 in Korean). The media is kind of a vehicle to reinforce the peculiar publicness of MCT. The Korea Land Corporation (KLC) was also keen on developing a new town, according to an interviewee (Government research institute, researcher, 2 January 2009), because it is a good way to sustain itself with 3,000 employees. Pro-growth interests and agendas are ideologically buttressed by the Korea Housing Institute and the Construction & Economy Research Institute of Korea, which were founded by the private developers' associations such as the Construction Association of Korea and the Korea Housing Builders Association.

The local governments involved in new town development are also likely to belong to the pro-growth side. An interviewee in the central government (MCT, former director, 5 January 2009) explained that this is because local governments make income by receiving acquisition tax and registration tax, which come mainly from housing not from industry. The government of Gyeonggi province wanted deregulation of Seoul metropolitan area, on the one hand, and autonomy for the development, on the other hand. For industrial land allocations, it argued in expansive terms for 3,305,800 m² for IT industry, but later a figure of one-fifth of this was agreed.

On the anti-growth side, the ME, civic organizations and progressive scholars criticized private developers as well as those governmental organizations which take enormous profits from new town developments. They also argued that even if more housing units were provided in Pangyo, it would not relieve the housing price in Gangnam because the housing supply would stimulate more speculation in the area (Presidential Committee, former director, 29 December 2008). Their activities challenged and pressurized the MCT. Particularly under the Kim Dae Jung administration (1998–2002), which had struggled for democracy, a number of people from civic organizations got positions in the central government. Besides, environmentalist organizations raised a voice against the development and motivated the Minjoo Party to go against the development.

The ME played an important role in raising environmental issues within the central government, but its position in the power structure was weaker than MCT. Environmentalists were strongly against the development in the beginning because of the green space in Pangyo, which, in ecological perspective, should be preserved. They also argued that low-income residents, who should be protected by housing policy, would be disadvantaged. Environmentalists effectively pressurized the Kim Dae Jung government (1998–2002) not to convert land use (MCT, former director, 5 January 2009). Cooperation between academic professionals and civic organizations was witnessed also in 2000, which is not likely to happen at present. During the Roh administration,

2003–08, the Blue House listened to civic organizations but the current regime is much less interested in discussing with civil society (Government research institute, former researcher, 10 January 2009). Another interviewee who works in a civic organization defined the Pangyo new town development a failure of the governmental real estate policy (Voluntary organization, executive manager, 5 January 2009).

Density and morphology of development

Despite the strong voices from the ME and environmentalists against the development plan, the development was first approved in 2001 by the MCT that 9.3 km^2 of Pangyo area would be developed as a new town. To negotiate with the anti-development groups, the pro-growth groups, especially the MCT, suggested a development idea involving low density and plenty of green space (64 people per hectare). Given that Bundang has 198 people per hectare and Gwachun's density is 274 people per hectare (MCT, 2001), this was a significantly lower density that was being proposed. The planned population was 59,100, and the total number of planned housing units was 19,700 including 3,400 single family housings, 1,800 attached housings and 14,500 apartments. Someone who was a former central government official confirmed the crucial role of MCT (Presidential Committee, former director, 29 December 2008): 'People in Ministry of Construction and Transportation first persuaded the Blue House...suggesting that Pangyo be developed in an environment-friendly way'. According to an interviewee in academia (Government research institute, researcher, 2 January 2009), the MCT agreed on 64 people per hectare in order to please the ME without serious consideration. However, the MCT later realized later that development cost of such residential densities was too high for them to provide affordable housing. They asked the Korean Research Institute of Human Settlement (KRIHS), which is a key national research agency for land use policy formulation to consult for a density plan. The KRIHS suggested that more small housing should be provided, and the advice was taken by the MCT although there was a disagreement within the ministry.

Based on KRIHS' suggestion, the density plan was re-negotiated between MCT and the majority party without the ME and announced in 2003 by MCT that the density would go up into 96 people per hectare. The numbers of housing units would also be increased to 29,700, and the land area allocated to industrial uses was also increased. The increased density and exclusive process caused serious conflicts between the MCT and ME, and the ME refused to accept it. Civic organizations also submitted an opinion against the population density increase. The ME insisted maintaining 64 people per hectare and postponed a discussion on Environmental Impact Evaluation in order to hinder the process. A research fellow in one research association said the MCT had been criticized by the Office for Government Policy Coordination regarding the conflicts between the two ministries. For a solution, both ministries opened a forum, inviting environmental organizations, and agreed that the density should be within (86 people per hectare) and the increasing housings should be given to the low income residents as public housing (Gyeonggi et al, 2003). It was also agreed that experts on environmental issues and environmental organizations should be involved for consultancy and monitoring in the implementation of the development plan. This shows that the tensions over density were spilt into civic groups and private sector, and the role of the civic group was very crucial in resolving the tensions.

It should be noted, however, that civic organizations' argument was not as prominent later as the development plan stimulated the real estate market. As severe public criticism arose due to rising housing prices and speculation, the state, especially the president's group in the Blue House, began to limit private sector involvement, and the August 31 Housing Policy was released as a response. The conflicting discourses appeared again when the whole plan was re-made. The MCT and private developers argued for the increase of big apartments while the Blue house, the ME and civic organizations such as the Citizen's Coalition for Economic Justice (CCEJ) supported more increases of public housing and small-sized apartments.

According to a former director in the Presidential Committee (Presidential Committee, former director, 29 December 2008), by Presidential Degree, the Roh President blocked the sale of apartment units led by private sectors and put on the market 20,000 new apartment units in Pangyo simultaneously in November to prevent overheated competition for the units among buyers, shifting from its initial plan to divide the sale into four rounds over the next two years. To prevent possible speculation on apartments in Pangyo, the president and his group imposed tighter measures to curb illegal transactions and increased the share of public housing units and small-sized apartment units. Eventually, 10,168 public apartment units and 24,191 private apartment units were provided. Among 24,191 private units, small-sized units (below 60m^2) were 403, medium-sized units (between 60m^2–85m^2) were 7,274, and large sized units (above 85m^2) were 6,343 (Byeon, 2005). The presidential group also introduced a new type of price control over all units below 85m^2 for low-income home buyers. The Blue House's leading power was most visible in Pangyo's case. Stopping the whole process right before sale and increasing the number of public housing units was what only the Blue House was able to do.

Due to the August 31 policy, the private sector's profits became increasingly constrained. Prior to this Presidential intervention in the case of Pangyo, private developers could use their brand for the surface of the apartments that they built. However, after the August 31 policy, it was decided that only the brand of Korea Housing Cooperation, Humansia, was to appear. This was then re-negotiated through the Ministry of Land, Transport, and Maritime (MLTM) – the new name of MCT under the current Lee Administration – so that both brands can be used (Daily Newspaper, reporter, 26 February 2009). Before the August 31 policy, the private sector's involvement was larger than the public sector's, but the public sector's involvement increased to match that of the private sector (Presidential Committee, former director, 29 December 2008).

Although the Blue House returned into publicness by suggesting the 31 August Policy, which supported the ME and the civic organizations, it was criticized by both, the pro-growth and the anti-growth side. A former-staff's remark in the Blue House confirms this, 'We [the Blue House] pondered what to do, being stuck between the two arguments, and were criticized by both sides' (Presidential Committee, former director, 29 December 2009).

The degree of self-containment

The sustainability of Pangyo new town was a hot issue between local governments and the central government. Local governments including Gyeonggi province government and the Sung-nam city government aimed to have self-sustaining business facilities while the central government wanted to provide more housing units in order to make the real estate prices stable.

In spite of a long history of extensive developmental state involvement in land and housing development, the state began to divest itself of public land development and management to local governments since the 1990s. In line with this devolution trend, as mentioned before, as restrictions on construction expired by 2001, Sungnam city called for the necessity of well planned development. For well planned development, Sungnam city designated some parts (694 ha) of the Nam Dan Green Area as the expected residential development area, based on its Basic City Planning in 1998. Sungnam city submitted its original plan, which aimed to build an Eco-Knowledge Town Pangyo, to the Gyeonggi province. But, Gyeonggi Province gave it back to Sungnam city and took independent action to make Pangyo a Venture District (1,000,000 pyeong) for the future industry. Although Sungnam city and Gyeonggi province disagreed over the size of the venture district, they shared a vision to have self-sustaining business facilities to avoid becoming a dormitory town for Seoul.

However, the MCT wanted to develop Pangyo as residential complexes so as to supply affordable houses, fight against real-estate inflation and stabilize housing markets in the Seoul metropolitan area. MCT argued for 100,000 pyeong as a venture district in its first plan. In the revised plan between the MCT and Sungnam city, a venture district was reduced to 550,000 pyeong. Gyeonggi Province reacted against the revised plan between the MCT and the city government and argued for 733,000 pyeong as a venture district. As a final decision-maker for the new town creation, the MCT finally allocated 200,000 pyeong as a venture district in its third amendments after several negotiations with Gyeonggi Province. This shows that local governments emerged as significant actors in land and housing development processes, but the state, especially the MCT, was still decisive in determining one key element contributory to the self-containment of Pangyo new town.

13.5 Conclusion

Through the case study of the South Korean new towns, we illuminate that the emerging new towns in the Seoul metropolitan area are developing closer to and more interrelated with Seoul without the accompanying de-urbanization of Seoul. The contemporary urbanization processes in South Korea are still under the state's control and management due to the legacies of the developmental state despite the strong tendency toward deregulation and marketization after the 1997 crisis. Through the construction of multiple new towns, the polycentric city-region is forming under the developmental state politics in the Seoul metropolitan region. These new towns in the polycentric city-region are contrasted to suburbanization associated with low-income groups in Southeast Asia as well as to massive suburban sprawl led by the local governments and private sectors in the US.

Despite their seemingly clear differences, both cases commonly demonstrate the emergence of increasingly complicated governance issues. In both cases, emerging new actors are involved in the politics of city-region development. They form a new governance of city-region development and discourse politics that is not reducible to simple privatization. Rather, it is a reflection of the struggles that the public sector, the private sector, and civil society have in order to shape developments. Although it is beyond the scope of this study to generalize if divergence or convergence is happening among different contexts, any similarity implies the need of careful investigation of micro- and macro- politics of city-region development.

Another important point to be raised is the nature of 'publicness'. The publicness of the public sector is traditionally considered as public welfare-providing, social equality-aware, and tax-based. However, the public sectors in different societies have various characteristics that could be far from the ideal type. As argued in Peterson's *City Limits* (1981), in North American cities, local government is limited to pursue urban growth rather than redistributional policies for social welfare. Compared to local government, the publicness of the central government is close to the ideal type of the public sector. However, if the central government in developmental states is considered, it is again a different story. Increasing variety within the public sector and the intertwined relationship between the public and the private sectors make it hard to define what the publicness is that only the public sector owns. What makes this publicness more complicated are various types of collaboration between the public sector and the private sector. The public sector could have a lack of publicness if these reflect innate limits as a city government, if it is entrepreneurial in a neoliberal response to global or national environment changes, or, if the public sector is entrapped or outweighed by the private sector in public debate.

14
Conclusion: Post-suburban Worlds?

Fulong Wu and Nicholas A. Phelps

14.1 Introduction

At the beginning of this book, we attempted to distinguish 'post-suburbia', asking whether it signalled a new era, a new settlement space or new actors and forces in suburban development. Now after the completion of the journey through many places, we might suggest that the answer is a bit of each to some extent. What emerged at the outset and in the subsequent chapters was that post-suburbia does not embody a clean break with suburbanization. We see the primary value of the term in focusing attention on the multi-faceted, and multi-scalar, nature of transformations affecting metropolises. In this conclusion chapter, we deepen the discussion of the prefix of 'post-' in the concept of post-suburbia and ask, in what sense is there a post-suburban world?

Just as Beauregard (2003) criticizes the use of prototype categories in urban studies, so our aim is not to distil a generic model out of diverse cases. Rather, our conclusion will remain comparative – this is also our intention when speaking of 'post-suburbia' rather than using terms such as 'edge cities' or 'edgeless cities' with their specificity to the North American setting. Recognizing the process of suburbanization has a different starting point from that in the United States (US), we discuss post-suburbia not in a temporal sense. For example, recent Chinese mass suburbanization is accompanied by post-suburban elements of employment dispersal, luxury residential development and new town development (Wu and Phelps, 2011). Accordingly, when we revisit the findings in this conclusion chapter, we maintain a fairly detailed account of key points made by contributors. In such a way, we seek to promote a broader understanding of processes of suburbanization and post-suburbanization.

14.2   Post-suburbia: History, form and politics

Our review begins with the history of post-suburbia. Jon Teaford (Chapter 2) provides a historical tour which presents post-suburbia as the ultimate expression of footloose activities in the metropolitan region. He reviews the origin of suburbia in terms of increasing mobility but also reformist approaches to decongesting cities and enhancing the quality of life. Twentieth-century suburbia firmly established itself in the post-war construction of new housing, epitomized by well-known Levittown outside New York City. Subsequent out-migration of business and retail opened up a new era where the suburbs perhaps are no longer dependent on or subservient to downtown economies. Garreau's (1991) 'edge city' concept describes the beginning of post-suburbia. Teaford summarizes a wide range of observations in North America and Europe, arguing that while the edge city is no longer a dormitory for the centre, the end product of post-suburbia is 'simply suburbanization carried to the extreme'; a result of 'two centuries of continuous deconcentration of metropolitan population'. His view serves as something of a common denominator to the contributions in this volume in the sense that 'continuity, rather than discontinuity, characterized the incremental shift from suburbia to post-suburbia'.

Chaves et al (in Chapter 3) examine the restless landscape of 'metro-burbia' (Knox, 2008). They focus on conspicuous consumption, asking how this is achieved through manufactured suburban development and alight on the process of 'enchantment' including poetic naming and signature designing of residential products. They reveal how this process of enchantment has been produced from the marketing tactics of developers to increase profit margins. The interesting point they made is that this particular element of post-suburbia, epitomized by residential 'vulgaria', is not just a result of increasing demand for ostentatious houses and homeownership in suburbs but rather a cultural value contributing to neoliberalism and its consumption form. McMansions are not just big houses but also an ensemble of material and social practices which include the retreat from community and civic mindedness in contrast to suburbia as we have come to regard it. Chaves et al suggest that post-suburbia represents a changing material and social practice – in that the rise of 'private master-planned developments exempt from most municipal land-use planning regulations' have been 'deepening sociospatial divisions within metropolitan region as a whole', 'seriously impeding any attempt at regional and metropolitan-wide planning'. This consumption perspective captures a different aspect from what Jonas (in Chapter 5) describes as the new regionalism in the US, and instead resembles some elements of the privatization and private governance emerging most recently in the outer suburbs of Latin American city-regions (discussed in Chapters 6 and 7).

Turning to city-region politics, Roger Keil and Doug Young (in Chapter 4) examine how suburbanization and fragmentation of cities has also created problems at the metropolitan scale. They analyse the Frankfurt and Toronto regions and reveal how the attempts to regulate metropolitan expansion creates a new dynamic within regional politics – a politics of the 'in-between' cities. They refer extensively to the literature on new regionalism (see also Jonas in Chapter 5) and suggest that the various spillovers of individual cities create a new politics beyond the central city-suburban dichotomy. In Toronto, a new in-between city has sprung up between the centre and periphery. In Frankfurt, this produces more complex governance at different scales. Different from the local growth machine in the US, the German version involves more actors in institutionalized networks at the regional scale as well. Post-suburbia as manifest in the form of 'in-between cities' therefore raises important questions regarding the need for regulatory capacity in new settlement spaces that straddle traditional old and new suburbia. Issues of marginality in these in-between spaces can be pressing. Low-wage service and manufacturing industries have emerged in the in-between city while there is the concentration of immigrants in tower blocks in old suburbs in Toronto. Keil and Young examine in detail the politics in in-between cities, concluding that the in-between city represents a 'messy mix of public and private' interests at work. To them, post-suburbia may lead to a new politics of in-between cities. Compared with the previous chapter on consumption and social practices by Chaves et al, Keil and Young emphasize the politics of infrastructure and housing development in these spaces which are left uncovered by existing dynamics of urban and suburban development.

14.3   The Americas

Instead of examining metropolitan forms, Andrew Jonas (in Chapter 5) focuses on the politics of development characterizing a possible new phase of post-suburbia. The traditional view of suburbs is that they are spaces for local exclusionary politics where suburban residents wish to preserve the local tax base and exclude unwanted uses. In this chapter Jonas asks whether the new regionalism means the end of suburban exclusionary politics. He uses the cases of Greater Los Angeles (the

Inland Empire region) and Greater Boston (the I-495 region) to show that there is a continuation of exclusionary politics and metropolitan fragmentation but at the same time there are attempts to develop regional cooperation. The links between suburbs themselves are becoming stronger and thus in the literature a concept of new regionalism, which focuses on metropolitan governance beyond the central city-suburbs relation, has been proposed (Jonas and Pincetl, 2006). For example, post-suburban spaces self-organize themselves into a web of specialized and yet collaborated employment locations with the potential for region-wide growth coalitions to emerge. Both the California and Boston cases show some increasing interest in regional coordination for the sake of economic development. There is a sense here in which an identifiable post-suburban politics as a marriage of enduring local exclusionary tendencies with emergent economic development and public infrastructure realities registers itself at a regional scale.

Moving from North America as the locus of much received theory and terminology regarding suburbia and post-suburbia to Latin America, the two chapters by Dirk Heinrichs, Michael Lukas and Henning Nuissl and by Sonia Roitman and Nick Phelps (Chapters 6 and 7 in this volume) explore the governance of outer suburbs and residential development. Not surprisingly they both focus on large-scale private development processes and their connection to a privatization of governance. Clearly, the prevailing neoliberal policy orthodoxy after structural adjustment continues to define the key parameters of Latin American urban development. The periphery of metropolitan regions is now at the frontier of neoliberal urbanism – a place of gated communities, sports and shopping and employment complexes. Recent megaprojects have begun to push urban development boundary into exurban locations. These developments import something of the Anglo-North American sensibility of retreat from the city into outer suburban contexts which have typically housed the poor in their attempts to approach the city and its employment opportunities. So in what sense can we label recent urban expansion in Latin America as 'post-suburbia'? As private actors have gained paramount importance, it is the shift of the 'mode of production of urban space' (Heinrichs et al, in Chapter 6) that evidently stands out. The development of gated communities through megaprojects in exurban locations is driven by investors and real estate companies, forming 'private governance' which excludes the traditional role of local authorities and civil society found in suburbia.

Roitman and Phelps (in Chapter 7) present similar findings in the case of the city of Pilar. Although synonymous with the 'country clubs' catering to elites living in the central city since the 1930s, the concentration of these gated residential communities in this favoured outer suburb of Buenos Aires metropolitan area has been a superimposition upon what was traditionally a municipality with poor populations. These gated communities as well as industrial development in Pilar together with new migrant populations have created demand for services and also stimulated the development of private hospitals, universities and hotels. These developments might be taken to signal the urbanization of suburbia but they in fact have fragmented Pilar into dual suburb. In such a context, municipalities are often unable to extract much in the way of 'planning gain' or wider economic benefits to improve services outside gated communities, according to Roitman and Phelps. These post-suburban elements are detached from and exist alongside traditional suburbia, forming a distinctive set of spaces separate also from the city centre. Thus the case of Pilar together with that of Santiago de Chile reported by Heinrichs et al in Chapter 6 are simply extreme examples of the more general manner in which land extensive suburban and post-suburban development often has regressive fiscal impacts on local communities (Burchell, 2005).

14.4   Post-suburbia and Europe's compact cities

In continental Europe, cities were traditionally more compact than their North American counterparts. Suburbanization was a more managed process, often associated with the Keynesian welfare state and the development of the periphery for public housing. However, as Marco Bontje and Joachim Burdack (in Chapter 8) suggest, there are significant variations between countries, especially between the Western and Central and East European countries. In recent decades, new suburban office complexes, R&D and business parks and out-of-town retail outlets began to emerge, to such an extent it is felt appropriate to apply the notion of post-suburbia to characterize these phenomena. These new developments are not necessarily agglomerated or confined to traditional suburban towns but rather occupy 'in-between places' – the *Zwischenstadt* proposed by Sieverts (2003) and also deployed by Keil and Young in Chapter 4 – and as such remain closer to historic city centres than their North American counterparts. The notion of *Zwischenstadt* was developed specifically in continental Europe, but there are interesting partial parallels to sought in the term *desakota*, (in which desa means village and kota means town in Indonesian) used to describe the fabric of extended metropolitan areas in East Asia (McGee and Robinson, 1995). These concepts also appear to resemble the concept of 'edgeless cities' proposed by Lang (2003). Although each of these concepts have been developed independently there is enough to suggest, as Dick and Rimmer (1998) argue, that important processes of convergence are at work in these post-suburban forms.

After closely examining six cities in continental Europe – Paris, Amsterdam, Frankfurt, Zurich, Helsinki, Budapest and Prague, Bontje and Burdack acknowledge the variation of these cities in terms of urban dispersal and in a sense there might not be a single European model of post-suburbia. If there are some commonalities between continental European cities, these might centre on the more compact and less sprawled post-suburban tendencies, and that post-suburbia and historic city centres are 'becoming complementary parts' of city-regions. So, in what sense can we give a 'post' denomination to European's suburbia? These case studies of European cities seem to suggest that post-suburban elements have been central both to planning visions for and the *de facto* replacement of monocentric cities with polycentric city-region.

The question of whether post-suburbia can be said to exist in the UK is raised by Allan Cochrane (in Chapter 9). He poses the question at a scale beyond London and its traditional suburbs out into the greater southeast of England. Echoing Jonas's post-suburban regionalism in America, Cochrane examines the development of sustainable communities and their role in a larger region. The sustainable community plan in the region foresaw the places as rather free-standing but connected to each other. These sustainable places are not dependent upon the central core for employment and services, and in this sense they could be said to be post-suburban – departing from earlier new towns and the dispersal of populations across the region to commuter or dormitory places. However, the history of previous experiments with self-contained new towns to cater for population and economic growth in the region leads Cochrane to argue that an overwhelmingly suburban character to settlement patterns remains across this most complicated of English 'regions'.

In the context of post-socialist transition, Oleg Golubchikov, Nicholas Phelps and Alla Makhrova (in Chapter 10) examine the transformation of a satellite 'closed' city – Khimki – near Moscow to something approximating an edge city of Moscow. The city of Khimki was developed initially as a military-industrial complex under the socialist plan-led regime. It was more like a company town than the dormitory new town of Moscow because it was more self-contained in terms of job and service provision. In the US, the federal government's support to freeway construction plays a pivotal role in mass suburbanization of Khimki. The suburbs under the centrally-planned regime were characterized by self-contained industrial-complexes and their enterprise towns in a vast hinterland of scattered second homes for season living with mass suburbanization commuting being limited in socialist-era city-regions. Now, market mechanisms have dramatically transformed the landscape of self-containment. Developments, no longer following top-down, sectoral, plans, are opportunity-led with suburban territories being prime locations for all manner of development projects. Yet, the planning system is severely undermined in its attempt to mould these development pressures in a way that contributes to the cohesion of municipalities such as Khimki. As Golubchikov, Phelps and Makhrova in Chapter 10 comment, development is 'fuelled by a variety of spontaneous and opportunistic profit-making initiatives that are characterised by short-termism'. Thus the meaning of 'post-' suburbia in the post-socialist context is not quite the same as in the context of post-mass suburbanization in the US, but rather represents a dissolution of self-contained suburbs with the massive release of pent up demand for suburban housing retail, office warehousing and manufacturing sites. In its appearance, such rapid and chaotic growth has superficial similarities with the growth machine (Logan and Molotch, 1987) dynamic driving edge cities but ought to be distinguished from it.

14.5   Varieties of post-suburbia in East Asia

For Southeast Asian cities, McGee observed long ago that urbanization extended beyond the city boundary under the model of export-oriented growth (McGee and Robinson, 1995). He divided the so-called extended metropolitan region (EMR) into three regions: the city core, peri-urban and *desakota* which is a mix of urban and rural uses. More recently he and his collaborators (McGee et al, 2007) applied this model to Chinese cities. The description of the Southeast Asian model has been almost entirely disconnected with the US phenomenon of edge and edgeless cities. Nevertheless, Dick and Rimmer (1998) tried to develop a framework in association with American style suburbanization and privately developed towns, arguing that globalization is likely to bring new convergence between Western and Southeast Asian cities. Others questioned such a proposition based on the specificity of geographical contexts and historical path-dependency (Ma and Wu, 2005). While it might not be entirely proper to 'transplant' a US edge city model to East and Southeast Asian cities, some changing mechanisms of suburban development have been witnessed. For example, in terms of Chinese cities, there has been: a change from government-led to a more market-oriented suburbanization process (Feng et al, 2008); the development of polycentric city-regions, even beyond the municipal jurisdiction, in large cities such as Beijing and Shanghai (Wu and Phelps, 2008) and; the growth of suburban office and industrial parks under state entrepreneurialism (Wu and Phelps, forthcoming).

Turning to the Jakarta metropolitan area, Tommy Firman (in Chapter 11) observed extensive conversion of farmland into industrial estates and new towns in the fringe areas. Despite a slowing down of large-scale residential development after the Asian financial crisis in 1997, land management has been weak. Some new trends can be found. In particular, it is evident that the Jabodetabek EMR became a multiple-core city-region. Government policy sponsored low-cost housing development and granted private developers to carry out large-scale residential development in new towns. Large private companies play a critical role in the development of these new towns, creating packaged or bundled development in which amenities, services and residential uses are collected together. The fringe areas have also attracted foreign and domestic capital and developed into manufacturing zones. In the context of Southeast Asian cities, if we see the phenomenon of *desakota* as a unique face of suburbanization, the meaning of post-suburbia can be understood in two ways: first the transformation from an earlier mix of urban and rural land uses dominated by the city core to a city-region of multiple cores and second, these new cores developed through new towns led by private companies.

The meaning of post-suburban development in Japan presents us with a meaning that has perhaps been less in evidence in any of the discussions so far including that in our introduction to this volume. André Sorensen (in Chapter 12) describes different stages of suburbanization, reurbanization and disurbanization in Tokyo and argues that post-suburbia in Japan is a process reversing earlier suburbanization. As a prime example of a developmental state, the central government of Japan retains remarkable authority over local plans but not over private land and property markets in which there are fine-grained patterns of land-ownership. Starting in the 1980s, Tokyo did see fine-grained urban expansion. This expansion with mixed land uses is due to the land ownership of small family farms in the suburbs and special tax exemption given to them. As a result, we do not see large plots converted in suburbs but rather the 'melting' of urban and rural areas into each other, leading to a condition similar to *desakota* in Southeast

Asia. The pattern of suburbanization changed in the mid-1980s, when the property boom and bubble economy led to the massive development of automobile-oriented resorts (such as golf courses and hotel complexes). The deregulation of retail resulted in large-scale stores in exurbs along the arterial highways. However, the demographic change in Japan – into an aging society with an increasingly rapidly declining population – is coupled with a significant trend of reurbanization, i.e. people moving back to the central cities because declining land prices and deregulation of high-rise residential development have made inner-city living more affordable (Sorensen et al, 2010). This is also producing a growing trend of vacant housing and housing plots in the outer suburbs that is adding to the fiscal distress of those municipalities and raising the spectre of spirals of decline and deurbanization in those areas. Sorensen thus adds a twist to the concept of post-suburbia – using it to denote the end of suburbanization as we knew it in Japan and raising questions regarding scenarios of suburban decline that we avoided in our discussion in Chapter 1 in favour of viewing post-suburbia in terms of various aspects of suburban growth. While Japan may be a special case other countries such as South Korea and Russia are also facing imminent population decline, and many cities, for example in Eastern Europe are experiencing shrinking populations, so one aspect of post-suburban development may be the various phenomena associated with shrinkage and absolute population loss in some metropolitan regions.

In contrast to more deregulated development in post-socialist cities and neoliberal approaches in Southeast Asia, South Korea is known for its long standing developmental state model. The state still holds significant institutional capacities in new town development. Yong-Sook Lee and HaeRan Shin (in Chapter 13) examine the politics of new town development in South Korea, using an example of Pangyo in Seoul metropolitan area. They describe the origin of new town programs under the developmental state and the process of constructing a polycentric city-region in which the state plays a pivotal role in land and housing development. The new town project started from the political target to expand housing provision. The first five new towns were built through a mix of public and private housing in the 1980s. But the Asian financial crisis forced South Korea to start a process of deregulation. The second generation new towns started against this background, of which the city of Pangyo is a case. What remains a striking feature is the extent of state control, which constrains the profitability of the private sector in the development, as well as controlling the brand of new town housing. Because of the state capacity, South Korea does not show a sprawled pattern led by US growth coalition, nor the peri-urban slums and informal settlement in other South and Southeast Asia cities. South Korea's new town post-suburbia, if such it can be called, demonstrates the strong continuities and legacies of the developmental state. Here, the meaning of 'post-' perhaps reflects a more complicated form of governance that now exists – especially the deepened and contested involvement of public corporations in new town development.

To compare East Asian cities, at this point it is useful to bring in the experience of Chinese cities, though this volume does not have a dedicated chapter to the case. There is an extensive literature on China's rapid urban expansion and suburbanization (e.g. Zhou and Ma, 2000; Feng et al, 2008; Wu and Phelps, 2008; Zhou and Logan, 2008), suggesting a period of mass suburbanization but with a difference from US consumption-driven mass suburbanization. Few have spoken of the dispersal of employment that has been associated with post-suburbia in the US, though factory relocation has been a driving force in earlier suburbanization in the 1980s. It has been noted in the literature that the development of economic and technological development zones (ETDZs) at the periphery (Deng and Huang, 2004) and the emergence of gated communities (Wu, 2005) have led to the expansion of built-up areas. Using Beijing ETDZ, Wu and Phelps (2011) discuss how the place has evolved from a rural market town, to a development zone, and finally to a more comprehensive new town, forming a significant new node within the polycentric metropolis of Beijing. They note the state plays an important role but this is not through a developmental state fashion as in the South Korea new towns example presented by Lee and Shin in Chapter 13. Rather, new development zones are promoted through a development arm – similar to a land development corporation – of the municipality. State entrepreneurialism is behind the development of Beijing's outskirts into an edge-city style space. Inserting such an entrepreneurial development device into rural areas created a complicated jurisdictional structure. While these new places may not be akin to the sort of edgeless city found in the US, they nevertheless create tensions between different governing bodies and challenges to governance. In a sense, new dynamics are created, forcing the entrepreneurial development corporation to take over social functions and transforming it into a quasi-local government. In this sense, the term post-suburbia in the Chinese case means a new form of settlement space, involving new actors and new governance from state-planned suburban development to market-driven dispersal of population and economic activities.

14.6   Conclusion and research directions

As we can see from the chapters concerned with cases from different parts of the world, the contributors do not agree on a singular definition of 'post-suburbia'. What they agree is that we are in a post-suburban world, different from the process of suburban development as we knew it decades ago. This world registers itself in multiple ways, reflecting aspects of change in these different places. In some instances post-suburbia can embody qualitative changes in the nature and degree of self-containment of particular suburban settlements, in others it is signalled by new forms of politics and governance driving urban development at the urban edge, while in others it encompasses the complex assemblages of governmental power that weave suburbs together into post-suburban metropolitan regions.

Table 14.1 tries to summarize and compare some of the key traits discussed in the partial survey represented by the foregoing chapters. What the table makes clear is that it is difficult to compress the sorts of contemporary changes being experienced by suburbs old and new into a single concept. Thus despite its breadth as an umbrella term, post-suburbia in this sense is different from labels such as 'edge cities' or 'edgeless cities', as its value is not as a singular prototype of urban development but rather in signalling a variety of processes of potential change at the periphery of our metropolises.

At the outset in Chapter 1 we presented a summary of potential trajectories within the city-regions of a second modernity (see Table 1.1). Our emphasis, and that in many of the contributions to the volume, has been on what might be regarded as the more positive aspects of economic and demographic and political change implied by the term post-suburbia, albeit a critical emphasis. Andre Sorensen's chapter in particular, however, raises the intriguing question of whether future research on the value of the label post-suburbia might usefully just as well be focused on aspects of economic and demographic change that imply some sort of *decline* or challenge for existing suburbs. To date, what we have seen is rather different bodies of literature, often with contrasting epistemologies, speaking to post-suburban growth, suburban stasis and suburban decline within what can be regarded as heavily urbanized city-region systems of specialized settlements.[1] The value of greater dialogue here can hardly

---

[1]Quite some part, though by no means all, of the literature on post-suburbia is imbued with post-modernist sensibilities. The literature on suburban stasis seems almost exclusively to focus on urban morphology. The literature on suburban decline is arguably more empirical in orientation.

Table 14.1 Contrasts in post-suburbia

Geographic location	Features of Post-suburbia
Americas	
North America	• Edge cities, edgeless cities, in-between cities, • New regionalism, territorial politics beyond localism, governance transcending the city and suburbs dichotomy • Conspicuous consumption, 'vulgaria', civic disengagement
Latin America	• From poor suburbs to dual or polarized suburbs • Gated communities, mega projects and private governance
Europe	
UK	• Complex and evolving polycentric settlement patterns in greater South East of England • Monocentric core cities alongside regionalism outside of the South East of England • The ambiguous role of new towns and sustainable communities in relation to urban cores
Continental Europe	• Edge location employment, airport cities, polycentric cities • More compact cities as concentrated version of edge cities • Diverse governance relations, involving public and private partnership
Post-socialist Europe	• Evolving from industrial satellite cities to more integrated metropolitan suburban/edge cities • Deregulation and opportunity oriented development
East Asia	
Japan	• Aging and population decline • Reversal of suburbanization, re-urbanization • Fine-grained suburban extension
South Korea	• Government-sponsored new town program • Developmental state but involving private sector participation
Southeast Asia	• Deregulated and private-sector dominated new towns • Gated residential projects • Bundled or semi-bundled cities
China	• State entrepreneurialism and land centred development • Mass suburbanization accompanied by post-suburban elements • Polycentric metropolis with new town and development zones • A mix of private governance (gated communities) and local entrepreneurialism

be understated since socio-economic polarization across city-regions represents a pressing challenge for the reworking politics and government in all national settings.

We also signed-off our introduction with the thought that whether, in an increasingly integrated international economy, we ought not to take more seriously commonalities in patterns of urban development. This is more intriguing than it at first seems since, Beauregard's (2006) claim that the export of the idea of US-style suburbia has only begun in earnest after decades of its purely domestic import, poses important questions of an emergent mixing of all kinds of suburban and post-suburban elements – imported US low-density detached housing appearing alongside domestic traditions of high-rise mass suburban housing, together with post-suburban elements of 'vulgar' niche residential provision, gated residential communities, new town mega-complexes and rapid decentralization of office, retail and leisure facilities. This is certainly the feel that one gets when one visits the burgeoning urban edges of China where the geographical and temporal boundaries between what is suburban and what can be regarded as post-suburban become blurred (Wu and Phelps, 2008).

Finally, and following on from the above, all of this serves to highlight the very real methodological difficulties of disentangling what is unique and what is general about suburban and post-suburban development. Whilst it is true that US suburbia is probably at present one of the dominant formats of development being exported around the world, there is ample evidence of models of urban and real estate development travelling from other points of origin (see King, 1984 on the bungalow, and Bunnell and Das, 2010 on Singapore's reach within Asia). Moreover, such models are significantly transformed in the process incorporation by, to name but two, the specifics of the stage and speed of the urban transition reached, and the systems and cultures of urbanization and planning and land-use regulation in different settings. Further study of the contemporary travel and adaptation of such models could usefully inform our understanding of our post-suburban world.

References

Adams, J.T. (1931) *The Epic of America* (New York: Blue Ribbon Books).

Alden, J.D., Hirohara, M. et al. (1994) 'The impact of recent urbanisation on inner city development in Japan', in P. Shapira, I. Masser and D.W. Edgington (eds) *Planning for Cities and Regions in Japan* (Liverpool: Liverpool University Press), pp. 33–58.

Ali, S.H. and Keil, R. (2006) 'Global cities and the spread of infectious disease: The case of severe acute respiratory syndrome (SARS) in Toronto, Canada', *Urban Studies*, 43(3), 491–509.

Allen, J. and Cochrane, A. (2007) 'Beyond the territorial fix: Regional assemblages, politics and power', *Regional Studies*, 41, 1161–1176.

Allen, J., Massey, D. and Cochrane, A. (1998) *Re-thinking the Region* (London: Routledge).

Allon, F. (2005) 'Suburbs for sale: Buying and selling the great Australian dream', in K. Anderson, R. Dobson, F. Allon and B. Neilson (eds) *After Sprawl: Post-Suburban Sydney*, E-Proceedings of 'Post Suburban Sydney: City in Transformation' Conference, no page numbers [online] available from <http://future/wws.edu.au/_da...ile/0017/6911/Allon_ Final.pdf> [11 August 2008].

Althubaity, A. and Jonas, A.E.G. (1998) 'Suburban entrepreneurialism: Redevelopment regimes and coordinating metropolitan development in southern California', in T. Hall and P. Hubbard (eds) *The Entrepreneurial City: Geographies of Politics, Regime and Representation* (Chichester: John Wiley), pp. 149–172.

Amin, A. (2004) 'Regions unbound: Towards a new politics of place', *Geografiska Annaler*, 86B, 33–44.

Amin, A., Massey, D. and Thrift, N. (2003) *Decentering the Nation: A Radical Approach to Regional Inequality* (London: Catalyst).

Amin, A. and Thrift, N. (2007) 'Cultural-economy and cities', *Progress in Human Geography*, 31(2), 143–161.

Andrusz, G. (1984) *Housing and Urban Development in the USSR* (London: Macmillan).

Aravena, A. (2006) 'Prólogo', in A. Galetovich (ed.) *Santiago: ¿Dónde estamos y hacia dónde vamos?* (Santiago de Chile. Centro de Estudios Públicos), pp. xv–xxviii.

Aring, J. (1999) *Suburbia – Postsuburbia – Zwischenstadt. Die jüngere Wohnsiedlungsentwicklung im Umland der großen Städte Westdeutschlands und Folgerungen für die regionale Planung und Steuerung* (Hannover: ARL (Akademie für Raumforschung und Landesplanung Arbeitsmaterial 262).

AS&P (Albert Speer und Partner) (2009) *Frankfurt für Alle: Handlungsperspektiven für die internationale Bürgerstadt Frankfurt am Main* (http://www.frankfurt-fuer-alle.de/; accessed 17 March 2009).

Badyina, A. and Golubchikov, O. (2005) 'Gentrification in Central Moscow – a market process or a deliberate policy? Money, power and people in housing regeneration in Ostozhenka', *Geografiska Annaler B*, N 87(2), 113–129.

Bae, Y. and Sellers, J.M. (2007) 'Globalization, the developmental state and the politics of urban growth in Korea: A multilevel analysis', *International Journal of Urban and Regional Research*, 31(3), 547–560.

Bähr, J. and Mertins, G. (1995) *Die lateinamerikanische Großstadt. Verstädterungsprozesse und Stadtstrukturen* (Darmstadt: Wissenschaftliche Buchgesellschaft).

Ballerup Commune (n.d.) *Made in Ballerup* (Denmark: Ballerup Commune).

Banham, R., Barker, P., Hall, P. and Price, C. (1969) 'Non-plan: An experiment in freedom', *New Society*, 338, 20 March.

Barker, P. (2009) *The Freedoms of Suburbia* (London: Frances Lincoln).

Barrow, H. (2004) '"The American dream of growth": Henry Ford and the metropolitanization of Detroit, 1920–1940', in R. Lewis (ed.) *Manufacturing Suburbs: Building Work and Home on the Metropolitan Fringe* (Philadelphia: Temple University Press), pp. 200–220.

Barsky, A. and Vio, M. (2007) 'La problemática del ordenamiento territorial en cinturones verdes periurbanos sometidos a procesos de valorización inmobiliaria. El caso del Partido del Pilar, Región Metropolitana de Buenos Aires', IX Coloquio Internacional de Geocrítica: 'Los problemas del mundo actual. Soluciones y alternativas desde la geografía y las ciencias sociales' Porto Alegre, 28 May–1 June, Universidade Federal do Rio Grande do Soul.

Bater, J.H. (1980) *The Soviet City: Ideal and Reality* (London: Edward Arnold).

Bater, J.H., Amelin, V. and Degtyarev, V. (1998) 'Market reform and the central city: Moscow revisited', *Post-Soviet Geography*, N 39, 1–18.

Beauregard, R.A. (1993) *Voices of Decline: The Post-war Fate of U.S. Cities* (Cambridge, MA: Blackwell).

Beauregard, R.A. (2003) 'City of superlatives', *City & Community*, 2(3), 183–199.

Beauregard, R. (2006) *When America Became Suburban* (Minneapolis: University of Minnesota Press).

Beck, U. (1992) *Risk Society: Towards a New Modernity* (London: Sage).

Beck, U., Bonns, W. and Lau, C. (2003) 'The theory of reflexive modernization', *Theory, Culture and Society*, 20, 1–33.

Béland, D. (2007) 'Neo-liberalism and social policy', *Policy Studies*, 28(2), 91–107.

Benfield, F.K., Raimi, M.D. et al. (1999) *Once There were Greenfields: How Urban Sprawl is Undermining America's Environment, Economy, and Social Fabric* (New York: Natural Resources Defence Council).

Bennett, J., with Hetherington, D., Nathan, M. and Urwin, C. (2006) *Would You Live Here? Making the Growth Areas Communities of Choice* (London: Institute of Public Policy Research).

Bertolini, L. and Le Clerq, F. (2003) 'Urban development without more mobility by car? Lessons from Amsterdam, multimodal urban region', *Environment and Planning A*, 35(4), 575–589.

Bhabha, H. (1994) *The Location of Culture* (New York and London: Routledge).

Blakely, E.J. and Snyder, M.G. (1997) *Fortress America: Gated Communities in the United States* (Washington, D.C.: Brookings Institution and Lincoln Institute of Land Policy).

Bloch, R. (1994) *The Metropolis Inverted: The Rise of and Shift to the Periphery and the Remaking of the Contemporary City.* Unpublished dissertation. University of California, Los Angeles.

Bloom, N. (2004) *Merchant of Illusion: James Rouse, America's Salesman of the Businessman's Utopia* (Columbus: Ohio State University Press).

Bogart, W.T. (2006) *Don't Call it Sprawl: Metropolitan Structure in the Twenty First Century* (Cambridge: Cambridge University Press).

Bölling, L. (2004) Zwischenstadt lesen. Spurensuche zwischen 'Downtown Eschborn-Sossenheim' und 'Airportcity Rhein-Main', in L. Bölling and T. Sieverts (eds) *Mitten am Rand* (Wuppertal: Müller and Busmann), pp. 94–113.

Bontje, M. (2004) 'From suburbia to post-suburbia in the Netherlands: Potentials and threats for sustainable regional development', *Journal of Housing and the Built Environment*, 19(1), 25–47.

Bontje, M. (2005) 'Der Amsterdamer Südraum – eine dynamische Wachstumszone', in J. Burdack, G. Herfert and R. Rudolph (eds) *Europäische metropolitane Peripherien* (Leipzig: Leibniz-Institut für Länderkunde), pp. 193–205.

Bontje, M. and Burdack, J. (2005a) 'Edge cities European style: Examples from Paris and the Randstad', *Cities*, 22(4), 317–330.

Bontje, M. and Burdack, J. (2005b) *Economic Poles in the European Metropolitan Periphery and Sustainable Development* (Leipzig: Leibniz-Institut für Länderkunde, Forum IfL series, nr. 1).

Bontje, M. and Musterd, S. (2009) 'Creative industries, creative class and competitiveness: Expert opinions critically appraised', *Geoforum*, 40(5), 843–852.

Bördlein, R. (2001) 'Region Rhein-Main: Region ohne Grenzen', in K. Brake et al. (eds) *Suburbanisierung in Deutschland* (Opladen: Leske & Budrich), pp. 175–186.

Borsdorf, A. (2004) 'Commercial areas in the outskirts of European cities: Location and structures', in A. Borsdorf and P. Zembri (eds) *European Cities: Insights on Outskirts – Structures* (Paris: METL/PUCA), pp. 129–148.

Borsdorf, A. (2004) 'On the way to post-suburbia?: Changing structures in the outskirts of European cities', in A. Borsdorf and P. Zembri (eds) *European Cities Structures: Insight on Outskirts* (Blanchard Printing), pp. 7–30.

Borsdorf, A., Bähr, J. and Janoschka, M. (2002) 'Die Dynamik stadtstrukturellen Wandels in Lateinamerika im Modell der lateinamerikanischen Stadt', *Geographica Helvetica*, 57(4), 300–310.

Borsdorf, A. and Hidalgo, R. (2005) 'Los Mega-Diseños residenciales vallados en las periferias de las Metrópolis Latinoamericanas y el advenimiento de un nuevo concepto de ciudad. Alcances en base al caso de Santiago de Chile', in *Scripta Nova, Revista Electrónica de Geografía y ciencias socials*, 9, 194(3) (Barcelona: Universidad Barcelona).

Borsdorf, A. and Hidalgo, R. (2008) 'Der Urban Sprawl in Europa und Lateinamerika: Ein Vergleich der Entwicklungen europäischer und lateinamerikanischer Agglomerationen', *Mitteilungen der Österreichischen Geographischen Gesellschaft*, 150(S), 229–250.

Borsdorf, A., Hidalgo, R. and Sanchez, R. (2007) 'A new model of urban development in Latin America; the gated communities and fenced cities in the Metropolitan Areas of Santiago de Chile and Valparaíso', *Cities*, 24(5), 365–378.

Boudreau, J.-A., Hamel, P., Jouve, B. and Keil, R. (2007) 'New state spaces in Canada: Metropolitanisation in Montreal and Toronto compared', *Urban Geography*, 28(1), 30–53.

Boudreau, J.-A., Keil, R. and Young, D. (2009) *Changing Toronto: Governing Urban Neoliberalism* (Toronto: University of Toronto Press).

Bourdieu, P. (2005) *The Social Structures of the Economy* (C. Turner, trans.) (Cambridge UK: Polity Press).

Brenner, N. (1998) 'Between fixity and motion: Accumulation, territorial organization and the historical geography of spatial scales', *Environment & Planning D, Society & Space*, 16, 459–481.

Brenner, N. (2002) 'Decoding the newest "metropolitan regionalism" in the USA: A critical overview', *Cities*, 19, 3–21.

Brenner, N. and Theodore, N. (2002) 'Cities and the geographies of "actually existing" neoliberalism', *Antipode*, 34, 349–379.

Browder, J., Bohlen, J. and Scarpaci, J. (1995) 'Patterns of development on the metropolitan fringes: Urban fringe expansion in Bangkok, Jakarta, and Santiago', *Journal of the American Planning Association*, 61(3), 310–327.

Bruegmann, R. (2005) *Sprawl: A Compact History* (Chicago: University of Chicago Press).

Bunce, M. (1985) 'Agricultural land as a real estate commodity: Implications for farmland preservation in the North American urban fringe', *Landscape Planning*, 12(2), 177–192.

Bunnell, T. and Das, D. (2010) 'Urban pulse – A geography of serial seduction: Urban policy transfer from Kuala Lumpur to Hyderabad', *Urban Geography*, 31(3), 277–284.

Burchell, R.W. (2005) *Sprawl Costs: Economic Impacts of Unchecked Development* (Washington, D.C.: Island Press).

Burdack, J. (2004) 'Die Ville de Lumières und ihre Schatten. Wirtschafts- und sozialräumliche Differenzierungen in der Pariser Metropolregion', *Geographische Rundschau*, 2004(4), 32–39.

Burdack. J., Dövényi, Z. and Kovács, Z. (2004) 'Am Rand von Budapest – Die metropolitane Peripherie zwischen nachholender Entwicklung und eigenem Weg', *Petermanns Geographische Mitteilungen*, 148(3), 30–39.

Burdack, J., Herfert, G. and Rudolph, R. (eds) (2005) *Europäische Metropolitane Peripherien*. Leipzig: Leibniz-Institut für Länderkunde (Series 'Beiträge zur regionalen Geographie' nr. 61).

Burns, N. (1994) *The Formation of American Local Governments: Private Values in Public Institutions* (New York: Oxford University Press).

Butterfield, E. (2008a) 'Builder 100 over the years', *Builder Online*. Retrieved from http://www.builderonline.com/housing-data/builder-100-over-the-years.aspx

Butterfield, E. (2008b) 'Builder 100: Painful year', *Builder Online* [online] available from <http://www.builderonline.com/business/painful-year.aspx> [March 30, 2009].

Byeon, C.H. (2005) 'The characteristics of Pankyo New Town and new approach for the housing development and supply', *Land Studies*, 16(2), 55–71 (in Korean).

Caldeira, T. (2000) *City of Walls: Crime, Segregation and Citizenship in Sao Paulo* (Berkeley: University of California Press).

Calthorpe, P. and Fulton, W.B. (2001) *The Regional City: Planning for the End of Sprawl* (London: Island Press).

Campi, M., Bucher, F. and Cardini, M. (2001) *Annähernd perfekte Peripherie. Glattalstadt/Greater Zurich Area* (Basel: Birkhäuser).

Carasso, A., Bell, E., Olsen, E.O. and Steuerle, C.E. (2005) *Improving Homeownership Among Poor and Moderate-Income Households* (Washington, D.C.: The Urban Institute).

Carrefour SA (n.d.) [online] available from <http://www.carrefour.com> [20 November 2008].

Carrel, F. (1999) 'Mickey, une ombre sur la ville', *L'Humanité*, September 25, 1999.

Cauvin, H.A. (2009a, March 26) 'Woman pleads guilty in mortgage fraud scheme', *The Washington Post*, p. B3.

Cauvin, H.A. (2009b, April 29) 'Woman pleads guilty to money laundering', *The Washington Post* [online] available from <http://www.washingtonpost.com/wp-

dyn/content/article/2009/04/28/AR2009042803320.html?hpid=sec-metro> [April 29, 2009].

Central Bureau of Statistics (CBS, 1991) *Population of Indonesia: Result of the 1990 Population Census* (Jakarta: CBS).

Central Bureau of Statistics (CBS, 2001) *Population of Indonesia: Result of the 2000 Population Census* (Jakarta: CBS).

Central Bureau of Statistics (CBS, 2006) *Economic Indicators: Monthly Statistical Bulletin.* February (Jakarta: CBS).

Cervero, R. (1989) *America's Suburban Centers. The Land Use-Transportation Link* (Boston: Unwin Hyman).

Cervero, R. (1998) *The Transit Metropolis: A Global Inquiry* (Washington, D.C.: Island Press).

Chamberlin, E. (1874) *Chicago and Its Suburbs* (Chicago: T.A. Hungerford and Co.).

Champion, T. (2001) 'Urbanization, suburbanization, counterurbanization and reurbanization', in R. Paddison (ed.) *Handbook of Urban Studies* (London: Sage), pp. 143–161.

Charlesworth, J. and Cochrane, A. (1994) 'Tales of the suburbs: The local politics of growth in the South-East of England', *Urban Studies*, 31(10), 1723–1738.

Charlesworth, J. and Cochrane, A. (1997) 'Anglicising the American dream: Tragedy farce and the "postmodern" city', in S. Westwood and J. Williams (eds) *Imagining Cities. Scripts, Signs, Memory* (London: Routledge).

Chatterjee, P. (1998) 'A new economic reality on Asian city street', *Urban Age*, 5(4), 5–9.

Christie, L. (2009) 'Mortgage deductions: Wealthy on the losing end', *CNNMoney. com.* Retrieved from http://money.cnn.com/2009/02/27/real_estate/mortgage_ interest_deduction_slashed

Chu, C.W. (2000) 'The evaluation of the five-year two million housing unit construction plan (1988–92)', in A. Yeh and M.K. Ng (eds) *Planning for a Better Urban Living Environment in Asia* (Burlington: Ashgate), pp. 172–187.

CIPPEC (Centro de Implementación de Políticas Públicas para la Equidad y el Crecimiento) (2005) 'Diagnóstico para la Planificación. Caso Municipio de Pilar', Octubre 2005.

Citizens' Coalition for Economic Justice (2006) *Annual Announcement Report for Bursting the Bubble in Sales Price of an Apartment* (in Korean).

Clapson, M. (1998) *Invincible Green Suburbs: Brave New Towns. Social Change and Urban Dispersal in Post-War England* (Manchester: Manchester University Press).

Clapson, M. (2004) *A Social History of Milton Keynes: Middle England/Edge City* (London: Batsford).

Cochrane, A. (2006) 'Looking for the South-East', in I. Hardill, P. Benneworth, M. Baker and L. Budd (eds) *The Rise of the English Regions* (London: Regional Studies Association/Routledge), pp. 227–244.

Collier International (2005) *Jakarta Property Market Overview, September* (Jakarta: Collier International).

Commission on Sustainable Development in the South East (2005) *Final Report* (London: Institute of Public Policy Research).

Cox, K.R. and Jonas, A.E.G. (1993) 'Urban development, collective consumption and the politics of metropolitan fragmentation', *Political Geography*, 12, 8–37.

Cox, K.R. and Mair, A.J. (1988) 'Locality and community in the politics of local economic development', *Annals of the Association of American Geographers*, 78, 307–325.

Coy, M. and Pöhler, M. (2002) 'Gated communities in Latin American megacities: Case studies in Brazil and Argentina', *Environment and Planning B – Planning and Design*, 29(3), 355–370.

Croydon Business (n.d.) 'Croydon 2020' [online] available from <http://www.croydonbusiness.com/croydon2020.html> [23 July 2008].

Croydon Council (n.d.) 'Considering the future of central Croydon: Summary of the issues & options' [online] available from <www.croydon.gov.uk> [30 July 2008].

Crutsinger, M. (2009) 'Home construction drops far more than expected', *The Washington Post*. Retrieved from http://www.washingtonpost.com/wp-dyn/content/article/2009/02/18/AR2009021800896_pf.html

Cushman, T. (2009) 'Battening down the hatches', *Builder Online*. Retrieved from http://www.builderonline.com/business/battening-down-the-hatches.aspx

Daein Sun (2005) 'Jypgap geopoom Ttubadchineoun Geonsul 5 gag goojeo Haeboo' [The analysis on the 5 angles structure that supports the housing price bubble] http://blog.daum.net/cityhiro/1775517, accessed on 11 May 2009.

Daniels, T. (1999) *When City and Country Collide* (Washington, D.C.: Island Press).

Danielson, M.N. (1976) *The Politics of Exclusion* (New York: Columbia University Press).

Darmstädter Echo (2009) 'Wohnen unter Tragflächen', *Darmstädter Echo*, April 28, 14.

Davis, J.S., Nelson, A. et al. (1994) 'The new "burbs": The exurbs and their implications for planning policy', *Journal of the American Planning Association*, 60(1), 45–59.

Davis, M. (1990) *City of Quartz* (London: Verso).

Davison, G. (1995) 'Australia: The first suburban nation?', *Journal of Urban History*, 22(1), 40–74.

De Mattos, C.A. (1999) 'Santiago de Chile, globalización y expansión metropolitana: lo que existía sigue existiendo', *EURE*, 25(76), 29–56.

De Mattos, C.A. (2004) 'De la planificación a la governance: implicaciones. para la gestión territorial y urbana', *Revista Paranaense de desenvolvimento*, 107.

De Mattos, C.A. (2005) 'Santiago de Chile: modernización capitalista y transformación metropolitana', in M. Carmona (ed.) *Globalización y grandes proyectos urbanos. La respuesta de 25 ciudades* (Buenos Aires: Ediciones Infinito).

De Mattos, C.A. (2007) *Globalización, negocios inmobiliarios y transformación urbana. Nueva Sociedad 212*. Noviembre/Diciembre 2007. www.nuso.org/upload/articulos/3481_1.pdf (accessed 5 August 2008).

De Mattos, C.A. and Hidalgo, R. (eds) (2007) *Santiago de Chile: Movilidad Espacial y Reconfiguración Metropolitana*. Serie GEOlibros 8, Insitituto des Estudios Urbanos y Territoriales, Pontificia Universidad Católica de Chile, Santiago de Chile.

Dear, M. (2000) *The Postmodern Urban Condition* (Malden, MA: Blackwell).

Dear, M. (ed.) (2002) *From Chicago to L.A. Making Sense of Urban Theory* (Thousand Oaks, CA: Sage).

Dear, M. (2004) 'The Los Angeles school of urbanism: An intellectual history', *Urban Geography*, 24, 493–509.

Dear, M. and Dahmann, N. (2008) 'Urban politics and the Los Angeles School of Urbanism', *Urban Affairs Review*, 44, 266–279.

Dear, M. and Flusty (1998) 'Postmodern urbanism', *Annals of the Association of American Geographers*, 88(1), 50–72.

Deng, F.F. and Huang, Y. (2004) 'Uneven land reform and urban sprawl in China: The case of Beijing', *Progress in Planning*, 61, 211–236.

Dharmapatni, I. and Firman, T. (1995) 'Problems and challenges of mega-urban regions in Indonesia', in T.G. McGee and I. Robinson (eds) *The Mega-Urban Regions of Southeast Asia* (Vancouver: The University of British Columbia Press), pp. 296–314.

Dick, H.W. and Rimmer, P. (1998) 'Beyond the third world city: The new urban geography of Southeast Asia', *Urban Studies*, 35, 2303–2321.

Dick, H. and Rimmer, P. (2009) *The City in Southeast Asia: Patterns, Processes and Policy* (Singapore: National University of Singapore Press).

Dijkgraaf, C. (2000) 'The urban building sector in Indonesia before and after the crisis of 1997', Paper presented to the Workshop 'The Indonesian Town Revisited', University of Leiden, 6–8 January.

Dingell, J. (2008) 'How the changes in the mortgage interest rate deduction might work?' Retrieved April 4, 2009, from http://www.house.gov/dingell/summary_detail.shtml#

Dodson, J. (2006) 'The "roll" of the state: Government, neoliberalism and housing assistance in four advanced economies', *Housing, Theory and Society*, 23(4), 224–243.

Dorling, D. and Thomas, B. (2004) *People and Places: A 2001 Census Atlas of the UK* (Bristol: The Policy Press).

Douglass, M. (2000) 'Mega-urban regions and world city formation: Globalisation, the economic crisis and urban policy issues in Pacific Asia', *Urban Studies*, 37(12), 2315–2335.

Douglass, M. and Jones, G. (2008) 'The morphology of mega-urban regions expansion', in M. Douglass and G. Jones (eds) *Mega-Urban Regions in Pacific Asia: Urban Dynamics in a Global Area* (Singapore: National University of Singapore Press), pp. 19–37.

Dövényi, Z. and Kovács, Z. (2004) 'The post-socialist metropolitan periphery between "catching up" and individual development path', *European Spatial Research and Policy*, 13(2), 23–41.

Downs, A. (1973) *Opening Up the Suburbs* (New Haven: Yale University Press).

Downs, A. (1981) *Neighborhoods and Urban Development* (Washington, D.C.: The Brookings Institution).

Dreier, P. (1996) 'Billions for the rich, pennies for the poor', *Where We Stand*, 85, n/a. Retrieved from http://www.nhi.org/online/issues/85/wherewestand.html

Dreier, P., Mollenkopf, J. and Swanstrom, T. (eds) (2001) *Place Matters: Metropolitics for the Twenty-First Century* (Lawrence, KS: University Press of Kansas).

Duany, A., Plater-Zuberk, E. and Speck, J. (2000) *Suburban Nation. The Rise of Sprawl and the Decline of The American Dream* (New York: North Point Press).

Dubois-Taine, G. (2004) 'Outskirts of European cities. Understand better, in govern better', in G. Dubois-Taine (ed.) *From Helsinki to Nicosia. Eleven Case Studies and Synthesis* (Paris: METL/PUCA (COST Action C10 'Outskirts of European Cities'), pp. 7–55.

Dubois-Taine, G. and Challas, Y. (eds) (1997) *La ville émergente* (La Tour d'Aigues: Editions de l'Aube).

Ducci, M.E. (2000) 'Santiago: territorios, anhelos y temores. Efectos sociales y espaciales de la expansión urbana', in *EURE*, 26(79), 5–24.

Ducci, M.E. (2004) 'Las batallas urbanas de principios del tercer milenio', *Urbared*. *Recuperado* el 2º Febrero 2007, de http://www.urbared.ungs.edu.ar/recursos_bibliografia_trabajos_consul.htm (accessed 7 May 2009).

Ducci, M.E. and Gonzáles, M. (2006) 'Anatomía de la expansión de Santiago', in A. Galetovic (ed.) *Santiago: Dónde estamos y hacia dónde vamos* (Santiago de Chile: Centro de Estudios Públicos), pp. 123–146.

Dyer, J. (2008) 'Manufacturing prosperity: Region's education, land resources provide support for jobs, salaries', *The Boston Globe*, 21st September (Accessed June 2010 at: http://www.boston.com/jobs/news/articles/2008/09/21/manufacturing_prosperity/)

Eaves, E. (2007) 'The American dream – Don't buy that house', *Forbes*. Retrieved from http://www.forbes.com/2007/06/26/home-ownership-negatives-biz-dream 0607_cx_ee_0626house_print.html

Ebner, M. (1982) '"In the Suburbes of Toun": Chicago's North Shore to 1871', *Chicago History*, 11(2), 66–77.

Echenique, M. (1995) 'Frenar la expansión de Santiago arriesgaría el desarrollo nacional', in *El Mercurio*. September 10th, Santiago de Chile.

El Nasser, H. (2009) 'Open house, anyone? 1 in 9 homes site empty', *USA Today*. Retrieved from http://www.usatoday.com/money/economy/housing/2009-04-09-vacanthomes_N.htm

Erlenbach, D. (2009) 'Furcht for sozialen Verwerfungen', *Darmstädter Echo*, April 28, 14.

Escolano, S. and Ortiz, J. (2007) 'Patrones espaciales de movilidad de la población: algunos efectos en la sociogeografia del gran Santiago', in C. de Mattos and R. Hidalgo (eds) *Santiago de Chile: Movilidad Espacial y Reconfiguración Metropolitana*. Serie GEOlibros 8, Instituto des Estudios Urbanos y Territoriales, Pontificia Universidad Católica de Chile, Santiago de Chile, pp. 53–66.

Espoo, City of (2008) *Espoo Pocket Statistics 2008* (Espoo, Finland: City of Espoo).

Evenson, N. (1979) *Paris: A Century of Change, 1878–1978* (New Haven: Yale University Press).

Feldman, T. and Jonas, A.E.G. (2000) 'Sage scrub revolution? Property rights, political fragmentation and conservation planning in Southern California under the federal Endangered Species Act', *Annals of the Association of American Geographers*, 90, 256–292.

Feng, J., Zhou, Y. and Wu, F. (2008) 'New trends of suburbanization in Beijing since 1990: From government-led to market-oriented', *Regional Studies*, 42(1), 83–99.

Filion, P. (2000) 'Balancing concentration and dispersion? Public policy and urban structure in Toronto', *Environment and Planning C: Government and Policy*, 18, 163–189.

Firman, T. (1998) 'The restructuring of Jakarta metropolitan area: A "global city" in Asia', *Cities*, 15(4), 229–243.

Firman, T. (1999) 'From "global city" to "city of crisis": Jakarta metropolitan region under economic turmoil', *Habitat International*, 23(4), 447–446.

Firman, T. (2000) 'Rural to urban land conversion in Indonesia during boom and bust periods', *Land Use Policy*, 17(1), 13–20.

Firman, T. (2003) 'Potential impacts of Indonesia's fiscal decentralization reform on urban and regional development: Towards a pattern of spatial disparity', *Space and Polity*, 7(3), 247–271.

Firman, T. (2004) 'New town development in Jakarta metropolitan region: A perspective of spatial segregation', *Habitat International*, 28, 349–368.

Firman, T. (2009) 'The continuity and change in mega-urbanization in Indonesia: A survey of Jakarta-Bandung Region (JBR) development', *Habitat International*, 33, 327–339.

Firman, T., Kombaitan, B. and Pradono, P. (2007) 'The dynamics of Indonesia's urbanization, 1980–2006', *Urban Policy and Research*, 25(4), 433–454.

Fishman, R. (1987) *Bourgeois Utopias: The Rise and Fall of Suburbia* (New York: Basic Books).

Fishman, R. (1991) 'The garden city tradition in the post-suburban age', *Built Environment*, 17, 232–241.

Fishman, R. (2002) 'Bourgeois utopias: Vision of suburbia', in S. Fainstein and S. Campbell (eds) *Readings in Urban Theory*, pp. 21–31, 2nd edition (Malden: Blackwell Publishing).

Flood, D.J. and Kablack, M.A. (2008) 'Affordable housing recap and forecast', *Massbuilder*, First Quarter, 22.

Foley, J. (2004) *The Problems of Success. Reconciling Economic Growth and Quality of Life in the South East*. Commission on Sustainable Development in the South East, Working Paper Two (London: Institute for Public Policy Research).

French, R.A. (1995) *Plans, Pragmatism and People: The Legacy of Soviet Planning for Today's City* (London: UCL Press).

French, R.A. and Hamilton, F.E.I. (eds) (1979) *The Socialist City: Spatial Structure and Urban Policy* (London: John Wiley).

Frisken, F. and Norris, D. (2001) 'Regionalism reconsidered', *Journal of Urban Affairs*, 23(5), 467–478.

Front, L. and Dingle, T. (1995) 'Sustaining suburbia: An historical perspective on Australia's urban growth', in P. Troy (ed.) *Australian Cities: Issues, Strategies and Policies for Urban Australia in the 1990s* (Cambridge: Cambridge University Press), pp. 20–38.

Fulton, W. (1997) *The Reluctant Metropolis: The Politics of Urban Growth in Los Angeles* (London: The Johns Hopkins University Press).

Fulton, W.B., Pendall, R. et al. (2001) *Sprawl Accelerates: Exploring and Explaining Urban Density Changes in the US, 1982–1997* (Washington, D.C.: Brookings Institution).

Galbraith, J.K. (1958) *The Affluent Society* (Cambridge, MA: The Riverside Press).

Galetovic, A. (ed.) (2006) *Santiago: Dónde estamos y hacia dónde vamos* (Santiago de Chile: Centro de Estudios Públicos).

Galetovic, A. and Jordan, P. (2006) 'Santiago: Dónde estamos. Hacia dónde vamos', in A. Galetovic (ed.) *Santiago: Dónde estamos y hacia dónde vamos*. Centro de Estudios Públicos, Santiago de Chile, pp. 25–72.

Garcia-Zamor, J.-C. (2001) 'Conundrums of urban planning in a global context: The case of the Frankfurt airport', *Public Organization Review*, December, pp. 415–435.

Gardiner, P. and Gardiner, M.O. (2006) 'Ecology of population dynamics in Indonesian metropolitan areas', Unpublished paper.

Gardner, A. (2006, September 24) 'Willisville still waiting for indoor plumbing', *The Washington Post*, p. T01.

Garreau, J. (1991) *Edge City: Life on the New Frontier* (New York: Doubleday).

Gauvin, M. (1992) 'Plateau de Saclay, recherche et haute technologie', *Regards sur l'Ile-de-France*, 18, 2–5.

Geis, A. (2002) 'Neue Konflikte durch kooperative Politikformen: Das Mediations-verfahren und das Regionale Dialogforum zur zukünftigen Entwicklung des Frankfurter Flughafens', in Stadtforschung aktuell, 87, 267–284.

Gentile, M. and Sjoberg, O. (2006) 'Intra-urban landscape of priority: The Soviet legacy', *Europe-Asia Studies*, N 58(5), 701–729.

Gillham, O. (2002) *The Limitless City: A Primer on the Urban Sprawl Debate* (Island Press).

Ginsberg, N. (1991) 'Extended metropolitan regions in Asia: A new spatial para-digm', in N. Ginsberg, B. Koppel and T.G. McGee (eds) *The Extended Metropolis: Settlement Transition in Asia* (Honolulu: University of Hawaii Press), pp. 27–46.

Glaeser, E., Kahn, M. and Chu, C. (2001) 'Job sprawl: Employment location in U.S. metropolitan areas', *Brookings Institution Survey Series* (May), 1–8.

Glaeser, E.L. and Shapiro, J.M. (2002) *The Benefits of the Home Mortgage Interest Deduction* (Cambridge, MA: National Bureau of Economic Research).

Golubchikov, O. (2004) 'Urban planning in Russia: towards the market', *European Planning Studies*, N 12(2), 229–247.

Goonewardena, K. and Kipfer, S. (2004) 'Creole city: Culture, capital and class in Toronto', in R. Paloscia (ed.) *INURA: The Contested Metropolis-Six Cities at the Beginning of the 21st Century* (Basel: Birkhäuser).

Gordon, I. (2003) 'Three into one: Joining up the Greater South East', *Town and Country Planning*, 72, 11.

Gordon, I. (2004) 'A disjointed dynamo. The Greater South East and inter-regional relationships', *New Economy*, 11(1), 40–44.

Gordon, I., Travers, T. and Whitehead, C. (2003) *London's Place in the UK Economy 2003* (London: London School of Economics for the Corporation of London).

Gordon, I., Travers, T. and Whitehead, C. (2004) *London's Place in the UK Economy 2004* (London: London School of Economics for the Corporation of London).

GOSE (2008) *Secretary of State's Proposed Change to South East Plan.* http://gose.lime-house.co.uk/portal/rss/pcc/consult Consultation Portal (accessed 18th July 2008).

Gottdiener, M. and Kephart, G. (1995) 'The multinucleated region: A com-parative analysis', in R. Kling, S. Olin and M. Poster (eds) *Postsuburban Cali-fornia: The Transformation of Orange County Since World War Two* (Berkeley, CA: University of California Press), pp. 31–54.

Goytia, C. (2005) 'Private residential investment growth: Implications on municipal revenues and socio-economic indicators. The case of the muni-cipality of Pilar', *Urban Research Symposium 2005, World Bank-IPEA*, April 4th, 2005.

Graham, S. and Marvin, S. (2001) *Splintering Urbanism: Networked Infrastructures, Technological Mobilities and the Urban Condition* (New York: Routledge).

Grange, A.L and Jung, H.N. (2004) 'The commodification of land and housing: The cause of South Korea', *Housing Studies*, 19(4), 557–580.

Green, M. and Soler, F. (2005) 'Santiago: de un proceso acelerado de crecimiento a uno de transformaciones', in C. De Mattos, M.E. Ducci, A. Rodríguez and G. Yáñez (eds) *Santiago en la globalización, ¿una nueva ciudad?* Colleción EURE Libros/Ediciones SUR, Santiago de Chile, 47–84.

Gruen, V. and Smith, L. (1960) *Shopping Towns USA: The Planning of Shopping Centers* (New York: Reinhold).

Gyeonggi Province, City of Sungnam, Korea Land Development Corporation and Korea National Housing Corporation (2003) *A Study on Master Plan and Development Demand Analysis of Sungnam Pangyo Development* (Gyeonggi-Do: Gyeonggi Province Government) (in Korean).

Gyourko, J.E. and Sinai, T. (2003) 'The spatial distribution of housing-related ordinary income tax benefits', *Real Estate Economics*, 31(4), 527–575.

Hack, G. (2000) 'Infrastructure and regional form', in R. Simmonds and G. Hack (eds) *Global City Regions: Their Emerging Forms* (London and New York: Spon Press), pp. 183–192.

Hall, P. and Pain, K. (eds) (2006) *The Polycentric Metropolis: Learning from Mega City-Regions in Europe* (London: Earthscan Publications).

Hall, P. with Gracey, H., Drewett, R. and Thomas, R. (1973) *The Containment of Urban England* (London: George Allen & Unwin).

Hamilton, D. (2002) 'Regimes and regional governance: The case of Chicago', *Journal of Urban Affairs*, 24, 403–424.

Hamilton, F.E.I., Pichler-Milanovic, N. and Andrews, K.D. (eds) (2005) *Transformation of Cities in Central and Eastern Europe: Towards Globalization* (Tokyo, New York, Paris: United Nations University Press).

Hanayama, Y. (1986) *Land Markets and Land Policy in a Metropolitan Area: A Case Study of Tokyo* (Boston: Oelgeschlager, Gunn and Hain).

Hanlon, B., Vicino, T. and Short, J.R. (2006) 'The new metropolitan reality in the US: Rethinking the traditional model', *Urban Studies*, 43, 2129–2143.

Harada, K. (1993) 'Railroads', in H. Yamamoto (ed.) *Technological Innovation and the Development of Transportation in Japan* (Tokyo: United Nations University Press), pp. 15–21, 49–60.

Harada, Y. (2002) 'How subsidies killed local autonomy', *Japan Echo* (December), 13–17.

Harney, K. (2007, August 25) 'Tax deduction under fire for "McMansions"', *The Washington Post*, p. F1.

Harris, R. (1996) *Unplanned Suburbia: Toronto's American Tragedy, 1900–1950* (Baltimore: Johns Hopkins University Press).

Harris, R. (2004) *Creeping Conformity: How Canada Became Suburban, 1900–1960* (Toronto: University of Toronto Press).

Harris, R. and Lewis, R. (1998) 'Constructing a fault(y) zone: Misrepresentations of American cities and suburbs, 1900–1950', *Annals of the Association of American Geographers*, 88, 622–639.

Harvey, D. (1985) *The Urbanisation of Capital* (Oxford: Blackwell).

Harvey, D. (1989a) *The Urban Experience* (Baltimore: Johns Hopkins University Press).

Harvey, D. (1989b) 'From managerialism to entrepreneurialism: The transformation of urban governance in late capitalism', *Geografiska Annaler B*, 71, 3–17.

Harvey, D. (2005) *A Brief History of Neoliberalism* (Oxford: Oxford University Press).

Hata, T. (2003) 'Improvement of railway system in Jakarta Metropolitan Area', *Japan Railway & Transportation*, 35, 36–44.

Haughton, G. and Hunter, C. (1994) *Sustainable Cities* (London: Jessica Kingsley Publishers).

Hawley, A.H. (1971) *Urban Society. An Ecological Approach* (New York: Ronald Press).

Hayami, Y. (1988) *Japanese Agriculture Under Siege* (New York: St. Martin's Press).

Hayden, D. (2004) *A Field Guide to Sprawl* (New York: W.W. Norton).

Hebbert, M. (1994) 'Sen-biki amidst desakota: Urban sprawl and urban planning in Japan', in P. Shapira, I. Masser and D.W. Edgington (eds) *Planning for Cities and Regions in Japan* (Liverpool: Liverpool University Press), pp. 70–91.

Hebbert, M. and Nakai, N. (1988) 'Deregulation of Japanese planning', *Town Planning Review*, 59(4), 383–395.

Herrington, J. (1984) *The Outer City* (London: Harper & Row).

Hidalgo, R. (2005) 'Post-suburbia ou post-urbia? Les mégaprojets résidentiels dans la périphérie de Santiago du Chili', *Revue Géographique de l'Est*, 45(3–4), 209–217.

Hidalgo, R., Borsdorf, A. and Sánchez, R. (2007) 'La expansion residencial amurallada en la reconfiguración metropolitana de Santiago de Chile', in C. de Mattos and R. Hidalgo (eds) *Santiago de Chile: Movilidad Espacial y Reconfiguración Metropolitana* (Santiago de Chile Serie GEOlibros 8: Insitituto des Estudios Urbanos y Territoriales, Pontificia Universidad Católica de Chile), pp. 117–136.

Hidayat, J.T. (2007) 'Urban sprawl phenomenon and sustainability of Jakarta fringe areas' (in Indonesian), Paper presented to Seminar 'Towards Sustainable Jakarta Metropolitan Area', Bogor, West Java, 6th September.

H.M. Treasury, Department for Business Enterprise and Regulatory Reform, Department for Communities and Local Government (2007) *Review of Subnational Economic Development and Regeneration* (London: H.M. Treasury).

H.M. Treasury, Department for Business Enterprise and Regulatory Reform, South East of England Development Agency (2008) *South East England Economy. A Joint Response to Changing Economic Circumstances* (Guildford: South East England Development Agency).

Hogan, T. and Houston, C. (2001) 'Corporate cities – Urban gateways or gated communities against the city? The case of Lippo, Jakarta', *Research Bulletin*, 47. Globalization and World Cities Study Group and Network.

Horan, C. and Jonas, A.E.G. (1998) 'Governing Massachusetts: Uneven development and politics in metropolitan Boston', *Economic Geography* (Special issue for the Annual Meeting of the Association of American Geographers), 74(S), 83–95.

Hornstein, J.M. (2005) *A Nation of Realtors: A Cultural History of the Twentieth-Century American Middle Class* (Durham, N.C.: Duke University Press).

Howard, E. (1965) *Garden Cities of To-morrow* (Cambridge, MA: MIT Press).

Huhdanmaki, A. and Dubois-Taine, G. (2004) 'Extension of Helsinki region – Inner city, edge city, outskirts', in G. Dubois-Taine (ed.) *From Helsinki to Nicosia. Eleven Case Studies and Synthesis* (Paris: METL/PUCA) (COST Action C10 'Outskirts of European Cities'), pp. 97–122.

Hulchanski, J.D. (2004) 'How did we get here? The evolution of Canada's "exclusionary" housing system', in J. D. Hulchanski and M. Shapcott (eds) *Finding Room: Options for a Canadian Rental Strategy* (Toronto: CUCS Press, Centre for Urban and Community Studies, University of Toronto).

Hull, A. and Neuman, M. (eds) (2010) *The Futures of the City Region* (London: Routledge).

INDEC – *Instituto Nacional de Estadísticas y Censos-*, Argentina, www.indec.gov.ar.

Inglis, R., and Thompson, J. (2009) 'Surprise! The rise and fall of the Western exurb', *High Country News*, *41.7*. Retrieved from http://www.hcn.org/issues/41.7/surprise/article_view?src=feat&b_start:int=0

Inkinen, T. and Vaattovaara, M. (2007) *Technology and Knowledge-based Development. Helsinki Metropolitan Area as a Creative Knowledge Region*. ACRE Report 2.5 (Amsterdam: AMIDSt, University of Amsterdam).

INSEE (Institut National de la Statistique et des Etudes Economiques) (2001) *Communes...Profils. Bases de données* (Paris: INSEE (CD-Rom)).

Irazábal, C. (2006) 'Localizing urban design traditions: Gated and edge cities in Curitiba', *Journal of Urban Design*, 11(1), 73–96.

Izsák, E. and Probáld, F. (2003) 'Le développement de l'agglomeration de Budapest: l'exemple de Budaörs', *Revue géographique de l'Est*, 12(1/2), 61–68.

Jackson, K.T. (1985) *Crabgrass Frontier: The Suburbanization of the United States* (New York: Oxford University Press).

Jacobs, J. (1961) *The Death and Life of Great American Cities* (New York: Random House) (Page references to Pelican edition (Harmondsworth: Penguin), 1964).

Janssen-Jansen, L. (2006) 'De tragedie van de kantoren', *Rooilijn*, 39(8), 442–457.

Japan Ministry of Economy, T.a.I. (2008). 'Outline of "Daiten-Ricchi Ho": Law concerning the measures by large-scale retail stores for preservation of living environment', D.I. Division. Tokyo, Ministry of Economy, Trade and Industry, pp. 1–5.

Japan Ministry of Foreign Affairs (2008) *Regulatory Reform: Japan Fact Sheet* (Tokyo: Ministry of Foreign Affairs).

Japan Ministry of Internal Affairs and Communications (2005) *Statistical Handbook of Japan Chapter 2 Population*. Retrieved November 13, 2005, from http://www.stat.go.jp/english/data/handbook/c02cont.htm.

John, P., Musson, S. and Tickell, A. (2002) 'England's problem region: Regionalism in the South East', *Regional Studies*, 36, 733–741.

Johnson, J.H. (ed.) (1974) *Suburban Growth: Geographical Processes at the Edge of the Western City* (London: John Wiley and Sons).

Jonas, A.E.G. (1992) 'Corporate takeover and the politics of community: The case of Norton Company in Worcester', *Economic Geography*, 68, 348–372.

Jonas, A.E.G. (1996) 'In search of order: Traditional business reformism and the crisis of neoliberalism in Massachusetts', *Transactions of the Institute of British Geographers*, 21, 617–634.

Jonas, A.E.G. (1997) 'Regulating suburban politics: "Suburban-defense transition", institutional capacities, and territorial reorganization in southern California', in M. Lauria (ed.) *Reconstructing Urban Regime Theory: Regulating Urban Politics in a Global Economy* (Thousand Oaks, CA: Sage Publications), pp. 206–229.

Jonas, A.E.G. (1999) 'Making edge city: Post-suburban development and life on the frontier in southern California', in R. Harris and P. Larkham (eds) *Changing Suburbs: Foundation, Form and Function* (London: E & FN Spon), pp. 202–221.

Jonas, A.E.G. (2002) 'Local territories of American government: From ideals to politics of place and scale', in J. Agnew and J. Smith (eds) *American Space/American Place* (Edinburgh: Edinburgh University Press), pp. 108–149.

Jonas, A.E.G. and Pincetl, S. (2006) 'Rescaling regions in the state: The new regionalism in California', *Political Geography*, 25, 482–505.

Jonas, A.E.G. and Ward, K. (2002) 'A world of regionalisms? Towards a US-UK urban and regional policy framework comparison', *Journal of Urban Affairs*, 24, 377–401.

Jonas, A.E.G. and Ward, K. (2007) 'Introduction to a debate on city-regions: New geographies of governance, democracy and social reproduction', *International Journal of Urban and Regional Research*, 31(1), 169–178.

Jonas, A.E.G., While, A. and Gibbs, D.C. (2010) 'Managing infrastructural and service demands in new economic spaces: The new territorial politics of collective provision', *Regional Studies*, 44, 183–200.

Jones, G. (2006) 'Urbanization in Southeast Asia', in T. Wong, B.J. Shaw and K. Goh, *Challenge Sustainability: Urban Development and Change in Southeast Asia* (Singapore: Marshal Cavendish Academic), pp. 247–267.

Jones, M. and MacLeod, G. (2004) 'Regional spaces, spaces of regionalism: Territory, insurgent politics and the English question', *Transactions of the Institute of British Geographers*, 29(4), 433–452.

Kaa, D.J. Van de (1987) 'Europe's second demographic transition', *Population Bulletin*, 42(1), 1–59.

Kartajaya, H. and Taufik, T. (2009) 'Jababeka industrial estate: A transforming city developer (in Indonesian)', *Kompas Daily*, 25 April, p. i.

KEG (Kommission der Europäischen Gemeinschaften) (1991) *Europa 2000. Perspektiven der künftigen Raumordnung der Gemeinschaft* (Luxemburg: KEG).

Keil, R. and Young, D. (2008) 'Transportation: The bottleneck of regional competitiveness in Toronto', *Environment and Planning C; Government and Policy*, 26, 728–751.

Keith, M. (2009) 'Figuring city change: Understanding urban regeneration and Britain's Thames Gateway', in R. Imrie, L. Lees and M. Raco (eds) *Regenerating London: Governance, Sustainability and Community in a Global City* (London: Routledge).

Kerwin, K. (2005, October 3) 'A new blueprint at Pulte homes', *Business Week*, p. 76.

Kim, C.H. and Kim, K.H. (2002) 'The political economy of Korean government policies on real estate', *Urban Studies*, 37(7), 1157–1169.

Kim, S.H. and Ahn, H.H. (2000) 'The peculiar "publicness" of housing in South Korea', in G.A. Dymski and D. Isenberg (eds) *Seeking Shelter on the Pacific Rim: Financial Globalization, Social Change, and the Housing Market* (Armonk, NY, London: M.E. Sharpe), pp. 211–231.

Kim, W.B. (1999) 'National competitiveness and governance of Seoul, Korea', in J. Friedmann (ed.) *Urban and Regional Governance in the Asia Pacific*. Institute of Asian Research, University of British Columbia.

King, A.D. (1984) *The Bungalow: The Production of a Global Culture* (London: RKP).

Kirby, A. (2008) 'The production of private space and its implications for urban social relations', *Political Geography*, 27, 74–95.

Kling, R., Olin, S. and Poster, M. (eds) (1995) *Postsuburban California: The Transformation of Orange County Since World War Two* (Berkeley, CA: University of California Press).

Knox, P. (1991) 'The restless urban landscape: Economic and sociocultural change and the transformation of metropolitan Washington, DC', *Annals of the Association of American Geographers*, 81(2), 181–209.

Knox, P.L. (1992) 'The packaged landscapes of post-suburban America', in J.W.R. Whitehand and P.J. Larkham (eds) *Urban Landscapes. International Perspectives* (London: Routledge), pp. 207–226.

Knox, P.L. (ed.) (1993) *The Restless Urban Landscape* (Englewood Cliffs, NJ: Prentice Hall).

Knox, P. (2008) *Metroburbia, USA* (New Brunswick, New Jersey: Rutgers University Press).

Kok, H. and Kovacs, Z. (1999) 'The process of suburbanisation in the agglomeration of Budapest', *Netherlands Journal of Housing and the Built Environment*, 14(2), 119–141.

Kooiman, J. (2003) *Governing as Governance* (London: Sage).

Kooiman, J. et al (2008) 'Interactive governance and governability: An introduction', *The Journal of Transdisciplinary Environmental Studies*, 7(1), 2–11.

Kraemer, C. (2005) 'Commuter belt turbulence in a dynamic region: The case of the Munich city-region', in K. Hoggart (ed.) *The City's Hinterland: Dynamism and Divergence in Europe's Peri-Urban Territories* (Aldershot: Ashgate), pp. 41–68.

Kravitz, D. (2009, March 31) 'Luxury enclave-to-be sheds a little cachet', *The Washington Post*, p. B1.

Kulcsar, L.J. and Domokos, T. (2005) 'The post-socialist growth machine: The case of Hungary', *International Journal of Urban and Regional Research*, N 29(3), 550–563.

Kunzmann, K.K. (2001) 'Welche Zukünfte für Suburbia? Acht Inseln im Archipel der Stadtregion', in K. Brake, J.S. Dangschat and G. Herfert (eds) *Suburbanisierung in Deutschland. Aktuelle Tendenzen* (Opladen: Leske & Budrich), pp. 213–221.

La Defense (n.d.) 'Everything about La Defense' [online] available from <http://www.ladefense.fr/culture...> [14 August 2008].

La Tercera (2003) *Rechazo a modificar Plan Regulador afecta inversión por US$ 5 mil millones*. May 3rd 2003, Santiago de Chile.

Lang, R. (2003) *Edgeless Cities: Exploring the Elusive Metropolis* (Washington, D.C.: Brookings Institution Press).

Lang, R. and Knox, P. (2009) 'The new metropolis: Rethinking megalopolis', *Regional Studies*, 43, 789–802.

Lange, B. (2000) 'Von Suburbia nach Postsuburbia? Neue Verstädterungsformen in der Stadt-Region Frankfurt-Main und deren raumordnerische Konsequenzen', in *Jahrbuch der Marburger Geographischen Gesellschaft* 1999 (Marburg: Marburger Geographischen Gesellschaft), pp. 315–319.

Laquian, A.A. (2005) *Beyond Metropolis: The Planning and Governance of Asia's Mega-Urban Regions* (Baltimore: The Johns Hopkins University Press).

Le Goix, R. (2005) 'Gated communities: Sprawl and social segregation in Southern California', *Housing Studies*, 20(2), 323–343.

Leach, D. (2004) 'The Arlington county case study: Rosslyn-Ballston Corridor', in H. Dittmar and G. Ohland (eds) *The New Transit Town: Best Practices in Transit-Oriented Development* (Washington, D.C.: Inland Press), pp. 131–154.

Leaf, M. (1994) 'The suburbanization of Jakarta: A concurrence of economics and ideology', *Third World Planning Review*, 16, 341–356.

Leaf, M. (1996) 'Building for the road for BMW: Culture, vision, and extended metropolitan region', *Environment and Planning A*, 28, 1617–1635.

Leaf, M. (2002), 'A tale of two villages: Globalization and peri-urban change in China and Vietnam', *Cities*, 19, 23–31.

Lee, B.S. (1998) 'Land use regulations and efficiency of Seoul's economy', Paper presented at the Seoul Metropolitan Fora 1998, *Sustainable Urban Competitiveness: Rethinking East Asian Cities*, 27–28 May 1998. Seoul, Korea.

Lehrer, U. (1994) 'The image of the periphery: The architecture of flexSpace', *Environment and Planning D: Society and Space*, 12(2), 187–205.

Leichenko, R. and Solecki, W.D. (2008) 'Consumption, inequity, and environmental justice: The making of new metropolitan landscape in developing countries', *Society & Natural Resources: An International Journal*, 21(7), 611–624.

Leisch, H. (2000) 'Structures and functions of new towns in Jabotabek', Paper Presented to *the Workshop of Indonesian Town Revisited*, The University of Leiden, 6–8 December.

Leitner, H., Pavlik, C. and Sheppard, E. (2002) 'Networks, governance, and the politics of scale: Inter-urban networks and the European Union', in A. Herod and M.W. Wright (eds) *Geographies of Power: Placing Scale* (Malden, MA: Blackwell), pp. 274–303.

Lewis, R. (1999) 'Running rings around the city: North American industrial suburbs, 1850–1950', in R. Harris and P. Larkham (eds) *Changing Suburbs: Foundation, Form and Function* (London: E & FN Spon), pp. 146–167.

Lewis, R. (2002) 'The industrial suburb is dead, long live the industrial slum: Suburbs and slums in Chicago and Montreal, 1850–1950', *Planning Perspectives*, 17(2), 123–144.

Ley, D. (1985) 'Cultural/humanistic geography', *Progress in Human Geography*, 9, 415–423.

Libertun de Duren, N.R. (2007) 'Gated communities as a municipal development strategy', *Housing Policy Debate*, 18, 607–626.

Lin, G.C-S. (1994) 'Changing theoretical perspectives on urbanization in Asian developing countries', *Third World Planning Review*, 16, 1–23.

Lin, G.C-S. (2002) 'The growth and structural changes of Chinese cities: A contextual and geographical analysis', *Cities*, 19, 299–316.

Lo, F.C. and Marcotullio, P.J. (2000) 'Globalization and urban transformations in the Asia Pacific region: A review', *Urban Studies*, 37, 77–111.

Lo, F.C. and Yeung, Y.M. (1996) *Emerging World Cities in Pacific Asia* (Tokyo: United Nations University Press).

Lo, F.C. and Yeung, Y.M. (1998), *Globalization and the World Large Cities* (Tokyo: United Nations University Press).

Loderer, B. (2001) 'Die heimliche Hauptstadt', *Hochparterre*, 10, 14–21.

Logan, J. and Molotch, H.L. (1987) *Urban Fortunes: The Political Economy of Place* (Berkeley, CA: University of California Press).

Lopez, E.J. (2006) 'Impacto del crecimiento del Gran Santiago en el deterioro funcional de sus espacios pericentrales', in H. Capel and R. Hidalgo (eds) *Construyendo la ciudad del siglo XXI. Retos y perspectivas urbanas en Espannã y Chile* (Santiago de Chile: Serie GEOlibros 6, Insitituto de Geografía, Pontificia Universidad Católica de Chile), pp. 337–350.

Lowe, M. (2000) 'Britain's regional shopping centres: New urban forms?', *Urban Studies*, 37(2), 261–274.

Lowenstein, R. (2006) 'Who needs the mortgage-interest deduction?', *The New York Times Magazine*. Retrieved from http://www.nytimes.com/2006/03/05/magazine/305deduction.1.html?pagewanted=1&ei=5090&en=e389e973631d2f3f&ex=1299214800&partner=rssuserland&emc=rss

Lucy, W.H. and Philips, D.L. (1997) 'The post-suburban era comes to Richmond: City decline, suburban transition and exurban growth', *Landscape and Urban Planning*, 36, 259–275.

Ma, L. and Wu, F. (2004) *Restructuring the Chinese City: Changing Society, Economy and Space* (London: Routledge).

Mack, K. (2009, February 15) 'Housing plan stirs working-class worry', *The Washington Post*, p. PW1.

MacLeod, G. (2001) 'The new regionalism reconsidered: Globalization, regulation and the recasting of political economic space', *International Journal of Urban and Regional Research*, 25, 804–829.

MacLeod, G. and Jones, M. (2007) 'Territorial, scalar, networked, connected: In what sense a "regional world"?', *Regional Studies*, 41(9), 1177–1191.

Majoor, S.J.H. (2008) *Disconnected Innovations, New Urbanity in Large-scale Development Projects: Zuidas Amsterdam, Ørestad Copenhagen and Forum Barcelona* (Delft: Eburon).

Makhrova, A. and Molodikova, I. (2007) 'Land market, commercial real estate, and the remolding of Moscow's urban fabric', in K. Stanilov (ed.) *The Post-Socialist City: Urban Form and Space Transformations in Central and Eastern Europe after Socialism* (Dordrecht: Springer).

Makhrova, A.G., Nefedova, T.G. and Treivish, A.I. (2008) *Moskovskaya Oblast Segodnya i Zavtra: Tendentsii i Perspektivy Prostranstvennogo Razvitiya* (Moscow Oblast Today and Tomorrow: Tendencies and Perspectives of Spatial Development) (Moscow: Novyy Khronograf).

Mamas, Si Gde Made and Rizky Komalasari (2008) 'The growth of Jakarta mega-urban region: Analysis of demographic, educational and employment changes', Conference on Growth Dynamic of Mega Urban Regions in Asia, Singapore, 24–25 June.

Marimow, A.E. and Spivack, M.S. (2008, December 10) 'Montgomery votes to scale back size of new homes', *The Washington Post*, p. B1.

Martens, M. (2006) 'Adaptive cities in Europe. Interrelationships between urban structure, mobility and regional planning strategies', PhD Thesis, University of Amsterdam.

Marvin, S., Harding, A. and Robson, B. (2006) *A Framework for City Regions* (London: Office of the Deputy Prime Minister).

Masotti, L.H. (1973) 'Prologue: Suburbia reconsidered – Myth and counter-myth', in L.H. Masotti and J.K. Hadden (eds) *The Urbanization of the Suburbs* (London: Sage), pp. 15–22.

Masotti, L.H. and Hadden, J.K. (1973) (eds) *The Urbanization of the Suburbs* (London: Sage).

Massey, D. (1994) 'A global sense of place', in D. Massey (ed.) *Space Place and Gender* (Cambridge: Polity), pp. 146–156.

Massey, D. (2007) *World City* (Cambridge: Polity).

McCann, E.J. (2002) 'The urban as an object of study in global cities literatures: Representational practices and conceptions of place and scale', in A. Herod and M. Wright (eds) *Geographies of Power: Placing Scale* (Malden, MA: Blackwell), pp. 61–84.

McCann, L. (1999) 'Suburbs of desire: The suburban landscape of Canadian cities, c.1900–1950', in R. Harris and P. Larkham (eds) *Changing Suburbs: Foundation, Form and Function* (London: E & FN Spon).

McGee, T. (1991) 'The emergence of *desakota* regions in Asia: Expanding a hypothesis', in N. Ginsberg, B. Koppel and T. McGee (eds) *The Extended Metropolis: Settlement Transition in Asia* (Honolulu: University of Hawaii Press), pp. 3–25.

McGee, T. (2005) 'Distinctive urbanization in the peri-urban regions of East and Southeast Asia: Renewing the debates', *Jurnal Perencanaan Wilayah dan Kota*, 16(1), 39–55.

McGee, T.G., Lin, G.C.S., Marton, A.M., Wang, M.Y.L. and Wu, J. (2007) *China's Urban Space: Development under Market Transition* (London: Routledge).

McGee, T. and Robinson, I. (1995) (eds) *The Mega-Urban Region of Southeast Asia* (Vancouver: University of British Columbia Press).

McKenzie, E. (1994) *Privatopia: Homeowner Associations and the Rise of Residential Private Government* (New Haven: Yale University Press).

Ministry of Construction and Transportation (MCT) (2001) *Development Ideas for the Pangyo Planned City* (Kwachon: MCT) (in Korean).

Ministry of Land, Transport and Maritime Affairs (MLTMA) (2008) *Announcement No. 2008-735* (Kwachon: MLTMA) (in Korean).

Molotch, H. (1976) 'The city as a growth machine – toward a political-economy of place', *American Journal of Sociology*, 82, 309–322.

Mori, H. (1998) 'Land conversion at the urban fringe: A comparative study of Japan, Britain and the Netherlands', *Urban Studies*, 35(9), 1541–1558.

Morio, K., Sakamoto, I. et al. (1993) 'Evaluation of actual "Kison Takuchi" system in Saitama prefecture', *Collected Papers of the Japanese City Planning Association Nihon Toshi Keikaku Gakkai Ronbun Shu*, 28, 253–258.

Mozingo, L. (2000) 'The corporate estate in U.S.A., 1954–64: Thoroughly modern in concept, but...down to earth and rugged', *Studies in the History of Garden and Designed Landscapes*, 20(1), 25–56.

Mulgan, A.G. (2000) *The Politics of Agriculture in Japan* (London and New York: Routledge).

Muller, E. (2001) 'Industrial suburbs and the growth of metropolitan Pittsburgh, 1870–1920', *Journal of Historical Geography*, 27(1), 58–75.

Muller, P. (1981) *Contemporary Suburban America* (Englewood Cliffs: Prentice Hall).

Muller, P. (1997) 'The suburban transformation of the globalizing American city', *Annals of the American Academy of Political and Social Science*, 551(May), 44–58.

Mummolo, J. (2009, February 1) 'Sick house, suffering family', *The Washington Post*, C1.

Murdoch, J. and Marsden, T. (1994) *Reconstituting Rurality* (London: UCL Press).

Musterd, S., Bontje, M. and Ostendorf, W. (2006) 'The changing role of old and new urban centres: The case of the Amsterdam region', *Urban Geography*, 27(4), 360–387.

Naranjo, G. (2006) 'Effectos del Plan Regulador Metropolitano de Santiago en el ordenamiento de los espacios periurbanes', in H. Capel and R. Hidalgo (eds) *Construyendo la ciudad del siglo XXI. Retos y perspectivas urbanas en Espanña y Chile* (Santiago de Chile: Serie GEOlibros 6, Insitituto de Geografía, Pontificia Universidad Católica de Chile), pp. 293–306.

Nas, P.J.M. and Houweling, T.A.J. (2000) 'Mega-urbanization in Southeast Asia', *Unpublished Paper*. Faculty of Social Sciences, University of Leiden.

Neiman, M. and Loveridge, R. (1981) 'Environmentalism and local growth control: A probe into the class bias thesis', *Environment and Behavior*, 13, 759–772.

Nicolaides, B. (2002) *My Blue Heaven: Life and Politics in the Working-Class Suburbs of Los Angeles, 1920–1965* (Chicago: University of Chicago Press).

ODPM (2003) *Sustainable Communities: Building for the Future* (London: Office of the Deputy Prime Minister).

Ogawa, N. (2005) 'Population aging and policy options for a sustainable future: The case of Japan', *Genus*, 61(3–4), 369–410.

Ohta, K. (1994) 'Transport problems and policies of the Tokyo metropolitan region', in *Contemporary Studies in Urban Environmental Management in Japan*. Dept. of Urban Engineering University of Tokyo (Tokyo: Kajima Institute Publishing), pp. 106–127.

Orange County Register (1996) 'Babbitt lauds endangered rat plan but some property owners protest', Orange County Register: Metro Section, 9th May, p. 5.

Orellana, A. (2007) 'La Gobernabilidad metropolitana: nuevos escenarios para el desarrollo urbano y territorial del área metropolitana de Santiago', in C. de Mattos and R. Hidalgo (eds) *Santiago de Chile: Movilidad Espacial y Reconfiguración Metropolitana* (Santiago de Chile: GEOlibros 8, Insitituto des Estudios Urbanos y Territoriales, Pontificia Universidad Católica de Chile), pp. 189–206.

Orfield, M. (2002) *Metropolitics: The New Suburban Reality* (Washington, D.C.: Brookings Institution).

Organisation for Economic Co-operation and Development (2007) *OECD Regions at a Glance* (Paris: OECD Press).

Ouředníček, M. (2005) 'New suburban development in the post-socialist city: The case of Prague', in F. Eckhardt (ed.) *Paths of Urban Transformation* (Frankfurt/ Main (a.o.): Lang), pp. 143–156.

Painter, J. (2008) 'Cartographic anxiety and the search for regionality', *Environment and Planning A*, 40, 342–361.

Pallot, J. and Shaw, D.J.B. (1981) *Planning in the Soviet Union* (London: Croom Helm).

Park, B.G. (1998) 'Where do tigers sleep at night? The state's role in housing policy in South Korea and Singapore', *Economic Geography*, 74(3), 272–288.

Parraguez Sanchez, L. (2008) *Emergent Social Movements in Santiago. Between the Defense of Spatial Identity and the Fight for City Rights. The Case of the Residents Assembly of José Mariá Caro*. Pontificia Universidad Católica de Chile, Santiago de Chile, Masters Thesis.

Paz Castro, C. (2006) 'Impacto de la dispersión urbana de la ciudad de Santiago en la calidad del suelo en la periferia norte: Colina y Lampa', in H. Capel and R. Hidalgo (eds) *Construyendo la ciudad del siglo XXI. Retos y perspectivas urbanas en Espannña y Chile* (Santiago de Chile: Serie GEOlibros 6, Insitituto de Geografía, Pontificia Universidad Católica de Chile), pp. 279–291.

Peck, J. and Tickell, A. (2002) 'Neoliberalizing space', *Antipode*, 34, 380–404.

Petermann, A. (2006) '¿Quién extendió a Santiago? Una breve historia del límite urbano 1953–2004', in A. Galetovic (ed.) *Santiago: Dónde estamos y hacia dónde vamos* (Santiago de Chile: Centro de Estudios Públicos), pp. 205–230.

Peterson, P. (1981) *City Limits* (Chicago: University of Chicago Press).

Phelps, N.A., Parsons, N., Ballas, D. and Dowling, A. (2006) *Post-suburban Europe: Planning and Politics at the Margins of Europe's Capital Cities* (Basingstoke: Palgrave Macmillan).

Phelps, N.A. and Wood, A.M. (2010) 'The new post-suburban politics?', *Urban Studies*.

Phelps, N.A., Wood, A.M. and Valler, D.C. (2010) 'A post-suburban world? An outline of a research agenda', *Environment & Planning A*, 42(2), 366–383.

Pierce, N.R. (1993) *Citistates: How Urban American Can Prosper in a Competitive World* (Washington, D.C.: Seven Locks Press).

Pile, S. (1999) 'What is a city?', in J. Allen, D. Massey and S. Pile (eds) *City Worlds* (London: Routledge).

Pirez, P. (2002) 'Buenos Aires: Fragmentation and the privatization of the metropolitan city', *Environment & Urbanization*, 14, 145–158.

Piron, O. and Dubois-Taine, G. (eds) (1998) *La Ville émergente. Constats pour renouveler les lignes d'action publiques* (Paris: PCA).

Planungsverband Ballungsraum Frankfurt/Rhein-Main (2005) *Frankfurt/Rhein-Main 2020 – die europäische Metropolregion. Leitbild fuur den Regionalen Flächennutzungs-plan und den Regionalplan Hessen* (Frankfurt: Planungsverband) (published together with Regierungspräsidium Darmstadt – Regionalversammlung).

Planungsverband Ballungsraum Rhein-Main/Frankfurt (2008) *Regionales Monitoring 2008* (Frankfurt: Planungsverband Ballungsraum Rhein-Main/Frankfurt).

Poduje, I. (2006) 'El globo y el acordeón: planificación urbana en Santiago, 1960–2004', in A. Galetovic (ed.) *Santiago: Dónde estamos y hacia dónde vamos* (Santiago: Centro de Estudios Públicos, Santiago de Chile), pp. 231–276.

Power, M. (2004a) 'Divided we stand', *Builder Online*. Retrieved from http://www.builderonline.com/business/divided-we-stand.aspx

Power, M. (2004b) 'Land wars', *Builder Online*. Retrieved from http://www.builderonline.com/business/land-wars.aspx

Publicountry, S.R.L. (2005) *Guía de Countries, Barrios Privados y Chacras* (Capital Federal, Argentina: Publicountry S.R.L.).

Raco, M. (2007) *Building Sustainable Communities. Spatial Policy and Labour Mobility in Post-war Britain* (Bristol: Policy Press).

Reiss-Schmidt, S. (2003) 'Zwischen Heimatgefühl und Weltstadtanspruch: Die Region Frankfurt/Rhein-Main In', *DISP*, 152(1), 80–86.

Robinson, P. (2004) *Going for Growth. Comparing the South East's Economic Performance*. Commission on Sustainable Development in the South East, *Working Paper One* (London: Institute for Public Policy Research).

Rodriguez, J. (2007) 'Paradojas y contrapuntos de dínamica demográfica metro-politana: algunas respuestas basadas en la explotación intensiva de microdatos censales', in C. de Mattos and R. Hidalgo (eds) *Santiago de Chile: Movilidad Espacial y Reconfiguración Metropolitana* (Santiago de Chile: Serie GEOlibros 8, Insitituto de los Estudios Urbanos y Territoriales, Pontificia Universidad Católica de Chile), pp. 19–52.

Roitman, S. (2003) 'Barrios cerrados y segregación social urbana', *Scripta Nova*, VII(146), Universidad de Barcelona.

Roitman, S. (2004) 'Urbanizaciones cerradas: estado de la cuestión hoy y propuesta teórica', *Norte Grande*, 32, Pontificia Universidad Católica de Chile, pp. 5–19.

Roitman, S. (2008) 'Urban social group segregation: The analysis of a gated community in Mendoza, Argentina', Unpublished PhD Thesis, University of London.

Roitman, S., and Giglio, M.A. (2010) 'Latin American gated communities: The latest symbol of historic social segregation', in S. Bagaeen and O. Uduku (eds) *Gated Communities: Social Sustainability in Contemporary and Historical Gated Developments* (London: Earthscan), pp. 63–78.

Romero, H. and Vázquez, A. (2006) 'La commodificación de los territorios urbanizables y la degradación ambiental en Santiago de Chile', in H. Capel and R. Hidalgo (eds) *Construyendo la ciudad del siglo XXI. Retos y perspectivas urbanas en Espanña y Chile.* Serie GEOlibros, 6, Insitituto de Geografía, Pontificia Universidad Católica de Chile, Santiago de Chile, pp. 263–278.

Roy, A. (2009) 'The 21st century metropolis: New geographies of theory', *Regional Studies*, 43(6), 819–830.

Rozenblat, C. and Cicille, P. (2003) *Les villes européennes: Analyse Comparative* (Paris: DATAR).

Rudolph, R. and Brade, I. (2005) 'Moscow: Processes of restructuring in the post-Soviet metropolitan periphery', *Cities*, 22(2), 135–150.

Rusk, D. (1995) *Cities Without Suburbs* (Baltimore, MD: Johns Hopkins University Press).

Rustiadi, E. (2007) 'Spatial analysis of development problems in Jakarta metropolitan area' (in Indonesian). Paper presented to Seminar 'Towards Sustainable Jakarta Metropolitan Area', Bogor, West Java, 6th September.

Sabatini, F. (2000) 'Reforma de los mercados de suelo en Santiago, Chile: efectos sobre los precios de la tierra y la segregación residencial', in *EURE*, 26(77), Santiago de Chile.

Sabatini, F. and Cáceres, G. (2004) 'Los barrios cerrados y la ruptura del patrón tradicional de segregación en las ciudades latinoamericanas: el caso de Santiago de Chile', in G. Cáceres, and F. Sabatini (eds) *Barrios Cerrados en Santiago de Chile: entre la exclusión y la integración residencial* (Santiago de Chile, Pontificia Universidad Católica de Chile – Instituto de Geografía and Lincoln Institute of Land Policy), pp. 9–43.

Salet, W. and Majoor, S. (2005) *Amsterdam Zuidas, European Space* (Rotterdam: 010 Publishers).

Salim, W. and Kombaitan, B. (2009) 'Jakarta: The rise and challenge of capital', *City*, 13(1), 20–128.

Saunders, P. (1979) *Urban Politics. A Sociological Interpretation* (London: Hutchinson).

Savitch, H. and Vogel, R. (1996) *Regional Politics: America in a Post-city Age* (Thousand Oaks, CA: Sage).

Savitch, H. and Vogel, R. (2004) 'Suburbs without a city: Power and city-county consolidation', *Urban Affairs Review*, 39, 758–790.

Schoon, N. (2001) *The Chosen City* (London: Spon).

Schubert, D. (2004) 'Theodor Fritsch and the German (volkische) version of the garden city: The garden city invented two years before Ebenezer Howard', *Planning Perspectives*, 19(1), 3–35.

Schumacher, M., Koch, M. and Ruegg, J. (2004) 'The Zurich Limattal. Steps of a servant valley towards emancipation', in G. Dubois-Taine (ed.) *From Helsinki to Nicosia. Eleven Case Studies and Synthesis* (Paris: METL/PUCA) (COST Action C10 'Outskirts of European Cities'), pp. 215–236.

Scobie, J. (1974) *Buenos Aires: Plaza to Suburb, 1870–1910* (New York: Oxford University Press).

Scott, A. (ed.) (2001) *Global City-regions: Trends, Theory, Policy* (Oxford: Oxford University Press).

Scott, A.J. and Roweis, S.J. (1977) 'Urban planning in theory and in practice: A reappraisal', *Environment & Planning A*, 9, 1097–1119.

SEEDA (1999) *Building a World Class Region. An Economic Strategy for the South East of England* (Guildford: South East Economic Development Agency).

SEEDA (2002a) *An Economic Profile of the South East of England* (Guildford: South East England Development Agency).

SEEDA (2002b) *Regional Economic Strategy for South East England 2002–2012* (Guildford: South East England Development Agency).

SEEDA (2006) *The Regional Economic Strategy 2006–2016. A Framework for Sustainable Prosperity* (Guildford: South East England Development Agency).

SEERA (2004a) *Integrated Regional Framework 2004: A Better Quality of Life in the South East* (Guildford: South East England Regional Assembly).

SEERA (2004b) *Perceptions of the South East and its Regional Assembly*. Report prepared by MORI for the South-East of England Regional Assembly, http://www. southeeast-ra.gov.uk/publications/surveys/2004/mori_report_july_2004.pdf

SEERA (2004c) *South East Plan Consultation Draft, November 2004* (Guildford: South East England Regional Assembly).

SEERA (2008) *Annual Report 2007–8* (Guildford: South East of England Regional Assembly).

Sennett, R. (1990) *The Conscience of the Eye: The Design and Social Life of Cities* (New York: Knopf).

Shearmur, R., Coffee, R., Dube, C. and Barbonne, R. (2007) 'Intrametropolitan employment structure: Polycentricity, scatteraton, dispersal and chaos in Toronto, Montreal and Vancouver, 1996–2001', *Urban Studies*, 44, 1713–1738.

Sheller, M. and Urry, J. (2000) 'The city and the car', *International Journal of Urban and Regional Research*, 24, 737–757.

Siavelis, P.M., Valenzuela Van Treek, E. and Martelli, G. (2002) 'Santiago: Municipal decentralization in a centralized political system', in D. Myers and H. Dietz (eds) *Capital City Politics in Latin America: Democratization and Empowerment* (Boulder CO: Lynne Rienner).

Sieverts, T. (1999) *Zwischenstadt. Zwischen Ort und Welt, Raum und Zeit, Stadt und Land* (Braunschweig: Vieweg).

Sieverts, T. (2003) *Cities Without Cities. An Interpretation of the Zwischenstadt* (London: Spon).

Sieverts, T. (2007) 'Von der unmöglichen Ordnung zu einer möglichen Unordnung im Entwerfen der Stadlandschaft', *DISP*, 169, 5–16.

Silverman, A. and Schneider, L. (1991) 'Suburban localism and Long Island's regional crisis', *Built Environment*, 17, 191–204.

Soja, E. (1980) 'The sociospatial dialectic', *Annals of the Association of American Geographers*, 70, 207–225.

Soja, E. (1989) *Postmodern Geographies: The Reassertion of Space in Critical Social Theory* (London and New York: Verso).

Soja, E. (2000) *Postmetropolis: Critical Studies of Cities and Regions* (Oxford: Blackwell).

Somashekhar, S. (2009, March 24) 'Affordable housing program reevaluated', *The Washington Post*, p. B5.

Sorensen, A. (2000) 'Land readjustment and metropolitan growth: An examination of land development and urban sprawl in the Tokyo metropolitan area', *Progress in Planning*, 53(4), 1–113.

Sorensen, A. (2001). 'Building suburbs in Japan: Continuous unplanned change on the urban fringe', *Town Planning Review*, 72(3), 247–273.

Sorensen, A. (2002) *The Making of Urban Japan: Cities and Planning from Edo to the 21st Century* (London: Routledge).

Sorensen, A., Okata, J. and Fujii, S. (2010) 'Urban renaissance as intensification: Building regulation and the rescaling of place governance in Tokyo's high-rise Manshon boom', *Urban Studies*, 47, 556–583.

280   References

Stanilov, K. (ed.) (2007) *The Post-Socialist City: Urban Form and Space Transformation in Central and Eastern Europe after Socialism* (Dordrecht: Springer).

Statistik Stadt Zürich (2004) 'Glatttalstadt' und 'Limmattalstadt' im Vergleich zur Stadt Zürich. *Info Statistik Stadt Zürich* 3/2004.

Steiner, K. (1954) 'Local government in Japan: Reform and reaction', *Far Eastern Survey*, 23(7), 97–102.

Stockins, P. (2004) 'Oferta y demanda de vivienda en la periferia santiaguina: los nuevos desarrollos inmobiliarios', in G. Cáceres and F. Sabatini (eds) *Barrios cerrados en Santiago de Chile. Entre la exclusión y la integración residencial* (Santiago de Chile: Lincoln Institute, Pontificia Universidad Católica de Chile).

Suarez, I., Overkamp, M. and Boersma, H. (2008) *Analyse atypische stedelijkheid in Haarlemmermeer* (Hoofddorp: Team Onderzoek, Gemeente Haarlemmermeer).

The Suburbanization of Retail Trade: A Study of Retail Trade Dispersion in Major U.S. Markets, 1958–1967 (1970) (New York: Columbia Broadcasting System).

Svampa, M. (2001) *Los que ganaron. La vida en los countries y barrios privados* (Buenos Aires: Biblos).

Swyngedouw, E. (1997) 'Neither global nor local. "Glocalization" and the politics of scale', in K.R. Cox (ed.) *Spaces of Globalization. Reasserting the Power of the Local* (New York: Guilford Press).

Sýkora, L. (1999) 'Changes in the internal spatial structure of post-communist Prague', *GeoJournal*, 49(1), 79–89.

Sýkora, L. (2007) 'Office development and post-communist city formation: The case of Prague', in K. Stanilov (ed.) (2007) *The Post-socialist City: Urban Form and Space Transformations in Central and Eastern Europe After Socialism* (Dordrecht: Springer), pp. 117–145.

Sýkora, L. and Ouředníček, M. (2007) 'Sprawling post-communist metropolis: Commercial and residential suburbanisation in Prague and Brno, the Czech Republic', in E. Razin, M. Dijst and C. Vàsquez (eds) (2007) *Employment Deconcentration in European Metropolitan Areas* (Dordrecht: Springer), pp. 209–233.

Takami, K. (2006) 'Car use and sustainability: Reflection on retail development control systems', in H. Tamagawa (ed.) *Sustainable Cities: Japanese Perspectives on Physical and Social Structures* (Tokyo: United Nations University Press), pp. 139–166.

Talen, E. (2001) 'Traditional urbanism meets residential affluence: An analysis of the variability of suburban preference', *Journal of the American Planning Association*, 67(2), 199–216.

Tasan-Kok, T. (2006) 'Institutional and spatial change', in S. Tsenkova and Z. Nedovic-Budic (eds) *The Urban Mosaic of Post-Socialist Europe: Space, Institutions and Policy* (Heidelberg: Physica-Verlag).

Teaford, J. (1979) *City and Suburb: The Political Fragmentation of Metropolitan America, 1850–1970* (Baltimore, MD: Johns Hopkins University Press).

Teaford, J. (1990) *The Rough Road to Renaissance: Urban Revitalization in America, 1940–1985* (Baltimore: Johns Hopkins University Press).

Teaford, J. (1997) *Post-Suburbia: Government and Politics in the Edge Cities* (Baltimore: Johns Hopkins University Press).

Teaford, J. (2006) *The Metropolitan Revolution: The Rise of Post-Urban America* (New York: Columbia University Press).

Teaford, J. (2008) *The American Suburb: The Basics* (New York: Routledge).

Thuillier, G. (2005) 'Gated communities in the metropolitan area of Buenos Aires, Argentina: A challenge for town planning', *Housing Studies*, 20(2), 255–271.

Tiebout, C.M. (1954) 'A pure theory of local expenditures', *Journal of Political Economy*, 64, 416–424.

Toder, A., Turner, M.A. et al. (2010) *Reforming the Mortgage Interest Deduction* (Washington, D.C.: Tax Policy Center, Urban Institute and Brookings Institution).

Tokman, A. (2006) 'El MINVU, la política habitacional y la expansión excesiva de Santiago', in A. Galetovic (ed.) *Santiago: Dónde estamos y hacia dónde vamos* (Santiago de Chile: Centro de Estudios Públicos), pp. 489–522.

Tsenkova, S. and Nedovic-Budic, Z. (2006) 'The post-socialist urban world', in S. Tsenkova and Z. Nedovic-Budic (eds) *The Urban Mosaic of Post-Socialist Europe: Space, Institutions and Policy* (Heidelberg: Physica-Verlag), pp. 349–366.

Tsuru, S. (1999) *The Political Economy of the Environment: The Case of Japan* (London: The Athlone Press).

UN Population Division (2008) *World Urbanization Prospects. The 2007 Revision* (New York: New York United Nations).

Upham, F.K. (1993) 'Privatizing regulation: The implementation of the large scale retail stores law', in G. Allinson and Y. Sone (eds) *Political Dynamics in Contemporary Japan* (Ithaca: Cornell University Press), pp. 264–294.

Urban Eden (undated) *Love Milton Keynes? Love Urban Eden*. http://www.urban-eden.org/ accessed 9 July 2010.

US Census (2006) *State and Metropolitan Area Data Book*. U.S. Census Bureau (Accessed July 2006 at: http://www.census.gov/compendia/smadb/SMADBmetro.html).

US Census Bureau (2009) American Community Survey, <http://www.census.gov/acs/www/>.

US Census Bureau (2010a) Historic Annual Characteristics of New Housing, 'Manufacturing, mining and construction statistics', US Census Bureau, Washington, D.C.

US Census Bureau (2010b) American Housing Survey, <http://www.census.gov/hhes/www/housing/ahs/ahs.html>.

Vaattovaara, M. and Kortteinen, M. (2003) 'Beyond polarisation versus professionalisation? A case study of the development of the Helsinki region', *Urban Studies*, 40(11), 2127–2145.

Vanolo, A. (2008) 'Internationalization in the Helsinki metropolitan area: Images, discourses and metaphors', *European Planning Studies*, 16(2), 229–252.

Verdecchia, C.R. (1995) 'Los Clubes de Campo', *Revista Arquis*, 5, 26–28.

Vidal-Koppmann, S. (2007) '*Transformaciones socio-territoriales de la Región Metropolitana de Buenos Aires en la última década del Siglo XX. La incidencia de las urbanizaciones privadas en la fragmentación de la periferia*', Unpublished PhD thesis, FLACSO Argentina.

Viehe, F. (1981) 'Black gold suburbs: The influence of the extractive industry on the suburbanization of Los Angeles, 1890–1930', *Journal of Urban History*, 8(1), 3–26.

Wacquant, L. (2008) *Urban Outcasts: A Comparative Sociology of Advanced Marginality* (Cambridge, U.K. and Malden, Mass: Polity).

Walker, R. (1981) 'A theory of suburbanization: Capitalism and the construction of urban space in the US', in M. Dear and A. Scott (eds) *Urbanization and Urban Planning in Capitalist Societies* (London: Methuen), pp. 383–429.

Walker, R. and Lewis, R.D. (2001) 'Beyond the crabgrass frontier: Industry and the spread of North American cities, 1850–1950', *Journal of Historical Geography*, 27(1), 3–19.

Walks, R.A. (2004) 'Suburbanization, the vote, and changes in federal and provincial political representation and influence between inner cities and suburbs in large Canadian urban regions, 1945–1999', *Urban Affairs Review*, 38(4), 411–440.

Ward, P. (1996) 'Contemporary issues in the government and administration of Latin American mega-cities', in A. Gilbert (ed.) *The Mega-city in Latin America* (Tokyo: United Nations University Press), pp. 53–72.

Warner, K. and Molotch, H.L. (1995) 'Power to build: How development persists despite local controls', *Urban Affairs Review*, 30, 378–406.

Weber, A. (1899) *The Growth of Cities in the Nineteenth Century: A Study in Statistics* (New York: Macmillan).

Webster, C. (2002) 'Property rights and the public realm: Gates, greenbelts, and gemeinschaft', *Environment & Planning B, Planning & Design*, 29, 397–412.

Webster, D. (1995) 'Mega-urbanization in ASEAN: New phenomenon or transitional phase to the "Los Angeles World City"', in T.G. McGee and I. Robinson (eds) *The Mega-Urban Regions of Southeast Asia* (Vancouver: University of British Columbia Press), pp. 27–44.

Webster, D. (2001) 'Inside out: Peri-urbanization in China', *Unpublished Paper, Asia-Pacific Research Center*, Stanford University, Palo Alto, California.

Wells, H. (1924) *Anticipations and Other Papers* (New York: Charles Scribners's Sons).

'West Edmonton Mall' (n.d.) WEM Trivia [online] available from <http://www.westedmall.com/about/wemtrivia.asp> [20 November 2008].

Whitehand, J. and Carr, M. (1999) 'England's interwar suburban landscapes: Myth and reality', *Journal of Historical Geography*, 25(4), 483–501.

Wijk, M. van (2007) *Airports as Cityports in the City-region. Spatial-economic and Institutional Positions and Institutional Learning in Randstad-Schiphol (AMS), Frankfurt Rhein-Main (FRA), Tokyo Haneda (HND) and Narita (NRT)* (Utrecht: KNAG) (Netherlands Geographical Studies nr. 353).

Wirth, L. (1964) *Louis Wirth on Cities and Social Life: Selected Papers* (Chicago: University of Chicago Press).

Wolch, J., Pastor, M. and Drier, P. (eds) (2004) *Up Against the Sprawl: Public Policy and the Making of Southern California* (Minneapolis: University of Minnesota Press).

Wong, T. (2006) 'Achieving a sustainable urban form? An investigation of the Kuala Lumpur mega-urban region', in T. Wong, B.J. Shaw and K. Goh, *Challenge Sustainability: Urban Development and Change in Southeast Asia* (Singapore: Marshal Cavendish Academic), pp. 146–174.

World Bank (1998) *Indonesia in Crisis: A Macroeconomic Update* (Washington, D.C.: World Bank).

Wu, F. (2001) 'China's recent urban development in the process of land and housing marketization and economic globalization', *Habitat International*, 25(3), 273–289.

Wu, F. (2005) 'Rediscovering the "gate" under market transition: From work-unit compounds to commodity housing enclaves', *Housing Studies*, 20(2), 235–254.

Wu, F. and Lu, D. (2008) 'The transition of Chinese cities', *Built Environment*, 34(4), 385–391.

Wu, F. and Phelps, N. (2008) 'From suburbia to post-suburbia in China? Aspects of the transformation of the Beijing and Shanghai global city regions', *Built Environment*, 34(4), 464–481.

Wu, F. and Phelps, N.A. (2011) '(Post-) suburban development and state entrepreneurialism in Beijing's outer suburbs', *Environment and Planning A*, 42(2), 366–383.

Yiftachel, O. (2009) 'Theoretical notes on "Gray Cities": The coming of urban apartheid?', *Planning Theory*, 8(1), 87–99.

Young, D. (2006) *Rebuilding the Modern City After Modernism in Toronto and Berlin*. Unpublished dissertation. York University, Toronto.

Young, D. and Keil, R. (2011) 'Seeking the urban in-between: Tracking the urban politics of infrastructure in Toronto', unpublished manuscript, The City Institute at York University.

Zegras, C. and Gakenheimer, R. (2000) *Urban Growth Management for Mobility: The Case of the Santiago, Chile Metropolitan Region*. Report, prepared for the Lincoln Institute of Land Policy and the MIT Cooperative Mobility Program.

Zhou, Y. and Logan, J.R. (2008) 'Growth on the edge: The new Chinese metropolis', in J.R. Logan (ed.) *Urban China in Transition* (Oxford: Blackwell Publishing), pp. 140–160.

Zhou, Y. and Ma, L.J.C. (2000) 'Economic restructuring and suburbanization in China', *Urban Geography*, 21(3), 205–236.

Zunino, H.M. (2006) 'Power relations in urban decision-making: Neo-liberalism, "techno-politicians" and authoritarian redevelopment in Santiago, Chile', *Urban Studies*, 43(10), 1825–1846.

Index